Old
Kiva

North
Plaza

THE CIVILIZATION OF THE AMERICAN INDIAN SERIES

María: THE POTTER OF SAN ILDEFONSO

María: THE POTTER OF SAN ILDEFONSO

By ALICE MARRIOTT

with drawings by MARGARET LEFRANC

UNIVERSITY OF OKLAHOMA PRESS

NORMAN

By Alice Marriott

The Ten Grandmothers (Norman, 1945)
Winter-telling Stories (New York, 1947)
María: The Potter of San Ildefonso (Norman, 1948)
Indians on Horseback (New York, 1948)
The Valley Below (Norman, 1949)
Greener Fields (New York, 1953; new edition, 1962)
Hell on Horses and Women (Norman, 1953)
Sequoyah (New York, 1956)
The Black Stone Knife (New York, 1957)
The First-Comers (New York, 1959)
Oklahoma: The Story of Its Past and Present (with Edwin C. Mc-
Reynolds and Estelle Faulconer) (Norman, 1961)

International Standard Book Number: 0-8061-0176-8

Library of Congress Catalog Card Number: 48-2101

In Memoriam
Nicolasa Peña Montoya
and
Hinda Wood Cunningham

Contents

Foreword   xi

    Part I: The Clay Is Shaped
1. The Pueblo   5
2. The Indian "Trader" (1886)   13
3. The Games (1886–1896)   20
4. The Pilgrimage (1890)   30
5. The Visit (1890)   39
6. The Withdrawing (1891)   52
7. The Storehouse (1892)   60
8. The Little Trees (1888–1892)   70

    Part II: The Bowl Is Polished
9. The Schools (1887–1898)   81
10. The Meeting (1899)   92
11. Time Together (1899–1903)   102
12. The Wedding (1904)   109
13. The Return (1904)   119

    Part III: The Bowl Is Fired
14. The Toilsome Spring (1907)   127
15. The Job (1907)   134
16. The Potsherd (1908)   149
17. The Whole Pot (1908)   158
18. The Firing (1909)   167
19. The Selling (1909)   175
20. Part of Living (1909–1910)   182
21. The Drinking (1909–1910)   189

22. The Black Pottery (1909–1912)   195
23. The Work Goes On (1913)   203
24. In the Business (1915)   210
25. The Invention (1918–1921)   217
26. The Signatures (1923–1926)   227

          Part IV : The Finished Bowl

27. The Breaking (1923)   239
28. The Breach in the Wall (1933)   249
29. Growing Away (1934–1939)   257
30. The Governor (1940)   267
31. The Parting (1943)   275

                Appendices
Table of Pottery as illustrated   283
Chronology of the Pottery-making of María Martínez   288
Bibliography   291

Foreword

María Montoya Martínez, or Marie Martínez, is a woman who has become in her own lifetime a legend. Her graciousness, charm, and beauty have been commented on many times by people who have known her well, and by people who have barely met her. Her strength of character and her skill as a craftsworker are immediately apparent, and have been spoken and written of frequently. The emphasis in speaking and writing has always been on her unusual qualities, on the facets of her character and disposition that seem to set her apart from humankind in general and from Pueblo womankind in particular.

The most striking characteristic that I have found in Mrs. Martínez, however, is that she does not regard herself as an exception to the general rule. Her life has been, as nearly as she could make it, the normal life of a woman of her culture. She herself is the first to say that San Ildefonso has other potters who are more skilled than she. Her charm and graciousness are not the natural, unstudied qualities of an unsophisticated woman, but arise from a conscious effort to meet and deal with situations that have become part of her daily life through no effort or desire of her own.

I, like many other Anglos, have come to regard Mrs. Martínez as a friend; and the foregoing statements are made to give greater credit where much credit is already given. It is my hope that the material here presented will show that Mrs. Martínez has met and overcome many problems which do not present themselves to the average Pueblo Indian woman, but that her method of overcoming obstacles has always been one which might have been predicted from a study of the group to which she belongs.

The material which follows is not in itself complete. It was gathered in 1945 and 1946, through several months of almost daily interviews with Mrs. Martínez, interspersed with attendance at those dances of San Ildefonso and other pueblos which were open to the public. Throughout the work a stream-of-consciousness method was employed in collecting data. During the interviews, informant and ethnographer were alone, in a room from which other members of the informant's family were excluded, at her request.

Subjects for discussion were seldom suggested; it was left to Mrs. Martínez to introduce a topic and to follow her train of thought to what seemed to her a natural conclusion. Many items of information, therefore, are given without rationalization or explanation. The informant took them for granted as facts and so presented them. A biographically chronological arrangement of material has been used as much as possible in the body of the book. When it has not been possible to determine the exact date of an event, the period of years in which the incident is known to have occurred is given in the chapter heading.

It is obvious from these statements that the book which follows is not a formal history of the pueblo of San Ildefonso or of the life of María Martínez. What has been attempted here is an exposition only of certain events. What happened is told informally, as a story, and as often as possible in Mrs. Martínez' own words.

Because of the conservative nature of the people of San Ildefonso and of the Pueblos generally, and their habit of preserving secrets with Masonic closeness; because of their fear that knowledge which the Pueblo Indians have guarded through the centuries might become public property, certain restrictions were placed on this work from its inception.

By order of the governor and the council of the pueblo, Mrs. Martínez was forbidden to discuss certain topics: the native religion of San Ildefonso, the clan and moiety systems in operation there, and such wholly masculine topics as the method of choice of the governor and the councilmen and their exact functions. The division within the pueblo which led to the establishment of a separate south plaza was also interdicted, as was anything connected with relations with the government agencies operating in the pueblos generally.

For this reason, the ethnologist and the sociologist will find blanks in the work at the very places where they most desire information. This is unfortunate. I find the same blanks myself, and regret their presence as bitterly as anyone can. The only consolation that I find, under the circumstances, is in the memory that negative evidence may be of equal value to positive evidence. Without resorting to trickery, or to the use of unreliable sources, the lacking information could not

Foreword

be supplied. The material, therefore, has been left in every regard as the people of San Ildefonso would have it presented to the reading public.

At the same time, I should like to mention a change in the character of the information which may be apparent to students of Southwestern pottery types. Over a period of years, the stories of the finding of a potsherd at one of the sites on the Pajarito Plateau and of the reproduction of the sherd in a whole vessel by Mrs. Martínez have become confused with the development of black-on-black pottery decoration by Julián Martínez.

The stories are told in full later in this book, but perhaps a brief summary here will be helpful to the reader. Excavation of the archaeological sites on the Pajarito Plateau was begun by the School of American Research, under the direction of Dr. E. L. Hewett, in 1907, and was continued through the summer of 1910. During these years Julián Martínez was one of the Indians employed as laborers on the digs. Dr. Hewett, in order to settle some of the technical questions that had arisen in connection with pottery excavated from the sites, asked Julián's wife, María, to duplicate a particular potsherd, using the method of pottery-making then employed in San Ildefonso. It is interesting to note that not one of the surviving members of the field party, including Dr. Hewett and Mrs. Martínez, was able to describe that particular potsherd when asked to do so in the summer of 1946.

The invention of black-on-black pottery came much later, possibly during the autumn or winter of 1919. The first positively dated specimen of the ware was described in *El Palacio,* the bulletin of the Museum of New Mexico, in July, 1920. Since the issue went to press in June, the piece (shown in the drawing on p. 219) must have been acquired by the museum during the spring of 1920. It was evidently an early piece, for the body of the vessel was painted a matte black, with the design appearing in shiny black against the duller surface. This use of the two blacks lasted for a few years, and was first supplemented and eventually supplanted by the style now in general use, in which the design appears in matte black on a shiny black surface. It is the latter style which is usually meant by the phrase "San Ildefonso black-on-black ware," although the expression could correctly be applied to either type of decoration.

There is a great deal of information available on the history of the Southwest. To some extent recapitulation may be unnecessary. However, there is no point in trying to visualize the life of a contemporary pueblo without some review of the historical factors that have made it what it is.

San Ildefonso belongs to the group of Tewa-speaking pueblos which are located on the upper Río Grande, not far from Santa Fé, in New Mexico. The Tewa name of the pueblo is *p' owo'ge,* which can be translated as meaning "Place Where The Waters Meet." Geographically, San Ildefonso is near Santa Clara, San Juan, and Tesuque pueblos. It has maintained some interest in and connection with them and with the nearly abandoned Tewa-speaking pueblos of Nambé and Pojoaque. There is much interest in, and a certain feeling of relationship with, the Keresan-speaking pueblos of Cochití, San Felipe, Ácoma, and Santa Ana. Pueblos farther south and west are known and sometimes visited, but are not felt to be closely related to San Ildefonso.

Except for the Jicarilla Apache to the northwest, the people of San Ildefonso have little interest in or knowledge of non-Pueblo tribes. Those tribes outside their immediate vicinity are grouped vaguely under the headings of "Plains Indians," "California Indians," and "them Navajos." Even the Hopi are considered so remote as barely to be recognized as Pueblos.

The Pueblo peoples generally must have come into the Southwestern area from the north, since there is a corridor open for migration between the main range of the Rockies on the west and the Sangre de Cristo Mountains on the east. Exact data on migrations into the area are still not available. The occupation must have taken place at a very early date, since it is at present postulated that the Pueblo peoples are descended from the Basket Makers, who are, in turn, supposed to have descended from the people of the Anasazi root culture. Descent, incidentally, in a cultural and not a physical sense.

Within the Southwest there developed, prehistorically, one of the great agricultural areas of the New World. Game was apparently never very abundant in the region, and the subsistence of the people was from an early period largely based on their gardens and field crops. Foods were grown in sufficient quantities to support sedentary populations living in large walled towns. Since the life of the prehistoric Pueblo Indians was materially as secure as any contemporary existence in North America, and since seasonal agriculture provided the people with ample time for such activities, there was a high development of religion and the arts in the Southwestern towns. Wall

Foreword

paintings; carvings in bone, stone, and wood; textiles, and, above all, pottery developed and flourished there.

At once too much and too little is known about prehistoric Southwestern pottery to make brief discussion possible. Until the sites at present known and excavated have been summarized, until the taxonomy and ecology of the subject have been studied, compared, synthesized, and simplified, condensation of the innumerable specialized site reports is almost impossible.

All too briefly it may be said that Southwestern pottery arose from undecorated mud-daubings applied to baskets to make of them fireproof cooking vessels. The craft developed through phases of imprinted and incised decoration on unsupported vessels and reached its ceramic peak in the fine painted wares of the Classic Pueblo period about 1100 A.D. The wares then retrogressed artistically but advanced technically to the use of glaze paints in the century preceding the Spanish conquest, and declined sharply in the years between 1540 and 1915. In the latter year, a revivalistic movement which had started about 1895 crystallized as an economically important factor when Indian pottery became salable in the white market. The great increase in economic activity in the craft largely owes its impetus to the efforts of María Martínez and her husband, Julián.

Prehistorically, religion was the focal point of all Pueblo activities. The government of the Pueblos was fundamentally theocratic; social organization was integrated with ceremonialism; and the finest of the art objects were those intended to be ritualistically used. Religion was a motivating and centralizing force, controlling and dominating the life of the Pueblo Indian from the cradle to the grave. How long this scheme of life might have lasted uninterrupted is a matter for conjecture. Certainly those parts of the old culture which have survived the Spanish conquest seem still to have great vitality. The hold of religion on the Pueblo Indian of today is as great as when it was first reported by Villagra in 1560.

The Spaniards came into the Pueblo area fresh from their conquests of Mexico and Peru. They were still filled with the excitement of great riches taken from briefly resisting peoples. Tales of wealth in the country to the north, heard in Mexico, had further excited them and increased their desire to conquer the whole unmapped, unknown continent. Thinking that gold for the king and themselves, and souls for the church, were to be had for the taking in the new lands, the *conquistadores* worked their way northward.

xv

The resistance which they met at the hands of the Pueblo Indians, after early hospitality had been repaid with blows, must have surprised the Spaniards. In the country north of Mexico their way was seldom cleared by legends of a bearded white god who would bring happiness to his people. The conquerors of New Mexico did not have the help of a native Indian woman as guide and interpreter. Instead, after a long and wearing journey through desert country, the Spaniards found themselves facing a people who wanted neither to be converted nor to be plundered, and who fought to protect their rights.

The Spaniards invaded the Southwest in 1540, conquered it in the following years, and held it until 1680. In that year the Pueblos revolted, and the Indians were able to hold their own against the Spaniards until 1695, when the country was finally reconquered.

Physical defeat at the hands of the Spaniards after the Rebellion of 1680 seems to have driven many phases of Pueblo life underground. The church attempted to dominate the ready-made theocracy which it had found in the villages by substituting priests for caciques. The attempt was unsuccessful. The ultimate solution was the existence of two systems of religion side by side; each giving lip-service to the other, and each consolidating with its own what it wished of the other's rituals. Neither religion existed unchanged; neither admitted that changes had taken place.

One of the most striking of the changes was in the substitution of Spanish for Indian names in many of the pueblos. Each pueblo, at the time of the conquest, was given a patron saint, and many of the villages were named for their patrons. The Spanish names were used in official documents. In time, the Indians themselves used the Spanish names to the exclusion of the native ones, and it became a matter of importance to conceal the Indian names of the villages from casual visitors.

That the imposition of a new religion was easy is obviously not true. That so much of the old beliefs managed to survive is amazing. The combination of faiths did not take place without conflict. How deep-rooted the religious dualism has become in the Pueblo Indian of today, no one but himself can be sure. Ask a resident of almost any one of the northern pueblos what his religion is, and he will tell you that he is a "good Catholic." Watch his attendance at and participation in the old religious dances of his pueblo, and you will begin to wonder of just what elements his Catholicism consists. The convention which, in our society, forbids discussion of religion with per-

Foreword

sons outside our own families is one which it is well to observe in any pueblo.

Materially, the Indians were greatly affected by the Spanish conquest, and by the later coming of the Anglos. Bows and arrows and atlatls were replaced by firearms; fire-making by friction, by the use of flint and steel and matches; hand-woven by machine-woven textiles; portage on human backs, carriage by beasts of burden, and wheeled vehicles. Pottery, to be specific, was largely replaced by utensils and containers of metal or of commercially made crockery.

In many ways the Spaniards were as much affected by the Indians as the Indians were by the Spaniards. Because the existing system of agriculture and the plants grown had been developed in the area, and because seeds and roots for plants of European origin were unobtainable for many years after the conquest, the conquerors largely adopted the diet of the conquered. They have retained it to this day. What is listed on restaurant menus throughout the Southwest as "Spanish food" is, actually, Indian. Spanish men, who came without their own women, took Indian women as housekeepers and cooks. The women brought with them to their new homes their own utensils for the preparation of foods, and the cooking equipment of the Spanish kitchen became as Indian as its cuisine.

The government of the pueblos, during the period of Spanish occupation, seems to have been left largely in the Indians' own hands so far as local matters were concerned. Tribute and lip service were exacted, but the remoteness of the pueblos from the centers of Spanish occupation served as a preservative for many features of the culture that might otherwise have been lost. The same situation existed during the later period of Mexican control of the Southwest, after the Spaniards had given up their New World possessions.

It was not until the coming of the Anglos, in 1846, that there was another significant change in the general pattern of Pueblo life. With the arrival of the new conquerors, who were accustomed to dealing with other Indians as enemies and who regarded all Indians as hostiles, the processes of change were accelerated. The reservation-enclosure system was not introduced into the Pueblo country, for with the already sedentary population it was not needed; but a definite program of governmental control was at once instituted and enforced.

The history of the United States Indian Service in the nineteenth century is one of petty looting without the spurious dignity of wartime raiding. The Indians were in the hands of the government agents, and the agents were not generally selected for their integrity or for their interest in their charges. Here and there a single man stands out, usually a Philadelphia Friend, who was as much missionary as administrator, and who made a conscientious and partially successful effort to improve the conditions under which the Indians lived.

The Pueblo Indians did not endure the periods of starvation and despair that suddenly assailed the peoples of the plains, the Mississippi drainage, and the Atlantic seaboard. Rather, the Pueblos were subjected to a prolonged process of attrition. Children were sent away to government schools in other parts of the country, where they were lumped as "Indians" with children of other tribes. The young people, returning from these experiences, were out of touch with the old centralized life of the pueblos, and with its controls. The medicine men were at best discouraged, at worst forbidden, to practice their beliefs. Meanwhile, new diseases, brought by the whites, reduced the Indian population in numbers and in strength.

Their lands indeed the Pueblos partially retained, but the whites steadily encroached on the country around the villages. The newcomers stripped trees from the watersheds to produce lumber and floods; plowed up the earth to raise grain crops and sandstorms; and turned a vast section of the Southwest, hitherto fertile enough for at least a subsistence economy, into outright desert.

The investigations of the Meriam Committee, and the publication of its report to Secretary of the Interior Work in 1928, focused attention on the conditions then existing in the Southwest. Public opinion demanded the correction of such evils. Change came slowly, but by 1934, with the passage of the Indian Reorganization Act, it seemed that something was about to be done.

However, the Indian Reorganization Act did not bring about the millenium. Indian Service employees continued to be human beings—one who was of them, and should know, speaks! At one point in the proceedings it seemed that the Indians had simply been provided with more, and not with better, government workers. The Indians found themselves being asked to revise a social system that had served them well for over a thousand years and was still applicable to their way of life, simply to bring it into line with an act of Congress.

In a way, World War II saved the day. It reduced the number of Indian Service positions available and the number of persons willing and able to fill them. More and more the Indians were thrown back on themselves; more and more tribal councils took over the control and direction of their own business and finances. The return of the younger men to the pueblos, following the war, has served as an incentive for the revival of old dances and ceremonies. Always conservative, the Pueblos have experienced an increase in conservatism from the very forces that might have been expected to bring about a decrease in that quality.

All of these factors and movements are reflected in the life of San Ildefonso Pueblo, and of one woman of that pueblo, during the past sixty-five years or thereabout. María Montoya Martínez was born, probably, in 1881; she has no positive record of the year. Her birth was in a small, remote village at a time when the population of the town was largely self-sustaining.

Part of her girlhood was spent in St. Catherine's Indian School in Santa Fé. Her young womanhood was a struggle for survival, with her husband working at such odd jobs as he could find. Then, through her mastery of the old Pueblo craft of pottery, she found an economic way out—first for her family and then for her village. Through the ensuing years, while the population of San Ildefonso declined from about 150 persons to not more than 80, she became the most economically secure person in her group. Her success, example, and assistance were the incentives through which other women gained skill as craftsworkers and other families became financially independent. The population trend changed for the better; today San Ildefonso has a population of about 200 souls and is steadily growing.

On the debit side of her life, there was the introduction of liquor, which ultimately wrecked Julián Martínez. There was dissension within the pueblo, leading finally to a complete break between the factions and the building of what amounts to a new pueblo beside the old one. And there was the unending succession of white people who invaded her home and interrupted her work.

The influence of tourists on the Southwest cannot be overstated. Tourists are a major industry. Their attitude towards the Indians varies from fear, through frank curiosity, to patronizing friendship. Few indeed are the tourists who take the time and the trouble to realize that they are dealing with human beings in approaching the Indians. Even fewer, it would seem, are those who realize that all human beings are entitled to certain privacies and reticences in their dealings with others.

In presenting the following material, I have tried hard to be fair all around. Like any working ethnologist, I am prejudiced in favor of the people with whom I have worked and from whom I have gathered information. Like any working ethnologist, I should like to see an Indian culture in which I have become absorbed preserved intact from outside influences for time and eternity. Like any working ethnologist, I should like to build a wall around that culture, so that no prying eye but my own should ever watch its workings. And, like a rank sentimentalist, I should like to think that all was sweetness and light in San Ildefonso before the highway was built and there were cars, and tourists could come and go in the village at will and random.

Realistically, I know that all these things are impossible. To put such wishful thinking into effect would be to hold back time. That the Pueblo Indians might be willing to see it happen, I do not doubt; that it might be the best thing for them, I do doubt. For after all, no Indian culture existed on this continent even in prehistoric times without experiencing outside influences from other Indian cultures. To try to withdraw all outside influence from any one of them at this late date would be as foolish as it would be futile.

My thanks are due to many friends, an unusual number of them members of my own culture. In dealing with statements from living white people about events in Mrs. Martínez' life in which they participated, I have tried to act as I would in dealing with similar statements from Indian informants. Where there has been a conflict of information, the final statement which I have accepted has been Mrs. Martínez' own. Dates as given in chapter headings are probably approximate, except where they can be associated with such definite landmarks as world's fairs. Lacking exact information on her own birth date, Mrs. Martínez—and I—cannot be more specific.

The accurate drawings of authentic pieces of pottery done by Margaret Lefranc were made from the vessels themselves. Full information about each piece, including its present owner who permitted its reproduction, is given in the "Table of Pottery Shown in the Illustrations" in the back of the book.

First of all, I should like to thank María Martínez; Dionicio Sánchez, the former governor of the pueblo; and Luis Gonzales, the present governor. They, alone, made the work possible. Then there is the Committee on Rockefeller Grants for the Preparation of Materials on the History and Life of the Southwest at the University of Oklahoma, who made research funds available, and I should like to give my whole-hearted thanks to both the University and the Rockefeller

Foreword

Foundation. I must also thank Kenneth Chapman of the Laboratory of Anthropology, Santa Fé; Jesse Nusbaum, of the National Park Service; John Evans, formerly superintendent of the United Pueblos Indian Agency; the late Dr. E. L. Hewett, of the New Mexico State Museum; F. H. Douglas, of the Denver Art Museum; Leslie Spier, of the New Mexico State University; Jacques Cartier, of Pojoaque, New Mexico; Miss Amelia Elizabeth White, of Santa Fé; Mr. Chester Faris, of Albuquerque; and Miss Bella Weitzner, of the Museum of Natural History, New York City; Dr. Bertha Dutton of the School of American Research of the Museum of New Mexico, Santa Fé; and Te-Ata (Mrs. Clyde Fisher) of New York City—all of whom have made their time and information available to me. Margaret Schoonover and Sydney C. Marriott have given me invaluable editorial help, and Mrs. Schoonover also assisted in the collection of data on dances given in San Ildefonso during the period of research. And I should like to thank one other friend, whose name I may not mention, for furnishing, from a store of close personal experience, many of the small, warming anecdotes that bring field notes to life.

ALICE MARRIOTT

Santa Fé, New Mexico

María: THE POTTER OF SAN ILDEFONSO

Part I: The Clay Is Shaped

1. The Pueblo

So these things happened in the pueblo of San Ildefonso. The name that the village has now is Spanish, and its Tewa name is seldom spoken. The old people will always know it by that Indian name, and perhaps sometimes they will speak it, but there are always many things that old people know and reluctantly speak. It is not a large pueblo, even as pueblos go. Once it was larger than it is now; then for many years it was smaller. Within recent years, because of the things that have happened there, the pueblo has begun to regain its greatest size. San Ildefonso flourishes, and with the passing of time it grows strong again.

With the passing of time, too, San Ildefonso has at once opened its gates and drawn within itself. Therein lies the strength of the pueblo. The people of San Ildefonso know how to keep their secrets; they know how much to tell each questioner without telling to anyone all that they know.

The village is on the upper Río Grande, below the junction of that river with the Chama. There are hills around the pueblo, and to the west of it is the great Pajarito Plateau. From the plateau and the hills, streams come down to the Big River, so there is water for the ditches to take to the crops. All these things are important, for they make life possible in the pueblo.

In early summer the country is dry; in late summer the rains come and the earth is moist. Again, the fall is dry, and there is a time of waiting for the moisture of the winter snows. The crops and the life of San Ildefonso are planned around the times of rain. The religion of the people is designed to bring the rain when moisture is needed; the government of the people is planned to distribute the water and the land on which the water is to be used. When the rains fail, the crops fail; and the religion must be called upon to supply the moisture which is lacking.

5

At the time when María began to remember, there were few towns of any sort near the pueblo. Santa Fé, the state capital, was twenty miles away to the southeast, but it was twenty miles of rough and rocky road over which to travel on foot or horseback or by burro or wagon or oxcart. All travel in those days was slow-paced. In going to Santa Fé from San Ildefonso then, one passed through the Spanish villages of Ranchos and Jacona and the Tewa villages of Pojoaque and Tesuque. Nambé Pueblo lay well off the main road, and could be visited only by a journey along a side track.

To the north of San Ildefonso was the town of Española, and beyond it were the pueblos of Santa Clara and San Juan. East from Española there were Santa Cruz and Chimayó and Cordova and Truchas—Indian towns in their beginnings, Spanish villages since the time of living memory. North again and northeast were Picurís and Taos, the last pueblo outposts against the Indians of the plains. South and west down the river valley, the country changed and opened and fell away to a low plateau. Here were other pueblos, speaking a different language from the northern Tewan and Tanoan towns, the Keresan villages of San Felipe, Santa Ana, Santo Domingo, Ácoma, and Cochiti. To the northwest of San Ildefonso was the country of the Jicarilla Apache, a people inhospitable and to be avoided by strangers.

Almost all the country, in those days, was in the hands of the Indians or the Spaniards. The Indians had lived there first and the Spaniards had come in upon them. The Indians had been forced over to make room for the Spaniards, but still it seemed that there was land enough for everyone. Few Anglos came into the country beyond Santa Fé. When they did come, it was on business; they were missionaries or teachers for the most part. A few ranchers who tried to run cattle and sheep in the high mountain country failed in the attempt and returned to the easier plains. Woodcutters came sometimes, but there were no sawmills and no large-scale logging as yet. No one traveled the land for pleasure; the existence of those who lived in this country was too difficult to tempt seekers of amusement.

It was a country in monochrome—the gray-brown-green of clay hills sparsely covered with sage, yucca, and cactus. On the mountains the green deepened somewhat, but the gray and the brown were still there, softening and dulling the tones of piñones and junipers. The sky and the distance made the color blue, but imperceptibly the blue of the sky merged through the gray-blue of the distance to the green-

6

ish-blue shades of the earth. It was impossible to know exactly where one color began and another ended.

What it lacked in colors the country gained in forms. Mountains had been shot out of the earth when disintegrating forces beneath its crust exploded. Wind and water had gashed into the mountainsides and had torn away their tops. Peaks rose beyond flat-topped mesas; mesas sprang from the plains beside the rivers. Two qualities all forms had in common in this land: they were high and they were clean in outline.

Water had shaped the earth from the beginning, and men had shaped earth and water to make their houses and the towns that were walled with houses. Because the towns came out of the earth and were part of it, they hardly showed against the countryside. From even a slight distance, if one did not know where the houses were, it was hard to see them. Men and their works were inconspicuous against the land, as inconspicuous as human life against the life of mountains.

This was what shaped the way men lived their lives. They knew the smallness of the single man. They knew that man's strength grew if it were bonded with the strength of his fellows, as the blocks of adobe were bonded with one another to make a wall. Men built their towns with continuous walls, not only as defense against their enemies but also to gain the strength that came from binding together the friends that the walls enclosed.

The bonding together of men's separate strengths was what made life within the pueblo possible. Without this union, the care of the ditches and the fields could not be accomplished; the ceremonies that needed the participation of whole towns to be complete could not be performed. Human life depended as much on unity within as on rain without; when either was lacking, the towns fell apart and the people died, as had happened at Pecos Pueblo.

Within their walls, the people of San Ildefonso hardly knew wealth or the lack of it in white men's terms. Most of the men were farmers, whose lands gave them what they needed to feed their families, with a little left over to sell to the Spaniards or to each other for work or goods or cash. In the village of San Ildefonso there was a single store, run by a Spanish man, where the Indians could purchase foods which they did not raise and could buy a few other items, such as yard goods and hardware. Large purchases were made in Santa Fé or Española.

The lands on which the people of San Ildefonso lived had come down to them from their fathers. Once, perhaps, all their lands had been held in common. Now, in the eighteen eighties, some fields were still community lands, while others were owned by individuals. Each man, with his family, worked his own plot. It was his, to pass by inheritance, as he had received it, into the hands of his children. All of the men worked together on the irrigation ditches that brought water from the river to the fields.

If a man needed land or more land, he could apply to the governor and the council of the village. They, after considering the matter carefully, assigned to him a share of the community lands. As long as he lived, and worked it, that field was his. If he abandoned the holding, the land reverted to the community. A man could pass on his lands received from the community to his children, however, and from the time of their inheritance the property belonged to the family. It was a rare occurrence for anyone to abandon a field; the earth was too precious to be lightly used and then deserted.

In the same way a family received its house. Within the village the houses belonged to the women, and a woman could bequeath her house to her daughters. She might leave it all to one child, or she might divide the rooms of her house among her several daughters. In this way, with each daughter adding more rooms as she needed them, the houses and the village grew.

Together, as part of their work for the community, the women cared for the plaza and the church. Cleaning and whitewashing the church was left altogether in their hands. Each woman swept the ground before her house daily, and, as a group, the women cleaned the plaza in preparation for the dances. This was good fun for them. All the women shared alike in this work, talking and laughing together as they labored, and the job was quickly done. Only age or sickness excused a woman from doing her full share.

The men cleaned the great round kiva, which belonged to everyone, and which stood in the fields just to the south of the village. The land around the kiva was fenced to keep animals away from the building, and within the fences the women kept the earth swept clean.

All of the work for the community was planned and directed by the governor and the council, under the direction of the cacique. The councilmen met as the need arose, to discuss the work to be done and the plans to be made for the village. In the council meetings it was decided whether or not a new room might be added to a house; that no brush shades might be built or trees planted in the plaza; and whose turn it was to walk the ditches, clean the wells, or round up

8

straying animals that might destroy the crops. All these things, when they had been decided, were announced to the people. A man with a clear, strong voice went through the village calling out the news and proclaiming the new rules and the assigned tasks. When the people had heard what was planned, they undertook their shares in the work.

The governor and the council decided, too, who should take part in the dances, as well as which dances should be given at what times.

In this way they acted as a religious council, besides being the governing body, politically, of the village. The people had chosen the councilmen, and the men who had been selected acted for the people in reaching and declaring important decisions of all sorts.

Whether the council met as a religious body or as a political one, it was on equal terms with the church. Once San Ildefonso had a great church and a monastery. Missionaries went out from the village to San Juan and Santa Clara pueblos and to some Spanish communities. Then, bit by bit, as the population of San Ildefonso grew smaller from the effects of the new diseases brought by the conquerors, the church there declined. First the monastery was closed; then the parochial

9

school was withdrawn; then the church itself was closed except on two Sundays a month, when a priest came from Santa Cruz to say Mass there. The only other times when the church was open were when the priest was sent for to hold a wedding or a funeral.

Some of the priests loved the Indians and were loved by them in return. Others felt no warming towards the strange people among whom they worked. Their indifference, too, was returned. Always, beyond the man who was the priest, was the feeling of the Indians for the church that was a part of their community life. Its services had become so blended with their own services held in the kiva that it was sometimes hard for them to distinguish one form of worship from the other. There were dances and Spanish music in the churchyard on Christmas Day; there were men who wore their rosaries as necklaces with their dance costumes.

Life was never easy in San Ildefonso, but in the old days it could be gay. The people of the town were relaxed and merry. They did not need stimulants to feel their enjoyment. Their happiness and pleasure came from within themselves, and from the feeling that all the people were together enjoying the same things. Again men walled themselves in, with their feeling of unity and oneness with each other.

When the Spaniards first came, they could bring no wines, for they came in haste and with difficulty over long distances. The soil of the country gave no root-hold for grapes, and native wines were unknown there. The Anglo-Americans brought whiskey into the country, but because it was hard to transport and they had only a little of it, they kept it to themselves and the Indians scarcely knew its taste.

It was after their lands and crops had suffered from the destruction wrought by the Anglos that the men of San Ildefonso began to leave their homes and look for work outside the walls that had protected them all their lives. Those who went into the towns found that liquor could be bought there, not cheaply or easily or legally, but it could be bought. Because they who were used to the shelter of the group found themselves for the first time alone, the men began to drink. To become quickly unconscious was to forget quickly their fears and their aloneness.

The council and the governor and the women fought against the new habit. They were frightened and offended by the effects that it produced. In the old days, they said, men did not have this thing, nor did they need it. Come back to your own place, away from the towns where you feel the need of this pretended protection; come back to your village and be safe.

Some of the men returned, and some of them brought back the habit with them. Anglo men and Spaniards, who knew the hold of liquor on these men, moved into the country around the village and opened cantinas near at hand. With the habit, the men had brought back money to satisfy it. When their money was gone, the habit remained. The men went out again, to earn more money to buy more whiskey and wine. The Anglos and the Spaniards became rich.

This was worse than the new diseases. Sickness struck at life, but drinking struck at the roots of life. A man who was drunk could no longer share in the work or the prayers of the community. For many years, a man who drank was barred from the ceremonies of the kiva and from membership in the council. He was a weak man, no longer whole, no longer able to share the responsibilities, as he could not share the work of the people. Decisions were made for him, but he had no part in their making.

The time came when even this protective rule could not be enforced. Too many of the men drank; they could not be excluded from the council if it were to have its full number of members. They could not be left out of the ceremonies if the ceremonies were to be performed. Rather than give up their community as a whole, the people gave up a part of it. They were not happy. A man who was drunk, or who had recently been drunk, could not dance or sing as he should, and the performances of the ceremonies suffered. Still, it was better than having no ceremony at all. As the rule against drinking broke down, other regulations and customs, too, gave way. The rule against divorces, established by custom and reinforced by the church, was abandoned. Strangers whom the young people met at school or at work were married and were brought to live in the pueblo. The old pattern of interlocking families and their relationships was threatened.

Then came the worst disaster of all, for the very walls of the pueblo gave way at last. There was anger and dissension within the group; men did not speak to their brothers, and sisters turned their faces away from each other. A family, and then another family, and then a third closed the houses where they had lived facing the plaza and built themselves a new plaza, with the old round kiva as its center. The new plaza stood on privately owned land; the people who built there could do as they liked with their own. So they built two-story houses, and *portales,* and put fences around their yards, and the old village solidity was lost. The two towns stood side by side, neither complete without the other, yet each apart.

What caused the break no one but the people of San Ildefonso will ever truly know. Bits of the story have been related here and there; one outsider or another knows a fragment and can tell it, but the whole unhappy history has not yet been told outside of the pueblo. Perhaps all of it has not been told outside the council meetings, for there are men and women in San Ildefonso who deny all knowledge of the cause of the break.

Passion was at the root of it, and passion was the quality to which all previous pueblo life had denied existence. It came with liquor and from the same sources—living and being alone. Passion is a thing that a man builds up within himself, though he must release it against others. Whatever the passion was—anger, or jealousy, or ingrown hate—it came when much had been destroyed, and it threatened to tear down what little was left.

And yet there is still a pueblo of San Ildefonso. It still has a governor and a council, and, hidden away somewhere, a cacique. It still has community lands and a community church and a kiva that is shared by all the people. There is a government nurse and a government doctor to care for the health of the people; there is a government school, and the children do not have to go away from home for book learning until they have finished the sixth grade.

There is even work for money in the pueblo for those who want to do it: painting and pottery-making, or field work for pay for the painters and pottery-makers. More children are born than die in San Ildefonso, and the young men have come home from war now and want to stay where they are. There are even signs in some of the dances that the break in the wall may be mended, or that the old walls may be rebuilt to include the new plaza. Life is coming back, and there is still hope.

So, as has been said, these things happened in the pueblo of San Ildefonso, and nowhere else. And they happened to one woman, and to her because she lived there. This is what made her life, up to today, the time of her telling of it.

2. The Indian "Trader"
(1886

It was Tuesday, and on Tuesday Mother made cheese. She started early in the morning, using milk that had clabbered overnight, and worked quickly so that the cheese would be finished before the heat of the day set in. Her wooden molds stood in a row on the table beside the fire, three big molds and six little ones. When the cheese was set, she turned it out of the molds on a clean board. Usually there was more cheese than the family could use before she made more, on Friday.

There was never any doubt in Mother's mind about what she would do with the extra cheese. She went to the door of the house and called to her second daughter, "María, come here. I need you."

María was a good little girl. She came quickly from her play place by the irrigation ditch, and stood before her mother. "What is it, Mother? The cheese?"

"Yes, the cheese. I have four big ones and three little ones to sell."

Together they went through the short hallway and back to the kitchen. Mother took a basket down from the rafters, where it hung by its handle, and lined it with a clean cloth. She folded other freshly laundered cloths about the cheeses, and put the packages in the basket.

"Here you are, María. Ten cents for the little ones and twenty-five cents for the big ones."

"A shirt size for the little ones and a skirt size for the big ones." The child nodded gravely, and took the basket. Quietly, she left the house.

Going down the hill from the house to the village seemed like a long walk for a little girl five years old. The slope of the ground was irregular, in long and short steps, and María walked slowly, balancing her basket in her arms. This was her second trip with the cheeses. The first had been a week ago, after her sister Ana had announced that she would rather help her father in the alfalfa field than go around to people's houses with things to sell. Ana liked outdoor things better than she did people.

Thus it had been María's turn to help her mother. Selling had been fun the first time, and María did not see why Ana minded it. This time, when María knew just what she was doing, she walked very straight and held her head like a grown-up lady's. She would have liked to balance the basket on her head like a water jar, but since it was too wide and flat for that, she held it firmly in her arms before her. When she tried to carry the basket by its handle, it dragged at her arm and hurt her.

Down the hill, across the cleared space where the round kiva stood alone, and through the Gonzales family's fields she went, to the south wall of the pueblo. Here there was a passageway from the kiva to the plaza. During dance times the passage was closed to all but the dancers, but on other days people walked through it freely. María went through the coolness of its shade and came out into the plaza before the big cottonwood tree that had always been there. She turned to the right, and knocked on the door of the first house.

The woman who answered her knock smiled when she saw the child. "There is the Indian trader," she said, and held the door open. "Come in."

"My mother sent me to sell these," said María, opening the cloth that covered one of the cheeses.

"They look nice," said the woman. "Reyes always makes good cheese. How much are they?"

"A shirt size for the little ones and a skirt size for the big ones," María answered.

The woman frowned a little, and shook her head. "That's too bad," she said. "I have no money in the house to pay you. Perhaps your mother would trade with me?"

"I don't know," said María doubtfully. Her mother had said nothing about trading, and when she had gone out before, the people had had their money ready to give her.

"I have some corn meal that I just ground," said the woman, thoughtfully. "Perhaps Reyes would like to have that in exchange for a cheese."

"Maybe," said María. "I don't know."

"I'll tell you what," said the woman. "I'll give you the corn meal. Then if Reyes doesn't want it, she can send you back with it; and

North Plaza, Looking West

when my husband comes in from the fields this evening, I'll get some money from him to pay her."

"Well, all right," María agreed. "I'll tell my mother what you say."

The woman went into her kitchen and came back in a moment with a measure of corn meal and a clean cloth. She laid the cloth on the floor of her house and poured the meal on the cloth. María watched the woman doubtfully. The measure of meal was larger than the measure of cheese, but she was not sure that it was as big as the meal measure she had seen the Spanish man use in his store. She was still thinking about this when the woman tied the corners of the cloth tightly together and handed the bundle to her.

"There," said the woman. "Now I'll take one of these nice little cheeses, and that will be all right."

María felt better when the woman said that she would take one of the little cheeses. She was quite sure that there was not enough meal in the cloth to pay for a big cheese.

"Don't forget," said the woman, as she opened the door for the child to go, "if your mother isn't satisfied, she can send the meal back this evening."

"All right," answered María. "Good-bye."

"Good-bye," said the woman, and closed the door.

At the next house the people did not want any cheese and at the one beyond it there seemed to be nobody at home. María knocked and knocked at the door, but no one came. The basket of cheese was slippery and hard to hold, especially now that she had to carry the bag

15

of corn meal too. She tried slipping the knotted corners of the cloth over her arm, and that made carrying it a little easier, but then she had to hold the basket with the other arm. The basket slipped and slid, and before she got to the door of the fourth house she almost dropped her load. Her arms were so full that she had to kick on the door with her toe instead of knocking with her hands in the polite way. The door was opened so fast that she was afraid the woman of the house must have seen her kick instead of knock.

"Good morning," said this woman. "Come in. What have you today?"

"My mother made some cheese to sell," said María. She was relieved because the woman had not called her a trader, so maybe she would not want to trade. The child set down the bag of corn meal and opened the cloth over the basket again.

"I think I'd like a big one," said the woman, looking at the cheese carefully. "Are they the regular price?"

"The big ones are twenty-five cents," María told her. This time she did not say anything about the shirt-sized and the skirt-sized coins. They called the money that at home because for ten cents one could buy enough material at the store for a blouse, but the cloth for a skirt cost twenty-five cents. Maybe other people had not heard money talked about in that way.

"That's the regular price," said the woman. "Here, I'll take this one." She lifted a cheese out of the basket and laid it on a plate. Then she folded the cloth carefully and put it back in the basket. María was glad the woman did that. The first woman had kept the cloth. Now that she thought about it, María wondered if she should have asked to have the wrapping back.

This woman reached inside the folds of her blouse and took out a cloth package. She unwrapped it carefully, and from its folds she took a coin purse. She saw María watching her, and smiled.

"Always wrap your purse up, child," she said. "Cloth sticks to cloth, but leather will slip. If you wrap your purse, you'll always be sure you have it."

María nodded gravely and watched the woman open the purse and take out a coin. It was a whole twenty-five cents.

"I'll tie it in the cloth that was around the cheese," the woman said. "Then, when you get home, you can count your cloths and your coins, and you'll know that you have something to show your mother for each cheese."

The Indian "Trader"

Again María nodded. It seemed a good idea to her. The woman refolded the cloth and laid it in the basket.

"There you are," she said. Then, as María picked up her other bundle, the woman asked, "What is it that you have there?"

"Corn meal," said María. "Mrs. Gonzales traded it to me for a cheese."

"That was a good idea," said the woman. She smiled. "You must be a good trader," she said. "How big a cheese was it?"

"It was one of the little ones," María answered.

"You are a good trader," said the woman. "You must have fifteen cents' worth of meal there."

"Thank you for telling me," said María. "I have a bigger piece of cloth than the cheese was wrapped in, too."

"That's just like Mrs. Gonzales," said the woman. "She'd give away anything she had. She never was a good bargainer."

"Thank you," said María. "Good-bye."

"Good-bye," replied the woman.

After that, selling went better. People were at home in the next four houses, and María sold a cheese at each one. Everybody was polite and kind. They all asked her in, and they all said nice things about the cheese and about the way her mother made it. At the last house, when she had only one small cheese left, María found the man of the family at home. His wife was away.

"I don't know," said the man doubtfully, when María told him why she was there. "That's woman's business. I don't know whether my wife needs any cheese or not."

María shook her head. She had hoped that the people in this house would buy her cheese so that she could go home. The bag of meal was getting heavier and heavier. If all of the cheeses were out of the basket, she could put the bag in it, and that would make the carrying easier.

"I'll tell you what," the man said, seeing how unhappy she looked. "I like cheese, and I believe I could eat that little one all by myself. I haven't any money with me, because my wife took it when she went to the store, but I'll trade you something for your cheese. Will you do that?"

"I guess so," María said. "I already made one trade today."

"Well, all right then," said the man. "That's what we'll do. I'll trade you a silver button for the cheese. It's a good Navajo button and it's made out of a ten-cent piece, so I know it's worth as much as the cheese is. I had two on my moccasins, but I lost one, so you can have the other."

"Well, all right," said María. "I guess my mother will like that."

"I think she will," said the man. "You wait here and I'll get it."

He must have had to cut it off his moccasin, for he was gone for some time. When he brought the coin back, there were still sinew threads hanging through the loop on the back of the button.

"Here it is," said the man. "Now you can give me the cheese."

"Have you a plate?" asked María. All of the ladies had known that cheese had to go on a plate, but the man seemed to think she could put it right into his hand.

"A plate?" asked the man. "Yes. I'll get it."

He made a lot of noise moving the dishes around before he came back with the plate. María unwrapped the cheese, and put it on the plate that the man held out to her. Then she tied the silver button in the wrapping, and put the cloth in the basket. Last of all, she put the meal sack in on top of the cloths. She picked the whole pile up in both arms.

"Good-bye," she said to the man, and started home.

María walked slowly, because the basket with the meal was so heavy that it seemed to press her bare feet down into the gravel. She set the basket down twice on the ground, and sat down beside it to rest before she went on. Once she tried to put the basket on her head, but her arms were too short to lift and hold it. It was a wide, flaring basket that her mother had got from a Jicarilla Apache woman, and it was just too big for María to handle easily.

Little by little, though, María went towards home. Once some of the Spanish children who lived just outside the wall of the village called to her to come and play, but she shook her head.

"I have to take this home to my mother," she said.

A little girl of about María's own age stuck out her tongue and called María by her middle name, which she hated. "Toñita, Toñita, you're red-headed mad!" the Spanish girl yelled.

María wanted to stick her own tongue out in return. She could think of worse things to say. But she was doing something to help her mother now, and she did not want to spoil it. Still holding the basket before her in both arms, she walked solidly up the hill to home.

She knew her mother was in the kitchen, for the front door was closed. María went to the back door and kicked at it with her toe. Mother came to open the door.

"Well," Reyes said, "you got back soon. Did you sell all the cheese?"

"All but two," María said. She was beginning to worry about telling her mother what had happened.

"Two didn't sell?" asked her mother. "What was the matter?"

"I traded for them," said María. "You didn't tell me to do it, but the people said they hadn't any money, and they wanted the cheese."

"What did you trade?" her mother inquired.

"Well," said María, slowly, "for one I got a Navajo button, and for the other I got this corn meal. Mrs. Gonzales traded me the meal, and that's her cloth it's wrapped in."

"Was it for a big cheese or a little one?" her mother wanted to know.

"A little one."

The mother smiled. "You're a good trader," she said. "Wasn't it heavy to carry?"

"Yes," María answered. "Sometimes I almost dropped it."

"Well," said her mother, looking at the silver button, "this was a good trade, too. When people trade you little things like this you can carry them home. But when someone trades you something big, like the meal, leave it. Then your father or Ana can go in the evening and get the things and bring them home. You can't carry all these bundles, not if you're going into the trading business."

She smiled again, and María knew her mother was pleased.

"Do you like to trade?" her mother asked.

"Yes," said María solemnly, "I like it. When I grow up, I'm going to have a trading post of my own and sell things all the time."

But this time her mother shook her head. "That's a lot of work for a woman. You'd better wait till you have a man to help you with it, before you start."

3. The Games
(1886–1896

There were different games for the different seasons of the year, and they followed each other in order, just as the dances did. Thinking it over when she was about eight years old, María decided that it was a good way for things to be. Nobody could be good at everything, but most people could be good at something. The different games, coming in succession, gave everybody an even chance to win.

In spring, when the blossoms were gone from the fruit trees and the weather was warm through the days, María and Desidéria began to think about making playhouses. Each year they made their playhouses a little better and stronger and more like their mother's big house. Each year more of the other children, both Spanish and Indian, came to play with them. Their play place was so good that they themselves almost never left it. The playhouses were on the bank of the *acequia,* the irrigation ditch, above the stream of water. The girls had really built a sisters' house, with a wall between their rooms, and a place for each of them to keep her family. In one corner of each room they built a fireplace. At first the fireplaces were just piles of mud and little stones. Later, when they had learned how to do it from watching Mother, they built real fireplaces with chimneys. The sisters always wondered if the fireplaces would draw, but as their mother never let them have any matches, they did not get a chance to find out.

Their *metates* were set in the floor next to the fireplaces. It usually took the girls a long, sunny Saturday to get the right stones to use for *metates* and *manos.* On the hill behind the big house there was a place where the water rushed down after the spring and autumn rains. When the water came, it carried stones with it, turning them over and over and grinding them against the earth and each other. Even the grown women of the pueblo went to that place to get flat round stones to use as *manos,* and it was a perfect place to go to find play *metates.*

For furniture, Mother let the girls take a stool apiece from the kitchen, if the stools were returned at night. In the playhouses the stools were tables or chairs or benches or stools, depending on what the children needed for their housekeeping. María always wanted to build a sleeping bench of adobe along one wall of her room, like the sleeping bench in Grandmother's house, but Desidéria said that it would slow down the game too much to do such a lot of work. They eventually decided to call the playhouses their living rooms and the big house their bedroom, which solved the problem satisfactorily.

Father made them brooms for their houses each year. Mother had seven different kinds of brooms in her house, each for a different purpose, but the girls were contented with a soft sagebrush broom to sweep inside the play house and a stiff rabbit-brush broom to sweep their yards. They always began their games by sweeping the playhouses, just as Mother began her day's work by sweeping the big house. On Sunday working games were forbidden, for it was as wrong to play work as to do work on that day. Then the girls took their dolls and played as quietly as they could, trying to remember the rules about how to behave.

One Sunday, after they had just finished building their playhouses for that year, they always remembered. Everything was done, and their rooms looked fine. The family had all said the Rosary together, for there was no Mass in the church that week, and they had all eaten their breakfast afterwards. Mother and Ana had washed and put away the breakfast dishes. Mother always said that dishwashing was a duty, and that even on Sunday you were not excused from doing your duties. Bed-making was another duty, but when María and Desidéria had finished their share of it, they took their dolls and went out to the playhouses to play a Sunday game.

María's doll was made of a squirrel skin, which Tío Tilano had given her the winter before. Mother had stuffed it with straw and had sewn red flannel patches on its face to make eyes and a mouth. When the little gray skin had been wrapped in blankets, with its arms hanging out like a real baby's, and its red flannel eyes peeping over the wrappings, it made the finest doll that María ever had.

Desidéria's doll was an ear of red corn, with the hair left on it and the husks stripped away. Mother had painted eyes and mouth on it with green house paint, and Desidéria called the doll "White," not

"Red" for the color of the corn, because the green eyes made the doll look like a white woman's baby.

The children carried the dolls out to the playhouses and laid them down on the stools, which were to be baby beds for the time being. María sat down on the floor beside her baby, and patted it.

"Lie still and don't cry, Tree Climber," she said. "Your father has gone away to trade with the Comanches, and when he comes back he'll bring you salt and buffalo hides. Then you can have good *atole* and some new blankets."

Desidéria got the idea of the game. "That's what your father's done, too, White," she said. "Maybe we'll have company today, though. Maybe my older sister will come to visit us."

"We'll just sit quietly at home today, Tree Climber," María went on. "I expect my younger sister will be coming over to get some advice."

"I don't know what I need advice about," said Desidéria to her doll. "I have just as good a house as my older sister, and I know how to take care of it as well as she does."

"Well, younger sisters always have to be advised by older ones," said María.

Desidéria set her mouth stubbornly. María could tell by looking at her that Desidéria did not want any advice and was not going out to ask for it. María herself was sure that a younger sister should visit an older one, so she set her own mouth and sat still, too. They sat that way all morning. Once María got up and started to sweep her floor; then she remembered that it was Sunday and sat down again. Once Desidéria went over to her *metates* and began moving the *manos* around, and then she remembered in her turn, and went back and sat down facing the *acequia* as María did. They grew drowsy and sleepy sitting there and paying no attention to each other or to anything else.

"Knock at the door," someone said, and María jumped a foot. Ana was standing before her, with a shawl-wrapped bundle on her back.

"Come in," said María. Playing this way with the younger girls was not like Ana, but it was fun for María. Ana came into the playhouse and sat down on the floor by the fireplace.

"I'm a Navajo lady from way over west," she said. "I can't herd sheep on Sunday, so I brought my baby and came to visit my Pueblo friends." She reached up over her shoulder and brought her doll out of the folds of her shawl. It was a store doll that Ana's Spanish godmother had given her, the only store doll that any of the sisters had ever had. The doll was dressed in cotton print, with ruffles, just like a white girl.

"My," said María, "you've got a fine baby there, Navajo friend."

"Yes," said Ana, "I got her at the trading post in Santa Fé when I was coming here."

"Santa Fé isn't west, it's east," objected María, letting go of the game for a minute.

"Well, I came by there anyway," replied Ana. "I wanted to get some presents to bring to my Pueblo friends."

"That's nice, thank you," María said. "I'm glad you came, because I was getting lonesome. I thought my younger sister would be coming over to see me to get some advice, but she hasn't got here yet."

That was a chance for Desidéria to get into the game. She picked up her doll and put it in her shawl. Then she came and stood in front of María, as Ana had.

"Knock at the door," called Desidéria.

"Come in," said María. "Hello, sister. This is our Navajo friend. She came to visit us and bring us presents."

"That's nice," said Desidéria. "What are they?"

Ana laughed and began taking things out of her shawl. There was a package of *tortillas,* wrapped in a clean napkin, a big piece of dried meat, and a jar of milk.

"Mother looked out of the window and saw you," Ana explained.

"She thought that if you could sit there quietly, like grown ladies, and remember that it was Sunday, you could eat lunch out here like ladies, too. She said she thought most girls would be quarreling, if they tried to sit around like that with nothing to do. So she sent these things out so we could all have a party together."

"Well," said María, "we weren't quarreling. We weren't even talking to each other, so how could we quarrel?"

After that, their mother let them eat lunch in the playhouses very often. Sometimes Ana joined them, and sometimes other children were there visiting and stayed to lunch, too. Often they were alone. Ana had told them that they should take turns and eat first in one house and then in the other. She warned them to be careful not to start quarreling, or Mother might not let them have any more parties.

It was the playhouse lunches that put the idea of dishes into María's head. Every grown-up house had its own dishes, and did not have to borrow them for meals. When she spoke about the dishes to Desidéria, her sister, too, was pleased with the idea.

They first tried to make the dishes all by themselves, with clay that they dug out of the *acequia.* The moist clay had made good fireplaces, and mortar for setting their *metates,* but the girls could not get the mud to work right when they started on the dishes. They tried again and again, but their bowls and jars always cracked in drying.

"I'm going to ask Tía Nicolasa," said María finally. "She's always making pottery for other people, and I'll bet she knows how."

They found Tía Nicolasa at her home in the village, sitting on the ground on the shady side of her house. María told her what the trouble was.

"Sit down and watch me," said Tía Nicolasa, when she had heard. "Just watch and keep watching, and then we'll talk about it." So they sat and watched her while she made four yeast bowls. By that time it was noon.

"Come in the house and have lunch with me," said Tía Nicolasa then. "We'll talk about your pottery while we eat."

"Well," said María, watching her aunt pour milk into their cups, "I think I know one thing. You made a *tortilla* for the bottom of your bowl, and then you coiled clay sausages around the edges of it. We started with the sausages, and coiled them around from the middle of the bottom out. We didn't make any *tortillas.* It was all right when the sausages were wet, but they didn't stick together when they got dry."

24

The Games

"Did you mix anything with your clay?" Tía Nicolasa asked, handing Desidéria another *tortilla*—a real one, not a clay one.

"No," answered Desidéria with her mouth full, "we didn't. It was just mud."

"Don't talk till you finish that bite, or you'll choke," Tía Nicolasa cautioned her. "Well, you've seen your mother mix plaster for the walls, haven't you? How did she make it?"

"She put in clay and water and straw," said María. She stopped and looked at her aunt. "That's what you mean? We ought to put straw in our mud?"

"Not straw," replied Tía Nicolasa, seriously. "That would burn out if you ever fired your pottery. But you do need something to separate the little bits of clay and spread them out so that the heat will get to them evenly. Sand is the best thing for that. Help me wash these dishes, now, and then I'll help you make some."

When they all went back outside, Tía Nicolasa's first act was to pick up all the things she worked with and carry them around to the other side of the house.

"If you make your pottery in the shade instead of in the sun, it will stay damp and dry out while you're working on it," she told them. "Now, each of you take a piece of clay, and make a *tortilla* for the bottom of a bowl."

When the *tortillas* were patted out, not too thin, but flat, Tía Nicolasa showed them the next step. She took a small piece of clay, and spun it between her hands as if she were twisting a cord to make it stronger.

"This part takes practice," she said. "You'll have to work to learn it. Your sausage should be just long enough to go around the edge of the *tortilla*. When you get it fitted right, and its ends joined, you put another one on top of it. You keep on going up as high as you want your bowl to be. Keep moving it around, so the joins won't show or all come in the same place up the side. Then I'll show you the next step."

"My," said María, beginning to make her sausage, "you're just like a school teacher, Tía. You know just what to do."

"I have taught a good many people," answered Tía Nicolasa. "A lot of the young women have come to me to learn, just the way that I learned from Grandmother. If you know how to do a thing, you can show other people. That's all teaching is."

"Did you ever say you wouldn't teach them?" María asked.

"I never did," her aunt assured her. "If you know something, it's wrong to hold it back from somebody else that wants to know, too. Remember that, if anybody ever asks you for help when you're grown up."

"I will remember," said María, solemnly. "My bowl's big enough now, I think. What do I do next?"

"Next you dip your fingers in water and smooth the bowl, inside and out, till none of the sausages show," said Tía Nicolasa. "When you get that done, you can take a piece of sharp stone and smooth the bowl some more. I use a gourd to scrape my pottery down, but you'd better use a stone first while you're learning. Be careful not to get a piece that's sharp enough to cut."

It took the girls all afternoon to make one straight-sided bowl apiece, but when they had finished, Tía Nicolasa said the bowls were good.

"The next ones will go more quickly," she assured them. "After you learn on these, you can start making bowls that are curved in at the top, but I think these are good enough for play dishes."

"May we fire them?" María asked.

"I don't think you'll need to," Tía Nicolasa replied. "Leave them out in the shade for two days and in the sun for two days, and I think they'll get hard enough to play with. Maybe later on, when you've made some more bowls for practice, you can learn to fire them."

Most of that summer the girls spent in making pottery. They practiced on the straight-sided bowls and then on the bowls with curved tops. After she had made several of the latter, María went to work one morning on a jar with a tall neck. She was surprised when it turned out just the way she wanted it to be. That afternoon she took the jar down to the village to show to Tía Nicolasa.

"It's fine," said Tía Nicolasa, "it's just fine. You're going to be a good potter when you grow up. This is a real jar, and I'm going to fire it with some of my pottery day after tomorrow."

"May I come and watch?" María asked. Her breath was short and quick with excitement. She was going to have a real jar fired. She had made a jar, and Tía Nicolasa was going to fire it.

"Yes," said Tía Nicolasa, "you have the right to help fire your own pottery."

That was how María learned to build a pottery fire, and how to sprinkle corn meal and to say a prayer before she lighted the cedar-bark kindling. It started as part of playing, but she was learning, too.

The Games

Her jar came out just right, though two of Tía Nicolasa's curved bowls were cracked down their sides.

"That's all right," said Tía Nicolasa, when Maria looked sad about the spoiled bowls. "We always count on losing one or two pieces in each firing. You'll always have good luck with yours, though, because your first piece turned out right. What are you going to do with it?"

"I'd like to give it to Mother," María replied, "that is, if she'd like to have it."

"I think she would," Tía Nicolasa assured her niece. "And I think that is the right thing to do with it, to give it away. And remember, María," she went on, "this isn't just a game. You may forget about it for a while, after school opens and the winter begins and it's too cold to work at pottery. But when summer comes, you should go back to it. You will make a good potter if you go on working."

"Yes, Tía," María said gravely, as she started to go home with her jar.

Mother was as pleased with the jar as Tía Nicolasa had been. She praised and admired it, and then she set it up in the *nicho* above the fireplace, where they could all look at it. María was happy about making something that her mother liked.

Soon afterward school opened again, and it was time for new games. The children played tag a lot, and the teacher taught them some games that white children played: hide-and-go-seek, and baseball, and blindman's buff. María did not like the last one very well, and Desidéria cried the first time they tied a handkerchief over her eyes. After a while the children just stopped playing that game and forgot about it.

The real fun that came in the winter was storytelling. You could hardly call it a game, because the older people took part in it and enjoyed it as much as the children. This was the part of the year when the farm work was finished, when the fruits and vegetables were dried and put away, and when everyone had time to sit by the fire in the evenings and to be happy together.

The best storytellers in the pueblo were old Jaime and his wife, Marta. Soon after the first snowfall of the winter, Mother would say, "Girls, go down to the village and ask the old people to come and visit us after supper."

Sometimes only one of the girls went; sometimes all three of the older sisters would run down the hill together, racing to see who could beat the wind to the shelter at the bottom of the slope. At the house in the village, old Jaime always said the same thing, "I'd like to go, but my wife's old and cranky, so maybe she won't let me."

And old Marta, when she heard him, would pout her lips together and blow her breath through them, and say, "He's so old himself he may not be able to walk up the hill, but I'll help him all I can."

Then the old people would both laugh, and Jaime would say, "We will be very happy to come. Please tell your mother so."

After dinner, when the dishes were washed, the whole family would sit down before the fire. Then Mother would get up and go over to the window and look out. "There they come," she would say. "I can see their torches shining as they walk up the hill."

When the old people came into the room, bringing the good smell of cold air with them, the first thing they did was to hand their pine-splinter torches to Father. He would knock the flames off into the fireplace and lay the torches on the hearth, where the old people could pick them up and use them again on the way home.

The stories that could be told at home in the winter evenings were different from the stories that could be told in the kiva. The home stories were about birds and animals, not about real men and women and gods. The home stories were called the "little stories," and each of them had songs to be sung as the story went along. Each story ended with a lesson for the children.

Old Jaime always told the first story and sang its songs. Then, when he had explained the lesson that went with the story, he would point with his lips at Father, and say, "You're next," and Father would tell a story in his turn. Then he would point at the next teller, but with Father you never knew who the next one would be. He might choose old Marta, or one of the girls, or Mother. It was always part of the fun to try to guess whom he would choose. Then, after three or four stories had been told, Mother would say, "That's enough for now. We'll have more later. Girls, come and help me."

That was the signal for them all to go into the kitchen and bring in bowls of popcorn, and plates of *biscochitos,* and a pot of coffee with milk and sugar in it. While the women of the family were bringing in their part of the food, Father usually went out to the storehouse and brought back one of the watermelons that he had saved for the winter. He never would cut the melon, though. He said that Mother did that better, and she did. She always made the slices come out even, and all just the same size.

After they had eaten the good food, old Marta always tied up her watermelon seeds in her handkerchief to take home to plant. She never had any luck raising winter melons, but she always tried. The girls would pick the hard kernels, that hadn't popped, out of the bottom of the popcorn bowl, and put them in their pockets to take to school in the morning to eat at recess. That, too, was part of the winter fun.

Then the storytelling would begin again, and go on until María and Desidéria began to nod by the fire, and Mother said, "That's enough for tonight. Everybody is getting tired. Too many good things to hear are like too many good things to eat. You should have just a few of them at a time."

"You're right, Reyes," old Jaime would answer, "and old people are just like children. They like to hear stories, but they like to sleep, too. Good night, and many thanks to everybody."

And the old people would pick up their torches and go down the hill towards home.

4. The Pilgrimage
(1890

All the time that María was sick, it seemed to her that there was something her mother was trying to tell her. Over and over again, through the heat of fever, she felt the voice in her mind rather than heard it in her ears. It was her mother's voice, but there was something different about it. The words came from far away, so far away that María could not distinguish them. She only knew that there was a thought that her mother wanted to give her. When María was getting better and the shapes of the furniture in the room became clear to her eyes, she asked her mother about the memory that had remained from her sickness.

"What were you trying to tell me all the time?"

Her mother looked at the child, queerly. "How did you know I was trying to tell you anything? You were too sick to know. You didn't even hear me when I tried to wake you to give you medicine."

"I knew," María said. "Maybe not about the medicine. But you wanted to tell me something else."

Her mother sat down quietly beside the bed. "Yes, I did. There was something I thought you ought to know."

"What was it, Mother?"

"I made a promise for you while you were sick."

María was excited. To have had a promise made for her meant that she must have been very sick. "Did I almost die, Mother? Was that what you made the promise about?"

"Hush," said her mother, sternly. "You don't know what dying is. Ten years old is too young to know."

"Yes, but I do know, Mother. It's like when the little puppy died last spring. When there isn't anything there to make him alive. Isn't that it?"

"That's it," said Reyes, "but you see, you didn't die. So you will have to keep the promise I made for you."

"Was it to dance?"

The Pilgrimage

"No, it wasn't to dance. It wasn't that kind of promise."

"What kind was it then, Mother?"

"It was to go to Chimayó. To the Sanctuario of the Santo Niño. He's the one that takes care of children and is good to them. I promised you would go there and make thanks to him yourself, as soon as you were able."

María was quiet, looking at her mother's face against the white wall. Dancing would have been fun. If people made a promise to dance, it meant going to another pueblo on its saint's day, and dancing with the strange people who lived there. A pilgrimage to Chimayó did not sound like so much fun, but it might be exciting.

"I never went to Chimayó. You and Father always leave us at home when you go there. What's it like?"

"It's in the mountains, a long way off. You'll see when you get there."

"When do we go?"

Her mother laughed. "Not yet. Not for a long while yet. Wait till you're strong enough to get out of bed, first, before you think about walking to Chimayó."

"Is Ana going, too?"

"Not with you. Not this time. This is your pilgrimage."

All the time that María was getting better, she thought about her pilgrimage. She had heard the older people talk of such trips, and she knew that when you made a pilgrimage, it was a special trip somewhere to say thanks to a saint who had helped you. What she did not know was what you did at the end of the pilgrimage. Her mother had said that she would walk to Chimayó. María was puzzled about what would happen at the end of the walk.

There was snow on the ground outside María's window, and she could lie in bed and see the footprints people passing by the house had made in the snow. María began to watch the marks, and they took on a sort of meaning for her that she did not tell to anyone. She would look out every morning, to see which way the first footprints of the day were pointed. They were always going north, so María knew that she would go to Chimayó. It was not until a long time afterwards that she realized that the footprints always pointed north because her father made them on his way to the well on the north side of the house.

As the snow melted, and María could no longer see the footprints in the snow, she grew better and stronger and more able to make footprints herself. The spotted sickness had left her without scars, and

31

she was sure that the Santo Niño had saved her from the marks. There was a man in the village who had had the same sickness so badly when he was a young boy that he had lost his eyesight. María was glad that had not happened to her. Not to have been able to see footprints in the snow, or the buds on the apple boughs, would have been the worst thing that could have happened.

After she was able to go outside and play, María began to forget about her pilgrimage. There were the new spring lambs and kids to play with, and she had a share of the garden work to do. Then the pueblo got ready for Easter, and there was the Easter dance, and time began to go on, with the days running into each other and melting, like the other days before she had been sick.

It was early June, with warm days and cool nights, when her mother reminded María of the pilgrimage. "I want you to say your Rosary tonight, and the next three nights, for sure," she said. "The fourth day will be Friday, and then we'll go to Chimayó."

"Who's going? All of us?" María wanted to know.

"You and your father are going," said her mother. "You two will walk. And Tío Tilano will drive me in the wagon, to meet you at the Sanctuario. The other girls will have to stay at home. This is your pilgrimage."

For the whole of the next three days, María felt that she was some-body a little special. She, not Ana or Desidéria, was going on the pilgrimage to Chimayó. Ana and Desidéria had not been sick. They had not nearly died. Mother had not had to make a promise about them. All those things had happened to her, and to nobody else. She wanted to tell people about it, particularly her sisters, but she was afraid that would not be polite. Instead, she told the Santo Niño about it privately, each night when she had finished her Rosary. It had to be private telling, for Mother was kneeling beside her, saying her Rosary, too. María knew what her mother thought about people who tried to be important, even to themselves. She hoped that the Santo Niño would understand and not think that she wanted to be rude to him.

On Friday morning, Mother wakened María very early. There was the beginning of color in the sky, but no real light yet showed.

"Come quickly and drink your milk," Mother said. "When you make a pilgrimage, you should fast from the time of sunrise till the ending of the day."

Father was sitting at the kitchen table, drinking coffee with milk in it and eating *tortillas*.

The Pilgrimage

"That's right for older people, Reyes," he said, "but not for this little one. She should eat now, and she should have something to eat while she's walking. We're making the pilgrimage because her life and health were saved, and we don't want her to get sick all over again while she's doing it."

"I can fast, Father," María said.

"I know you can," Father answered. "Anybody can fast if the need and the faith are great enough. But I think sometimes faith can be strengthened by eating a little."

Mother nodded. "I believe you're right," she said to Father. "We'll make it a fast of abstinence, not a total fast. She shall have bread and water to eat on the way, and nothing else."

"That will be right," Father said. "I'll make a total fast myself, in thanks to the Santo Niño. He's a good saint, and being a child himself, he understands that children get hungry."

They gave María milk with coffee in it, then, and white flour *tortillas,* and some of Mother's white whole-milk cheese. María finished her breakfast just as the sun rose, and went to dress. Mother told her to wear her best dress and the high white moccasin boots that were usually saved for Mass and for dances. Mother braided María's hair, and tied it in a knot at the back of her neck, like a grown-up lady's. Then Mother put three more white flour *tortillas* in a little basket with a bottle of water, and María and Father were ready to start out.

"Where is your rosary?" Mother asked as they reached the door, and María turned back quickly to get it. The rosary was the one thing she had almost forgotten, and the one thing she most needed to be a pilgrim. She shook her head a little, and then fell into step beside her father, who was carrying the basket on his arm.

They went along the east side of the village, and took the path that went through an arroyo on the east side of the Black Mesa. Parts of the path were stony, and parts of it were thick with sand. All of the way was uphill or downhill, over rough ground. Father walked steadily, without speaking aloud. He held his rosary in his hand, and his lips were making the movements of prayers. María held her own rosary and prayed, too. Presently Father began to repeat the prayers aloud.

So they went over the hard path, praying together in time like drumbeats. María walked carefully at first, so as not to soil her white moccasins, or catch her best purple dress on the cactus beside the trail.

Presently she forgot about her clothes, but the Santo Niño must have been with them, for nothing happened to spoil her dress or her boots.

When the rocks had drawn their shadows under them to mark the noon time, they came to an old tree.

"Here we can sit down," Father said.

When they were seated in the shade, he handed María the basket. "Now you can eat and drink."

"Is it right to, Father? Are you sure it's right?"

"It's all right," Father answered. "The kiva dancers are allowed to eat and drink at noon sometimes. What you are doing is like religious dancing. For you to eat and drink a little won't spoil your prayers."

"Will you eat something?"

"My prayers are different," said Father quietly. "They aren't a child's prayers. I have to follow other rules."

It was a little embarrassing at first, eating and drinking alone, sitting beside somebody else. But Father sat with his eyes on the hills before them and did not look at her, and presently the embarrassment went away. María finished all three *tortillas* and drank the water. Then she put the bottle back in the basket. Her father held out his hand for it.

"I can carry it for a while," María said.

Her father nodded. "All right. It's your basket. You can take your turn carrying it."

Through the afternoon heat they walked steadily, not too fast, but not too slowly. The sun was midway down the sky when they came to the town of Chimayó, and went along the road that edged its houses. The Sanctuario was at the east end of the town, and the road came in to it from the west. María wondered once if there were people watching them from the houses as they walked, but Father had started saying the Rosary again, and she joined him under her breath. Wrapped in their prayers, they never knew whether there were people in the town to look at them.

The wagon was waiting in front of the Sanctuario, under the great cottonwood trees that arched over its gate. Mother and Tío Tilano got down from its seat, and came to meet them. They, too, held their rosaries in their hands, and when they heard Father and María praying, they joined in. Together, they all four finished the Rosary. Then Mother held out her hand to María.

"I have things in the wagon for you," she said. "They are your offerings."

34

The Sanctuario

She took a bundle from the back of the wagon, and she and María went towards the carved doors of the old church. A small bell hung on a wire there, and Mother put out her hand and set the bell to ringing gently. It hardly rang, but the soft tap was enough. A Spanish man, so old that he was bent, came around the corner of the building.

"Do you want to go in?" he asked, and when Mother nodded, he took a bunch of keys that hung from his belt, selected one of them, and unlocked the door. Slowly one leaf of the door swung inward, and they went inside.

There were votive lights blooming like yellow yucca flowers on an iron stand before the altar, as the old man led María and her mother down the aisle. Then the man turned to his left and unlocked a grilled iron door beside the altar. There was darkness behind the door—darkness and a sense of depth. Mother drew María towards it. The child smelled an earthen dampness, like the darkness of the storeroom at home, and it surprised her. Most churches smelled of dry dust, not wet.

"There are steps going down," said Mother. "You must go down them. When you get to the bottom, take off all your clothes. Don't be afraid, because nobody can see you. Then take this holy medal and scrape off the earth on the sides of the hole. Rub the earth all over your body. That's what makes you well."

"Will you go with me?" María asked.

"Just you can go. This is your pilgrimage. After you have rubbed yourself with the sacred earth and dressed again, take the medal and dig out enough earth to fill your water bottle. That much you can take home with you, to drink there to make you well. While you are doing this, you should say your 'Our Father.' Don't think about any thing but your prayers and the Santo Niño."

So this was what you did at the end of a pilgrimage! María did not mean to think of other things or to disobey her mother and possibly be rude to the Santo Niño, but she was too surprised to stop thinking. She had not expected a hole in the ground or that she would have to go down into it alone. Carefully, feeling her way with her toes, she went down the four steps behind the grill. She knew she must be staining her white moccasins, but perhaps the stains of the sacred earth would not show when she came out.

"Say your prayers aloud so I can hear them," María heard her mother's voice say above her.

María never knew how long she stayed in the hole under the

church. She undressed and rubbed herself with earth and dressed again. She filled the water bottle, cautiously feeling along the wall with the medal to loosen the earth. Many people must have been there before her, for she could feel with the tips of her fingers the deep scratches they had left in the walls of the pit.

Her mother was waiting, kneeling just outside the grill when the child came out. The bundle lay on the ground beside the woman, and a dark shawl covered her head. When she saw María, Mother reached out, without rising, and opened the bundle.

"These things are your offerings," she said. "You can take them to the altar and leave them there."

The old Spanish man stood at the head of the church aisle. He nodded without speaking when he saw María coming towards him and led the way to the altar and its wreaths of blooming lights.

"You can put the things down here," he said in Spanish.

There was cloth in the bundle, purple cloth, like María's own best dress. There was a little black rosary and a big piece of buckskin, and there were three ten-cent pieces. The old man watched while the child laid down her gifts, and when he saw the money, he nodded.

"That's the best offering," he said. He seemed to be speaking to himself. "That's the offering that can be used for anything. The others you have to plan how to use, but that one you can fit into your plans."

María did not understand. She left the offerings and crossed herself in front of the carved and painted figure of the Santo Niño that stood on the great altar. Then she turned and walked back to her mother, who was kneeling now in the aisle of the church. From the side aisle on the left of the church, Father and Tío Tilano also rose. Together they all four went out into the sunset.

"Give me the bottle of earth, please," Mother said, and María handed it to her.

"What will you do with it?" she asked.

"You will have to mix it in water and drink it before breakfast every morning for the next four days," her mother answered. "This is good earth. The Indians knew about it and how to use it a long time ago. Then the padres came and learned about its power, and the Santo Niño came and told them what to do, so they built the church here. Everybody knows that the earth is good. It makes everyone well who drinks it, for the rest of his life."

The old Spanish man had come out of the church and stood

listening. He shook his head at Mother. "The Santo Niño makes the people well," he said. "He could do it on a mud-pile. He doesn't need any special Indian earth."

Father spoke quickly. "Both together make the people well," he said. He was a man who hated even a little quarreling. "Faith in the earth and faith in the Santo Niño go together, and both heal the sick. Each is good, but together both are better."

The old Spanish man nodded, doubtfully. "Well, the padres say that faith without works is dead," he answered. Then he looked at them directly. "Where will you all sleep tonight?" he asked. "You can't go back in the dark."

"We have friends here, up on the hill," said Father. "We plan to stay with José Trujillo and his wife."

"Go with God, then," said the old man. "José and his wife eat and sleep early. You'll have to hurry to catch them before they go to bed."

Tío Tilano lifted María into the back of the wagon, while the grownups crowded together on the seat. The child sat with her legs stuck straight out in front of her. Anxiously, she looked at the toes of her white moccasins. She had been right. The sacred earth had not left upon them a stain that showed to the eye.

5. The Visit
(1890

At the time when María made her pilgrimage to Chimayó, she was ten years old. It was really the first time that she had been away from home. She talked about it and talked about it after she got back to the pueblo, and Ana and Desidéria began to feel discontented and unhappy because they never had been anywhere and María had.

Mother and Father let the girls talk, without saying anything themselves, and after a while everybody began to forget about it. María and Desidéria played in their playhouses and learned to make pottery from Tía Nicolasa during the summer. Then it was fall, and school opened, and the children were busy about that. So the time went on, and the pilgrimage to Chimayó moved from the front to the back of María's mind. It became something that she thought about only a little, and then to wonder whether it had really happened.

So the family went through the year, and it was like any other year, till they came to the next spring. Then one morning Mother asked Ana, "When does the Easter school vacation start?"

Ana was surprised, because she thought that Mother knew when as well as the girls did, but she answered, "On Monday of Holy Week."

"Then we'll have time," said Mother, but she didn't say for what.

Palm Sunday was always exciting in the pueblo, because sometimes there was a dance and always there was a procession. The procession came during Mass, and the children loved it because then they could get up and march around the churchyard, singing. It made a good break in the long kneeling. When they went back inside the church, carrying green branches and waving them, everybody felt good and rested. When the Mass began again, it meant something extra.

After they had come home from Mass on Palm Sunday and were eating their feast-day meal of tamales and chili sauce, Mother added

39

to the general excitement of the day. She said, "Your father and I have been making a plan for this week. Since there is no school, we will all go up to Chimayó, and visit our Spanish friends there."

"Oh, Mother!" the children said, in chorus.

"We'll start tomorrow morning," Mother went on, "and we'll stay there until Good Friday. Then we'll come back that day, and have Saturday to get the house ready for Easter. We can have a good visit, and then everybody will have been to Chimayó."

"Are we going to the Sanctuario?" asked María. She felt as if she could not go to Chimayó without going to the old church. In some way the Sanctuario was especially hers.

"We'll go to see it, at least," Mother replied.

"What else will we do?" Desidéria inquired.

"Visit our friends," said Mother.

"What about the garden?" Ana demanded.

"Oh," said Father, "the garden can get along without us for a few days. Even I am willing to leave the garden right now, after the ditches have been cleaned and opened."

"All right," said Ana, but she said it a little doubtfully.

"What do we have to do to get ready, Mother?" María asked.

"Well," said Mother, "I'd like to take some dried meat and some corn meal for presents to our friends."

"Is the meal ground?" asked Desidéria.

"No," said Mother. "I don't like to work on Sundays, but I thought maybe I'd grind some of it this afternoon, and the rest early tomorrow morning before we start."

"Let us help you," María suggested. "We can do the coarse grinding anyway. Then it will all be ready sooner."

"That's good," Mother agreed. "Then it will be a present from all of us, because we will all have worked on it."

They hurried with the dishes. It was María's and Desidéria's turn to do dish-washing, and they had never worked faster. Mother took care of baby Juanita, and Ana started right in with the coarse *metate*, breaking up the corn and getting it ready for finer grinding. By the time the baby had been fed and washed and put back in her swing-cradle, María and Desidéria, like Mother, were ready to help Ana.

"You two younger girls can take turns with the middle *metate*," said Mother. "I'll take the fine one. That way the work will be evenly divided. María can grind first."

It was hard work grinding corn, but it was fun, too, because they all sang as they worked and the grinding kept time to the singing. That made the work go faster and more smoothly. By supper time they had a big sackful of ground meal, which Mother said was enough to take with them.

They had *atole* and milk for supper, and Mother sent the girls to bed early, while she filled a sack with dried meat. "We want to be ready to start right after breakfast," she explained.

Going to Chimayó by road in the wagon was very different from going there on foot through the back country, María discovered. Their father and mother rode on the seat of the wagon, Mother with Juanita on her lap or in her arms. The three older girls sat on the floor of the wagon, with the sacks of corn meal and dried meat and the two bundles of spare clothes that Mother had brought along for everybody.

When you were walking, María thought, the country unfolded and opened before you, and it was like opening a book one page at a time. Now, as she sat in the wagon and faced backwards, the country seemed to close itself together as she watched. You never saw new things beginning, but always saw them ending as they shut in on themselves. Watching the landscape made her a little dizzy, like starting at the end of a book and letting the pages fall together one at a time. Presently she turned around and sat facing the side of the wagon. Then it was better, because things moved from one side to the other before her eyes. They neither opened nor closed themselves, but passed before her and were gone.

They went on across the country. First there was the river-bottom road, and that was green and fertile and familiar, winding through Ranchos and Jacona and then to Pojoaque, with tree shadows making the family cooler and sun making them warmer as they moved. Then they came out on the main road that went straight across the country from Pojoaque to Santa Cruz. After a while they came to Santa Cruz itself, which was a bigger town than any they had seen so far on the trip. It was the biggest town María had ever seen.

There was a plaza in the middle of Santa Cruz, with the church and convent filling its west side, and houses around the other three. There were trees in the plaza, and Father stopped the horses under one of them. There they all ate their lunch and rested. María thought again about her pilgrimage to Chimayó, because they had *tortillas* and milk for lunch this time, too. She began to wonder if you ever ate anything but *tortillas* when you were going to Chimayó.

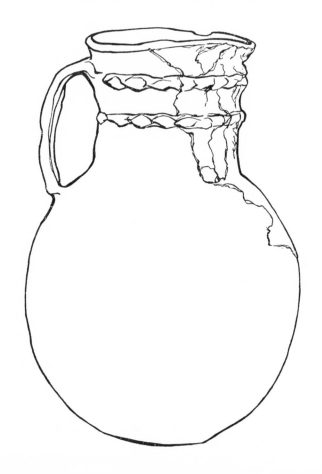

When they were rested and ready, they went on again. Now the road began to wind up into the mountains. There were houses by the roadside, not set close together like a village but strung out along the strip of land between the road and the hills on one side and the road and the river on the other.

There was nothing to see that María could recognize until they crossed a wide arroyo, and she remembered the place where she and Father had come out of the back road to the main one. María was sure this was the same spot, for on a hill directly facing the arroyo there was a square, solid building without windows, and with a great wooden cross standing before it. Nobody had told María what it was, and she had been too tired to ask about it before. Now her pride kept her from asking, for she did not want her sisters to know that she had

The Visit

failed to find out all about the town on the first trip. Ana saved her. She leaned forward and punched Father in the back, and said, "What's that, Father? That building up there on the hill?"

"That's a *morada,* or church," replied Father. "It belongs to the Penitentes."

"What are the Penitentes?" Ana insisted.

"It's their religion," said Father.

"Aren't they Catholics, like us?" Ana demanded.

"Yes, they're Catholics," Father answered. "But this is something besides that belief, the way the kiva is with us."

The children could all understand that part, and it explained things for them. The wagon went on past the *morada* and through the town of Chimayó, and out on the other side for about half a mile. Then there was a long adobe house, standing in an orchard well back from the road, and Father stopped the horses before its gate. Ana climbed down and opened the gate, and Father drove through and drew up before the house.

Right away there was a lot of excitement. An old lady and an old man came running out of the house. They were so old their shoulders were bent and their faces looked alike, like the faces of children who belong to the same family and have been together all their lives. The old lady held up her hands in surprise, but the old man held his out in greeting. "Good evening," they both said in Spanish. "Hello, there. Are you all well? Come in and be welcome."

"Thank you," said Mother, climbing down from the wagon seat. She and the old lady put their arms around each other and kissed one another's cheeks, while the men shook hands. Then the old lady took baby Juanita and held her, while the old man showed Father where to take the horses, and went with him to help take care of them. The old lady led the way indoors, and Mother and the girls followed her.

Inside, the house was very much like the houses in the pueblo. There was a fireplace in one corner and a pounded earth floor, like the ones they had at home. Pots and pans were hanging from the walls, and there were pottery storage jars in the corners—the kind of pottery that Tía Nicolasa said came from Nambé or Picurís or Taos. There was one thing that was different from the furniture the children were used to seeing. In a corner there stood a big, closed wooden cabinet. When she saw the girls looking at it, the old lady smiled at them, and said in Spanish, "That is a *trastero.*" She opened the cupboard and showed them that it was full of plates and dishes

43

and cups. María thought that she had never seen anything like them before. She wondered if she could have a *trastero* full of dishes when she was grown up and had a house of her own. She did not say anything about it, though, because she felt too shy.

"It's Holy Week," said the old lady going quickly about in her kitchen, "so I don't have meat or sweet things to give you. But I think we can manage to find some food anyway," and she smiled at all of them.

"Whatever you have will be all right," said Mother. "We know that you are a good cook."

Then Father and the old man came in, with the sacks and bundles from the wagon, and the old lady raised her hands again with surprise when she saw what they had brought.

"Thank you," she said over and over again. "Thank you a thousand times."

"It's nothing," answered Mother. "Just some little things we thought you might like to have."

"It's a great kindness and very thoughtful of you," said the old lady. "Now come sit down, and we'll eat our supper."

The old lady was a very good cook; Mother was right about that. They had fresh wheat bread from the outdoor oven, and beans and cheese, and stewed dried fruit.

"I made the bread and cheese this morning," the old lady said when Mother praised them. "They aren't as good as I usually make, but when they're fresh they're all right."

"They are very good," said Father, smiling.

After supper, Mother said, "Now we'll all help you with the dishes."

That was bad news for María. She had been thinking that if they went visiting, they would not have to do any housework. The old lady answered, "No, I don't want you to help me tonight. You're all of you tired from your trip, and you want to go right to bed. Tomorrow will be different." She looked at the children, and laughed. "See the little ones," she said. "They can hardly keep their eyes open. Come along, girls, and I'll show you where to sleep."

She took a fat pine splinter from the fire, for a light, and opened a door into the next room. The girls had never seen any room like this one. There were four beds in it, with an old homemade blanket on each of them. Over against the wall there was a low, square, wooden chest. The old lady went across to the chest and opened it.

Then she began taking out more and more of the old handmade covers. María could see that there were designs painted on the chest, but the room was too dark for her to make out what they were like.

It was very exciting to go to bed in a real bed instead of on an adobe shelf built along the wall. The striped blue and yellow and brown covers were exciting, too. There was a little narrow bed for each of the older girls and a big double bed for their parents. The old lady hung a rope and blankets from the *vigas,* to make Juanita the kind of hammock bed she was used to sleeping in at home.

After the light and the grown people had gone away, María lay and thought about the wonderful colors of the covers that were over her, and the wonderful designs that were painted on the chest. She could hardly wait for daylight so that she could see the beautiful things again. Sleep caught her and held her, though, and did not let her go until there was broad light shining through the lace curtains at the windows. She had been so excited about the other things that she had not noticed the window curtains the night before.

When she went out into the kitchen to wash her face, María found her mother and the old lady busy getting breakfast. They worked together easily and well. María thought that all went smoothly, like the corn grinding at home, when they were all working and singing. It seemed to take almost no time to put the toasted bread and milk and the coffee and honey and butter on the table. Then they all sat down and ate together.

After the meal, the old lady said, "Now you children can make your beds and then go out to play, while your mother and I see to things in the kitchen. Go on, now."

That was what María had been waiting for. She and Ana and Desidéria went back into the bedroom, and now she could look at the covers while they pulled them smooth on the beds, and admire the soft colors in the blankets. When the beds were all made and neat, María went over and looked at the chest.

Its background color was blue, so old and soft that it had faded nearly gray. The designs painted on the blue were in red and yellow and black. There were flowers and birds and hearts, all held together by twining vines. The painting was nothing like the designs that Tía Nicolasa sometimes used on her pottery; they were not like the designs on the Apache baskets Mother had for carrying food to the kiva on feast days; the only designs that María had ever seen that were like them were the designs on altar cloths and on the priest's robes at Mass. In some way, although they were not just the same, the designs on the chest were like those others.

María came back to the kitchen and stood close beside Mother until she was noticed.

"Mother," she said then, "the chest in the bedroom—who painted it?"

"Who painted your chest, *comadre?*" Mother asked their hostess.

"My father, years ago," was the answer. "He painted it when he and my mother were going to be married, for her to store her blankets in. All the brides had chests, in those days. Some of them even had the girls' names painted on them. My father never learned to read or write, so he couldn't do that, but he made the chest as beautiful as he could. Do you like it?" she asked María.

"Very much," said María. "Oh, very much. Could Father make one like it?" she asked her mother.

"I don't know," said Mother, laughing. "He's a better farmer than he is a carpenter, and I never saw him put designs on anything."

"Oh," said María, sadly, "I guess he couldn't, then. But it would be nice to have a chest like that to keep our clothes in, instead of laying them on the bed or hanging them on racks from the *vigas.*"

"Well," said Mother, "we've got along without a chest this long, and I guess we'll manage." She laughed a little. "Run outdoors and play with your sisters now."

María went out and found Ana and Desidéria watching some goats that were penned at the back of the house. There were four goats, and they were all of them white with yellow eyes. The slits in their eyes went sidewise instead of up and down. It seemed to María a part of this strange world that the slits in the animals' eyes were different. She had never noticed the eyes of the kids that they had at home. The Spanish goats rubbed against the sides of their pen and blatted plaintively. The goats were nicer than cows because they were not so big and frightening.

That day and the next passed quietly and well. The sisters played under the trees in the orchard, ate the good food that the old lady cooked for her guests, and were happy. On the third day, Thursday, the old lady said at lunch, "Well, tonight is the Penitente procession to the *morada.* Would you like to see it, Reyes?"

"I'd like to very much," said Mother. María remembered then what her father had said about the Penitentes, that they were Catholics but different.

"Is it like the Palm Sunday procession?" she asked.

"No," said the old lady. "It's different from that. My husband will be in it, and the rest of us can go and watch, if you like."

"All of us?" Ana asked.

"I think so," said Mother. She turned to Father. "Is it all right for the girls to go?" she asked him.

"If they are quiet and say their Rosaries," Father answered. "This is something holy, and they must be careful how they act while it is going on."

"Are you coming with us, Father?" Ana questioned him.

"I think I will go with my *compadre* and take part in the procession," her father told her. "He has asked me to do that, and it is a great honor to be invited. I don't want to refuse such an honor when it is offered to me. I never knew of any Indian man's being asked to do that before."

"No," Mother agreed, "I never heard of its happening, either. Will you be all right?" she asked, anxiously.

"I'll be all right," said Father. "It is religion, and that is all right."

María wondered why Father, who was so strong and able to do anything he started to do, should not be all right. But one of the things that she had been learning since she was a little girl was not to ask questions about religious matters. You waited, and when you were old enough, those things were explained to you so you could understand them.

"I think the girls should take a nap this afternoon," the old lady said. "They will be up late, if they go to the procession, and they should have some rest first. In fact, we all should take a nap."

"You women should do that," the old man agreed, "but Tomás and I will have to go up to the *morada* and help get things ready for tonight. We'll leave you until supper time."

"All right," said the old lady. "You can go, then."

They all went into the bedroom, after the men had left, and lay down to rest. María lay so that she could look across the room at the painted chest. At first it was just a chest, standing there; then the vines and flowers on it began to grow and twist and run into one another. Then she lost sight of it completely, and was asleep.

She was awakened by a hand on her shoulder. The old lady was bending over her. "Come along," said her hostess. "You've slept all afternoon. Come and have something to eat. Soon it will be dark, and we'll have to start."

María

They had just bread and milk for supper that night. The food surprised María, after the good meals they had eaten, until she noticed that her parents and the old people ate only one slice of bread apiece. Then she understood that it was a time of abstinence, and no one could eat more than a little.

Afterwards, when the dishes were washed, the old lady and Mother got their shawls and were ready to go. Mother hung the baby's hammock from a *viga* in the bedroom, and fastened little Juanita in it securely with soft cloths, so that she would not fall out. Then Mother said, "Wrap up as warmly as you can, all of you. It will be chilly up there on the hill."

"Wrap the blankets clear around you," said the old lady, smiling. "Then if anyone sees you, they will think you come from Taos."

They all laughed at that, and the girls each took a blanket and wrapped up in it. Then they all went outside, where there was a nearly full moon coming up over the mountains, and started walking back through the village towards the hill where the *morada* stood. They walked briskly, and María began to feel too warm, with the heavy blanket around her. She started to take it off, but Mother shook her head.

"Keep it around you," she said. "You'll need it more later on, but you won't feel the cold so much then if you're wrapped up now. Your body will keep the same warmth inside the blanket."

María did not understand what her mother meant, exactly, but she did as she was told. Afterwards, up on the hill, she decided that Mother must have been right, for she felt just the same warmth all evening. It was comfortable inside the blanket, though she could feel in the air on her face that the night was getting colder.

They climbed the hill slowly. They could hear other people moving near them, and the rustle of clothes and the whispering of breathings came clearly to their ears. They were on the shadowed side of the hill, and the other people were wrapped in blankets, too, so that they could not distinguish anybody. It was only by joining hands in the darkness that they could be sure they were all together.

When they reached the top of the hill, the old lady drew the family into a tight group around her. "This is where we will have to wait," she said. "This will be a good place to be near the procession. Sit down on the ground, and as soon as you see or hear anything, kneel down on your knees and say your Rosaries."

The Visit

"Keep your eyes down while you're praying," Mother added. "Don't look at anything, and don't talk or laugh. Remember, this is these peoples' religion. It is serious, and it means a lot for them. It's not like our dances, where everybody is supposed to be gay and happy, and religious, too."

"Yes, Mother," said María and Desidéria. Afterwards María remembered that Ana had not said anything at all.

They sat on the ground in the dark, then, and waited silently. María held her rosary in one hand and Mother's skirt in the other, so as to be ready for anything that happened. The moon moved up and up the sky, and their side of the hill became lighter as night went on.

What it was that she heard first, María never knew for sure. There was a sound in the air, but she felt rather than heard it. It was a sad, strange humming that filled her ears and got into her chest and made it hard for her to breathe. There was no pounding to the sound, as there was to the drums in the pueblo, and perhaps that was why she could not catch her breath. The drumbeats opened and closed your lungs for you, and all you had to do was to live to them. Beside her, María felt her mother stir.

"Kneel, all of you," Mother whispered, "and keep your eyes on the ground. They're coming now."

María rose to her knees, and she felt Desidéria, beside her, do the same thing. The sound was coming closer now, and as it drew nearer, it became more regular. The noise had a rhythm, but not a drum rhythm, to it. There were lights beginning to move along the ground. A man's voice was raised, chanting words María did not recognize. Other voices answered him; and, timed with the words of their chorus, came that strange, irregularly beating sound that was not like any other noise.

María clutched her rosary and closed her eyes and began to pray, hard. Then her eyes opened without her really wanting them to, and she could look along the ground. Before her, in the strange little light of lanterns, a row of men's feet was passing. They took three steps forward and one back, timed with the beating and chanting. There were all kinds of shoes: moccasins and sandals and store-made work shoes, and even cowboy boots like those the young men wore when they dressed up. Some of the feet that María could see were bare. She closed her eyes again. Somehow, more than anything else in the world right then, she wanted not to look at those feet.

49

The procession did not go on for very long, just long enough to say the decades through. Then the sounds were gone and the lights were gone, and Mother was moving again. This time she rose.

"Come along," she said to her daughters. "The part that we can see is over now. We'll go home and go to bed quickly."

They hurried as much as they could going down the hill, but over that rough ground it was hard to walk quickly. No one spoke at all until they were back at the house. Then Mother said, "Go to bed at once, girls. We'll have to start back early in the morning."

Without saying anything, the girls went into the bedroom and to bed. María was so sleepy and so stilled by what she had heard that she did not even look at the chest that night.

Mother called the children early, before light had come to the sky. She and the old lady had breakfast ready, and the girls ate mechanically, without thinking about the food that was given them. Father and the old man ate the same way. It was a silent breakfast. The last thing that María did, when everything was loaded into the wagon, was to go back into the bedroom and look at the chest. It was as strange and beautiful to her eyes as it had been the first time that she saw it. When María turned around, the old lady was standing just behind her.

"You like the chest, don't you?" the old lady asked.

"Oh, yes," said María. "I think it's beautiful."

"Nobody else has ever felt like that about it," said the old lady. "I think you ought to have it; I think it would be happy with you. I am going to tell my husband that when I die, the chest is to be given to you."

"Oh, thank you!" María exclaimed.

"You won't get it right away, you know," the old lady warned her. "Maybe you won't get it for a long time yet. As long as I live, I will use it, don't forget."

"That's all right," said María. "After I get it, I'll have it for a long time. I can wait."

"You'll get it before you're married, anyway," said the old lady. "You can count on having it for a bride's chest."

"Thank you," said María again.

"I'm not doing this for the other girls," the old lady went on, "so maybe you'd better not say anything about it to them."

"I won't," María promised.

María went out to the wagon carrying her secret in her heart like a bird in her hand. Like a bird, the secret fluttered and tried to free itself, but María held it softly and firmly. She told no one, not even her mother.

The journey back to San Ildefonso was very quiet, and slower than the trip to Chimayó had been. At noon, when they stopped to rest, Ana spoke for the first time.

"Father," she said, "why did they whip themselves?"

"What!" said Father. "Why do you ask that?"

"Because I want to know," said Ana, reasonably. "I want to know why they whip themselves."

"You aren't supposed to know that they do whip," said her father. "Reyes, didn't you tell the children not to look?"

"Of course I did," said Mother, frowning. "I told them to kneel down and say their prayers, and not to look at all."

"You are a disobedient girl," said Father to Ana. "You should mind your mother, and not do things you are not supposed to do."

"I did mind my mother," said Ana. Her face drew together, as if she were going to cry. "I did mind her. I kneeled down and said my prayers, and I didn't look until after I said all the decades."

Father nearly smiled, but not quite. "I'm glad you partly obeyed," was all that he said. "Next time be sure that you mind everything that you're told."

"Yes, father," said Ana, "but why do they whip themselves?"

"It's their religion," said Father. "It's different from the dances, in that way. The Indian religion is to be happy, but the Spanish religion is to be sad. That's why they are two different people."

6. The Withdrawing
(1891

Old Grandmother lived with Grandmother, Mother's mother, who was her daughter. Once the house where they lived had belonged to Old Grandmother, but as she grew older, she had lent it to Grandmother, and now they lived there together. The house was even older than Old Grandmother, because it had been built by her father. It was hard for María to think of Old Grandmother's having a father or mother, or any relatives older than she was, because she was so very old herself. Always, it seemed, she must have been older than anyone else in the village, and almost as old as time.

But there she was, living in the old, two-story house that her father had built at the west end of the pueblo when he was its governor. The house was so old that there were hatchways in the ceilings of the ground-floor rooms, where ladders went up inside the house in the old days. The ladders were inside so that the people who lived in the house could go from one level to another without being in danger from the Navajos or the Apaches, if they attacked the pueblo.

Once, people said, Old Grandmother had been a good-sized woman, tall and strong and broad-shouldered. Everybody told stories about how she could grind more corn than any other woman in San Ildefonso, and hoe a bigger garden, and dance harder and longer and more earnestly in the ceremonials.

Now that she was so very old, Old Grandmother had shrunk in on herself and had become as tiny as a little girl. She was not even as tall as Desidéria, and not nearly as large as María. Old Grandmother's hands and feet and face were shrunken, too, but the shrinking had made wrinkles in their skin, so that they were not like a child's except for their small size. Even Old Grandmother's voice had shrunken and become tiny and twittering like a little bird's. You had to bend your head down and listen close to her mouth to hear anything that she tried to say. Only her hair was like a grown woman's, except that it had turned white all over her head. None of the hair had fallen out, and it was still thick and straight and heavy. Old Grandmother and Grandmother were both of them proud of that hair. They kept it brushed and combed and cut as carefully as if it had been a young woman's.

María and Desidéria liked to go to visit Old Grandmother. Sometimes, when she felt like it, she could tell them wonderful stories about things that had happened a long time ago, or that she had seen or done when she was a little girl or a young woman. Sometimes she would play dolls with the children, and one time, when she was feeling very well, she made them each a doll dress. The dresses were made out of pieces of an old *manta;* and the dark blue, hand-woven cloth was stiff and stood away from the dolls' bodies as the women's *mantas* stood away from their bodies when they danced.

Often, though, Old Grandmother was tired. Then she lay on her bed on the floor, and looked out through the door at the fields and the Black Mesa, if it were summer; or across the room at the flames in the fireplace if it were winter.

"Why are you so tired, Old Grandmother?" María asked her once.

"I'm just tired from living," Old Grandmother answered in her tiny voice. Even bending down to the old lady's mouth, María could barely hear the words.

On days like that, when Old Grandmother was tired from living, Grandmother worked very quietly in her house. When her sons, the children's uncles, came in from the fields, Grandmother would hold up one hand to warn them to be quiet, too. Then the big grown men would tip-toe into the room where Old Grandmother lay and sit beside her for a while, one of them at a time, without saying anything. Afterwards they would get up and go away, as quietly as they had come. No one knew whether or not Old Grandmother realized that they were there.

One day one of the uncles came to Mother's house. "You must come down to the village," he said, when he and Mother had exchanged greetings. "Old Grandmother has sent for everybody. She says for you to bring the children, too. She wants to talk to everybody."

"How does she feel?" Mother asked.

"She feels very well," her brother answered. "That's why she has sent for all of us. She doesn't think she will feel this well again for a long time, if she ever does."

Mother got her shawl, and sent María for Father and Ana, who were working in the garden near the house. They all went quickly, and without speaking, down the slope to the village and across the plaza to Grandmother's house.

When they got there, Old Grandmother was lying in her bed on the floor, but she was not looking at the fireplace, although it was a chilly day and the door was closed. Instead, Old Grandmother was looking at the people who sat there in the room—her daughter, and her grandchildren, and their husbands and wives, and her great-grandchildren. Old Grandmother seemed to be studying their faces and to be thinking deeply about what she saw there. Not until everybody was in the room did the old lady speak. Then her voice was bigger and stronger than María could ever remember hearing it. The voice sounded as if Old Grandmother had been saving it up, so that she could speak one more time without whispering.

"I have called you all here to speak to you," Old Grandmother said. "I've come to the time now when I know I'll be going away from you pretty soon. That happens to all old people. It just hasn't happened to me as soon as it does to most."

She stopped talking and lay still again, waiting for her voice to be strong enough to go on speaking. Nobody else said anything, or moved.

"This is what I want to say," Old Grandmother continued. "I haven't very many things left. Most of the things I have had in my life have worn out, the way I have. Most of the things that didn't wear out I've already given away to different ones of you who needed them. But there are still a few things that I have left."

She stopped and waited again, and once more let her voice strengthen so that she could use it.

"This house is for my daughter," said Old Grandmother. "She has lived in it and taken care of it and loved it for many years. I should have given it to her long ago, but I didn't. Now I want you all to know that she shall have it for her own, and that she can give it away when she has finished with it and with her life. It is the same with all the woman's things that I am leaving in the house."

"Thank you, Mother," Grandmother said.

"There are my dance costumes," Old Grandmother went on. "I still have them, and the jewelry that belongs with them. Those I want to be divided among my granddaughters. I don't care which of them has what parts. All I want is for their mother, my daughter, to decide what they need, and to give it to them. If there are any things left over after my granddaughters have been taken care of, they can be given to my nieces. That is fair, I think."

"Thank you, Grandmother," said Mother. "We all think that is fair and right, and we will share the things with our cousins."

Old Grandmother rested once more, and when she spoke again, her voice was almost the whisper that you had to stoop to hear. Not

quite, though. She was a wise old woman, and she had saved her voice as she had saved other things, so that there was enough of it left for all the words she wanted to say.

"The last things that I have left are my pottery things," she said. "I don't know what is left of them. Pots break and wear out even worse than people, and when they are gone and only the pieces remain, then there is nothing anyone can do to make the pots useful again. So it may be that there are no pots left. If there are, I want them divided among my great-granddaughters, starting with the oldest ones, as long as there are any pots left. Some of you may not think that is fair, for it may mean that the little girls won't get anything, but that is the only way I know to divide."

"That is all right, Mother," Grandmother said. "There will be a piece of pottery for each of the great-granddaughters, even the littlest ones."

Old Grandmother lay still, with her eyes closed. They all waited, not sure whether she had said everything she meant to say, or whether there was more to come. The silence grew in the room like a plant; it grew until it seemed like something that was alive. Still they all sat and waited, and at last Old Grandmother opened her eyes to them again.

"That is all I have to say to you now," she said. "I don't think that I am going away right now, but I know that I will go soon. I wanted to do this before I went, so that you would be able to use my things and wouldn't have to throw them away just because I had finished with them, when some of you could use them. That is all I have to say. You may go home now."

She closed her eyes and lay still, like a tired child, and they all left the room silently. When they were walking, still silently, back to their own house, María pulled at her mother's shawl.

"Is Old Grandmother going to die?" she asked. "Was that what she meant, when she said she was going away?"

"That's what she meant," said Mother.

"When is she going to die?" Desidéria questioned.

"That we don't know," Mother replied. "People die when God is ready to take them to Him. Old Grandmother doesn't know when she will die any more than anyone else does."

"Why did she talk like that, then?" Ana demanded. "She talked as if she knew all about it."

"Sometimes old people who are near their time for going home know more than others would," said Mother. "Still, they don't know exactly. God doesn't tell us these things. He wants us to live always as if we were ready to die and to meet Him; and if we knew just when the time was coming, we might not do that until the last minute. That's why we don't know when we're going to die. Not ever, any of us."

Certainly Old Grandmother didn't know just when she was going to die, María thought. After all of her belongings had been divided so that people could use them after her death, the old lady even seemed to get stronger and better. She could sit up in her bed and look around the room. Grandmother piled pillows behind her as she sat, or came and took them away sometimes so that her mother could lie down, and things went on very much the way they did before.

The Withdrawing

There was only one change that María could notice. Little as Old Grandmother had spoken before and tiny as her voice had been when she did speak, she said even less now. It was as if Old Grandmother had used up almost all her words, and the strength for saying them, on the day when she gave her things away. But the old woman still smiled at the children when they came to the house, and she seemed to like to have them sit beside her on the floor. Once she stretched out her hand and touched María's hair.

"Nice hair," Old Grandmother said, in her tiny whisper. "Good hair. Pueblo woman's hair." Then she was silent again, and soon her hand slid from María's head as if it were too heavy to remain placed on the shiny, slippery hair.

By spring the children had almost forgotten the day when Old Grandmother had divided her possessions. At first they had talked about what pots they would like to have, if Grandmother allowed them to choose. Then they were busy with school and the dances, and they forgot. That was the year when Ana danced as the Montezuma's Daughter in the Matachines, and everybody was busy getting her white dress and veil ready for Christmas Day.

It was after the apricot trees had bloomed and at the beginning of the peach blossoms that Mother called María into the kitchen one day, and gave her a covered basket.

"Here," she said. "This is fine-ground meal that will make good *atole*. Take it down to Grandmother, to make some for Old Grandmother."

María went down to the village, walking carefully so as not to lose any meal. At Grandmother's house she knocked on the door and then went in without waiting to be called. Sometimes, when Grandmother was busy in the kitchen, she did not hear the children knock. Old Grandmother was lying as usual by the fire, looking at it, and María went over to her.

"Good morning, Grandmother," she said.

Old Grandmother did not move or speak. She only lay there with the covers drawn over her and her eyes closed, as she often did when someone spoke to her. María went on into the kitchen with her basket.

"Good morning," said Grandmother. She was kneeling by her *metate,* grinding meal.

"Good morning," María answered. "Mother sent this to make *atole* for Old Grandmother. She ground it extra fine, so it would be just right."

"That was good of her," said Grandmother. "Thank her for me." She shook her head a little from side to side. "I'm afraid we won't be making *atole* for Old Grandmother much longer. This morning she said to me, quite loud, 'I'm going home. My ribs have fallen in and will hold my heart from beating. I know today that I am going home.'"

"Mother says nobody knows," María hazarded. She did not like to contradict Grandmother, but this was something that Mother herself had said.

"Old people know sometimes," Grandmother answered. She got up from her *metate* and walked to the door with María. On the way she looked at Old Grandmother, still lying as she always lay, with the fireplace before her.

"I guess she's resting," Grandmother said. "Good-bye."

"Good-bye," María answered, and went home.

When she got there, Mother called to her to come help get lunch ready. They were going to have *posole,* and María and Desidéria washed and washed the grains of corn, getting them ready for Mother to cook. When the kettle with the corn and meat and chili was on the fire and beginning to steam, Mother said, "Someone is knocking at the door, Desidéria. Go and see who it is."

It was one of the uncles. He came into the house and sat down very quietly. They all waited for him to speak, in the same kind of silence they had felt on the day when Old Grandmother had sent for them to make her division. At last he looked up, with tears on his face.

"Old Grandmother has gone," he said. "She must have left us this morning. My brother went to see her, and when he spoke to her, she didn't answer. So he turned back her eyelids and looked at her eyes. She was cold and dead. She must have died just lying there."

Mother began to cry, silently. "That's the way it is," she said. "It comes to all of us. We all have to go. I can remember Old Grandmother as far back as I can remember anything. Now that she is gone, it seems that part of me has gone with her. Part of my childhood is gone."

"She did know that she was going, then!" María cried. She forgot that it was rude to interrupt her elders, and spoke right out. "She told Grandmother this morning that she was going home today. She did know."

"Hush," her mother said. "You don't understand these things. You're just a little girl. You couldn't know or understand."

The Withdrawing

"But she did," María insisted. "She did know. And she was right about it, too. This was the day she went."

"Maybe she did," the uncle said slowly. "Old people live near God, like little children. Maybe she knew, and María is right to believe her. Come along, sister. We need to help our mother get ready for the funeral."

7. The Storehouse
(1892

The storehouse at home was something that the children knew all about. It opened off the kitchen, and from time to time Mother sent her daughters into the small dark space to bring out supplies that were needed for cooking. Although no one went into the room very often, it was a part of their house like any other room.

Grandmother's storehouse was different. It opened off her kitchen, too, and Grandmother or someone else in the family often went into it for supplies. But there was a kind of secrecy about Grandmother's storehouse; you felt that it was something special, not just another room in the house. This may have been because, instead of having a door that swung on hinges like any other door, Grandmother's storehouse had a door that fitted tightly into its opening and had to be lifted in and out of the wall like an oven door. Then, too, the storehouse at Grandmother's was so old that it had a special kind of smell, a musty smell of dried squash and seed corn and sun-cured meat and adobe that was like no other smell, and that hurried out to meet you as soon as the door of the room was opened.

After Old Grandmother died, there seemed to be a great many tasks for everybody. Since the old lady had divided everything she had, they did not have to throw her belongings away. She was a good Catholic and had died in the faith of the church, so they had a church funeral and a Mass for her. Then Grandmother cleaned the house all over, replastering the walls with white clay and getting the place neat and pretty. That was so that she could call the relatives in and give them a share of the things Old Grandmother had left.

There was so much to do that they all had to help whenever there was time to leave their own work. Mother made time for herself and her daughters. She was a worker anyway, Mother. She always said that if God sent you work to do, He sent you the time to do it in, also; and that only lazy people tried to get out of working by saying that they did not have time. Mother made everybody get up just that much earlier so that they could finish their own work and go down to Grandmother's house, to help with what she had to do.

That was how it happened that María and Desidéria were there when the old storehouse was opened. They were helping their mother put the new white clay on the walls of the living room, when Grandmother came in and spoke.

"Reyes, I have laid out all the dance costumes and jewelry to divide, and they're all ready. But I just remembered that Mother wanted her pottery divided among her great-granddaughters. I've been trying to remember where she put it, and now I think I know. It must be in the old storehouse behind the one I'm using now. I know the pottery in the new storehouse is all mine. My sisters and I made it ourselves. The old storeroom is the only place I can think of."

Mother stopped working, and looked at Grandmother. "That must be it," she agreed. "It's been so long since the old storehouse was opened that I'd forgotten it was there."

"I think we'd better open it," Grandmother said. "It's bound to be dusty and dirty, and I'd like to get those old things out and clean them up before we start plastering the kitchen."

"All right," said Mother. "Just let me wash my hands, and I'll come help you. The girls can go on with this work. They know how."

"I think the girls had better come, too," said Grandmother. "The door of the old storehouse is so small it will be a tight fit for one of us to crawl through it. The children can manage better than we can."

"They can come, then," Mother said. "Put your tools away, girls, and wash your hands first."

"Where is the old storehouse, Mother?" María asked.

"Behind the one that Grandmother uses now," her mother replied. "You'll see."

"What's in it?" Desidéria wanted to know.

Grandmother laughed a little, and shook her head. "I'm not sure I remember," she answered. "It's been such a long time since that room was opened. My grandfather built it for a storehouse, and the room we use for a storehouse now used to be the kitchen. Then we added this kitchen when I was about fifteen, and used the old kitchen for a storehouse, and shut the old storehouse. I'm sure it's been used since then, but I don't remember when."

"Go wash your hands and get ready, girls," said Mother.

María did not see why they had to wash their hands. It seemed foolish to her, especially when they were going into a room that Grandmother herself said would be dusty and dirty. But as they had been taught to obey, she and Desidéria went out to the well for a bucket of water, and they all washed their hands, Grandmother first, then Mother, and then the two little girls.

"Now," said Grandmother, and, getting down on her knees before the storehouse door, she took it out of the door opening. The smell came out to meet them as it always did. Beyond the doorway the store-

room was dark, and María could just see the shapes of the big pots where corn and dried foods were stored. The jars at the doorway, where the light from the kitchen fell on them, had enough polish to reflect the light. María knew that there were other jars farther back in the storeroom, but those did not show at all.

Grandmother took an armful of fat pine fire sticks from the wood-box and began splitting them into fine fringes at one end.

"You can use these for lights," she said. "Be careful how you hold them, though, and don't burn yourselves." She lighted the first one at the fireplace, and handed it to María. "Go through the first room to the back wall," she said. "The door to the old storehouse is there. It's sealed with adobe, and you'll have to use this knife to loosen it.

The Storehouse

Desidéria can wait here till your light burns down, and then it will be her turn. You go first because you're older."

María felt important and excited as she stepped over the raised door-stone of the storehouse. Carefully, holding her light high in her left hand and the knife in her right, she walked between the rows of storage jars to the back wall. Some of the jars at the back of the room were smooth and polished and red like those near the doorway. Others were from Taos or Picurís or Nambé, and reflected the light in little sparkles, where there were scraps of mica mixed in the surface clay.

At first María could hardly find the doorway at the back of the room. The wall had been plastered almost smooth, and she had to feel all over it to find any unevenness in the surface. She was afraid her light might go out before she found the door. Then her sliding fingers went up and down and up again, and she knew that she had touched the crack around the door and the door itself. Holding the torch tightly in one hand, María began to dig with the knife she held in the other. The old plaster had set hard and was difficult to loosen. She had worked about a foot of the plaster loose, around the crack of the door, when her light went out.

Grandmother must have been watching closely from the other doorway. "Come out now, María," she said. "Let Desidéria have her turn."

Desidéria came right in with her torch, so she and María met in the middle of the outer storeroom.

"Here," said María, handing the knife to her sister, "You have to dig hard to get the plaster loose. It comes out if you keep on working, though."

"All right," said Desidéria, and she took the knife and went on through the storehouse to the back wall.

Mother had gone back to her plastering in the living room, but Grandmother was sitting by the door, cleaning beans, when María came out.

"Sit down and rest," said Grandmother. "Pretty soon it will be your turn again."

María sat down in the doorway beside her grandmother and waited. They could see the light of Desidéria's torch through the opening, and hear the chipping noise that she made with the knife against the plaster. It all seemed to go on for a long time: the waiting, and the chipping, and the flickering of the light. Then the light flared brightly, suddenly, once, and was gone.

"There," said Grandmother. "You can go in." She reached behind her for another torch, and, bending over, she lighted it from the fireplace. "Now you can go," she said.

María took the torch. "I hope Desidéria didn't get it all the way open," she said.

"I don't believe she did," Grandmother replied. "I believe she would have called to us, so we could all be there and see it opened, if that had happened."

"Yes," said María. "I guess she would have called us." Then Desidéria came crawling out of the opening. "Did you get it open?" María demanded.

"Not quite," Desidéria said. "Almost, not quite. You can do it, easy."

"There," said Grandmother, "I told you. Desidéria would have called us all to see, if she had opened it."

María said nothing more. She took the torch and the knife and went through the new storeroom again. The room did not seem as big now as it had the first time that she crossed it, and she did not think there were as many jars as before, or that they were so large.

"I guess I'm getting used to it," she thought to herself.

Desidéria must have worked hard at the old door, for it was almost loose. There was just about a quarter of the plaster left to be taken out. María went to work, quick and hard, until all but about an inch of the plaster was gone. Then she called, "Grandmother! Grandmother! I'm almost through! You'd better come now."

"Wait for us, then," said Grandmother. Then María heard her call, "Reyes! Reyes! María is ready to take the door out."

"I'm coming," María heard Mother's voice answer, and a minute later she, with Grandmother and Desidéria, came through the new store room. Grandmother was carrying an extra armload of torches. She reached out her hand for the light María was carrying, and with it started one of the new ones. Then she handed the torch to Desidéria.

"You stand here and hold the light," Grandmother said. "Your mother and I will stand on either side of the door, ready to catch it when it falls. Now, María, you take out the last of the plaster."

Very carefully, so that the door would not fall on Mother or Grandmother and hurt them, María chipped loose the rest of the plaster. Nothing happened. The door stayed right where it was.

"Well," said Grandmother, "I guess we'll have to pull it out. Stand back out of the way, girls, but hold your lights so we can see."

The Storehouse

Mother and Grandmother took hold of the edges of the door, and worked the ends of their fingers under it. Delicately, with just their fingers at first, and then with the whole strength of their hands, they pulled at the door.

"It's loosening," said Grandmother. "Just give it one good pull now, Reyes."

Mother must have given the door an extra good pull, for all of a sudden it slid out of the wall and landed with a crash on the floor.

"Look out!" cried Grandmother. "Are you hurt, Reyes?"

"No, I'm all right," said Mother, "What about you and the girls?"

"All, all right," answered Grandmother. "I think we'd better get out of here now. Sometimes when a room's closed a long time, the air in it gets bad and makes you sick when you breathe it. We'll stop and eat some lunch, and then we can come back."

They all went back out of the storeroom into the kitchen. One of the uncles was standing there.

"I heard you talking, but I couldn't see you," he said. "What were you doing?"

"Opening the old storeroom," answered Grandmother. "It must be time for lunch, if you're here."

"My stomach says it's lunch time," the uncle answered, laughing. "What did you want from the old storehouse, Mother?"

"The pottery that Old Grandmother said to divide," Grandmother replied. "We had to pry the door out first, with the girls' help."

"Well, if you're going to lift that old pottery out, you'd better let me help you," her son said. "It's probably pretty heavy."

"All right," said Grandmother. "Let's have lunch first, though."

Grandmother was a good cook, and even a picnic lunch like this was good at her house. They had *atole* with milk and honey, dried plums from Taos that were as sweet as the honey itself, beans, and *tortillas*. There was coffee for the grown people and milk for the children. When they had all finished their lunch and had rested for a few minutes, Grandmother said, "Well, let's get back to work."

She got up and prepared another armful of torches before she said to her son, "I think you'd better go into the old storeroom and lift things out through the door. Reyes and the girls and I will wait for you to hand them out, and then set them in the kitchen."

They all went back into the new storeroom, with Grandmother carrying two lighted torches. At the door, she handed one to the uncle, to carry into the storehouse with him.

"I don't think I can handle the light and the pottery at the same time," he said doubtfully. "One of the girls had better come along."

"María, you're bigger than Desidéria," said her mother. "You can go in and hold the light."

It was exciting to be chosen to go into Old Grandmother's storehouse. Carrying the torch, María crawled through the door to hold the light for her uncle. That was how it happened that she was the first person to go into the old room since it had been sealed. She looked around her and could make out the shapes of the jars and the gleams of reflected light on their sides, but at first she could not count how many there were, or tell just what they looked like.

"Is the air all right in there?" Grandmother called from the other room.

"It's better than you'd expect," her son replied. "I can see why. There are two little open ventilator slits in the wall, and they've let fresh air in all the time."

"Don't stay in there too long and get headaches," said Mother. Desidéria can hold the light when María gets tired."

"We'll be careful," promised the uncle. He turned to María. "We can start with these jars right here by the door," he said, "and then work back to the ones against the wall. Come and hold the light over here for me."

Now that she was used to the feeling of the old room, María could see better what it held. The first storage jar that her uncle took hold of, there by the door, was a big black one with small shiny spots.

"That came from Picurís or Nambé," María told herself, remembering something Tía Nicolasa had said about how pottery was made in those pueblos.

"Is there anything inside?" she asked her uncle.

He lifted off the flat, platelike lid that covered the mouth of the jar and peered in; then he shook his head. "Just dust, I think," he said. "That's what it looks like, anyway. Maybe it was corn meal a long time ago."

María was disappointed. She had hoped that there would be things in the jars; she didn't know exactly what kinds of things, but things of some sort that had been hidden away and forgotten as the storehouse itself had been. The jars were fine to have, but empty jars were not as exciting to her as full ones. Still there were a great many of the jars, full or empty. The uncle lifted them through the doorway one at a time.

The Storehouse

Once María heard her mother say, "I wish Nicolasa were here to see these. She'd appreciate them," and Grandmother answered, "We ought to get her here, to look at them."

"It's time María came out, anyway," Mother said, and she called, "María, come and change places with Desidéria, so she can have a turn. I want you to go and get Tía Nicolasa to come and see the old pottery."

When she crawled back through the hole and went into the kitchen to wash her hands, María saw the old pottery in the daylight. Grandmother had dusted off the jars and set them in a row along the wall, beside the fireplace. There were eight jars lined up there already, and María knew that there were still more to come. She stood and looked and looked at the jars.

"Why, Grandmother," she said, "they're all different!"

"Yes," answered her Grandmother, "all of them different kinds of pottery."

María was so anxious not to lose any of the excitement that she ran all the way across the plaza to Tía Nicolasa's house. When she got there, she was panting so hard that at first she could not speak. Tía Nicolasa led her inside the house and gave her some water to drink. When she had swallowed it, María could explain to her aunt what was happening.

"Grandmother thought maybe you would like to come and see," she said when she had finished. "She thought you would like to see all those different kinds of old pots."

"Yes, I would," said Tía Nicolasa. "Wait a minute till I wash my hands, and we'll go right back there."

"You don't need to wash your hands," María told her. "Grandmother dusted the pots, but they're still dirty. Your hands won't stay clean."

"Well, I may as well start with them that way," said Tía Nicolasa. "It won't hurt you to sit still for a minute while I wash them, either."

It seemed to María that she had never known anybody to take as long washing one pair of hands as Tía Nicolasa did that time. María sat on a chair and waited politely until her aunt had finished, but her mind was running ahead of her body across the plaza and through Grandmother's front door, and back into the kitchen where the row of jars stood. Finally, however, Tía Nicolasa said, "There. Now I'm ready."

It had not really taken as long as María had thought, for when they got back to Grandmother's house and she counted the jars, there were only two more than when she had left. One of them was plain dark red, but the other had black designs painted on a white background.

"That's a beautiful one," said Tía Nicolasa, going straight to it while they all watched her.

Most of the jars were bigger than any María had ever seen used in San Ildefonso, but there were a few small ones. Some of the jars were in plain colors, and some were decorated. There were a few of the ones that came from the northern pueblos, and there were two dark, smudgy brown ones of a kind that María had never seen before.

"Those came from the Apache country," said Tía Nicolasa, looking at them. "They haven't made any like those for a long time now."

"This one came from Santa Clara, I think," said Grandmother, putting her hand on a tall, polished black jar with a bear-paw design stamped on its side.

"And this from San Juan," said Mother, touching a squatty red one, almost a bowl, with its top-half polished and the bottom-half plain.

"Which ones were made here, Tía Nicolasa?" María asked.

"This one and this one and this one," said Tía Nicolasa. She pointed out two polished red jars, and the black-and-white painted one.

"How do you know?" María demanded.

"Partly because we have seen lots of pottery," said Tía Nicolasa, "and partly because each pueblo has its own way of making it. They don't ever all make it in the same way. Just as every woman does things a little bit differently when she works, so do all the pueblos do their work a little differently. That's the way we know."

"Don't they ever copy from each other?" asked María.

"Sometimes they copy colors or trade clays," said Tía Nicolasa, "but they wouldn't be likely to copy designs."

"But this one Mother said came from Santa Clara has a bear paw pressed on it, and this one you said was made here has a bear paw painted on it," María protested.

"One is pressed and one is painted," said Grandmother, "and that makes them different, just as Tía Nicolasa said."

"Oh," said María. "Mother, shall I go back now and hold the light?"

The Storehouse

"I think Desidéria is all right," her mother answered. "They've just about finished, anyhow."

There were sixteen jars, when all had been lifted out and dusted and set in line. "One for each of the fourteen great-granddaughters," said Grandmother, "and two left over. Reyes and Nicolasa, I want you each to have one."

"Thank you very much," said Mother. "Nicolasa, will you choose which one you want?"

"No, you choose first," said Tía Nicolasa, politely. Her eyes were fixed on the black-and-white jar, however, and she could not have chosen more plainly with words.

"I'd like the big Apache one," said Mother. "It looks as if it were good and strong, and would stand hard use."

"Then I'd like the painted one," said Tía Nicolasa. "I'd like to have it to use the design."

"All right," said Grandmother. "Now, María, you're next oldest. Which one do you want?"

"I'd like the old red one that was made here," said María. "It has a nice polish."

"And Desidéria?" asked Grandmother.

"I'd like the other old red one," Desidéria answered.

"Well!" said the uncle "It looks as if the other girls would have to take the jars from other pueblos. I think the best have been chosen. These girls worked hard, though, and earned the right to choose."

"What are you going to do with your jar?" Grandmother asked María.

"Put it in the storehouse at home and fill it with popcorn," said María promptly. "Then we'll have it ready for winter."

"I'm going to put blue corn in mine," said Desidéria.

"Well," said Tía Nicolasa, "those are both good jars that you have there. If you keep them filled with corn and use them right, they will last in your time as long as they have already. That's the good thing about pottery. If you use it right, it helps you right."

"Yes," said the uncle, "that's the way it is. Those are big jars for little girls to carry. Come along now, and I'll help you take them home. That way we'll get them there safely, and you'll be ready to fill them with corn when the harvest is in."

8. The Little Trees
(1888–1892

When Father and Mother were first married, they owned few fields, and those they had were near the pueblo. As time went on, however, and the family acquired more land, they found that much of what they owned was outside San Ildefonso. Father had to spend a good deal of his time away from home in the growing season, to take care of all his crops. Sometimes his family saw him only on Saturdays and Sundays, when he came back to the village to go to Mass and to get clean clothes. During the week, in summer, it was like not having a father at all.

As Ana grew up and became interested in making things grow and in taking care of the animals, she could help with the garden and with the small fields near the house. Father said that she was the best help he ever had. He and Ana thought a lot of each other in that way, and liked to work together with the crops.

In the big fields away from the village, though, Father had to trade work with his brothers. First, all four men would work in the fields that belonged to one of them. Then they would all move on, and work in the fields of the next brother. Taking it in turn, they got a lot of work done; but sometimes a field was gathered a little too soon or was left to stand a little too long, and part of the crop was spoiled.

"Each of you be sure to marry a good farmer," Father would tell his daughters at such times. "I need plenty of strong sons-in-law to help me with farming."

Ana always laughed, and reminded him that she could help.

"I know you can," her father would say, "but I need more men than you'll ever be to get things done."

Then he came home on a Saturday night in spring, and said, "Reyes, I've planted the field at Jacona in corn."

"That's farther away than any of the other fields," said Mother. "How are you going to take care of it? It was hard to care for even when you planted it to alfalfa."

70

"I know," said Father. "I have a plan for it."

"You and your plans!" said Mother. "Now what is this plan?"

"This is a good plan," said Father. "If it works, we can all be together the whole summer. We'll plant corn and a garden at Jacona. Those are our biggest fields. Then we'll plant the alfalfa here. We'll build a summerhouse over there and close this house for a while. The alfalfa will be in the fields near my brothers', so it can all be cut at the same time when theirs is, and we'll be living where our big fields that take steady work are located."

"Will your brothers be able to help you there?" Mother wanted to know.

"They can help with the harvesting," said Father, "and I'll help them. Some of the work at Jacona we can do ourselves, and some I'll hire a Spanish boy to help with. Then we'll be where we're needed, and everything will get done."

"That all sounds good," said Mother. "The girls are old enough to help with everything, and it will be fun for me to live in a summerhouse, where I don't have as much housework to do as here."

"That's what I thought," said Father. "We'll all go over in the wagon after Mass tomorrow and choose a place to build the summerhouse."

All the time their parents were talking, María and Desidéria had been listening. They were sitting in one corner of the kitchen, making string pictures. They had been playing with their strings since early in the spring, and had learned how to make some of the hardest pictures. All the girls played string games in the spring, but not all of them made as many or as hard figures as María and Desidéria. María had first learned to make the rope corral, and then the stars, and then the turkey's claws; and then she had gone on to the harder moving ones, like two women walking to meet each other and the shooting arrow. She and Desidéria wore their strings around their necks in school or when they were helping at home, so that every spare minute they had could be spent remaking old pictures and learning new ones.

"Put your strings away, girls," their mother said. "I need you to help me get supper."

"Just let us finish these, Mother," said María, but her mother told her, "No, I need you to help me. You can make them after supper."

Desidéria had gone on with her string while her mother and María were talking, and now she looked up and grinned. "I finished mine anyway," she said. "Look, it works!" And she showed them a perfect shooting arrow, going across her palm from one side to the other.

"Mind your mother, Desidéria," Father said sternly. "Put your string away."

Desidéria and María hung their strings around their necks without another word. Mother often scolded them, but Father seldom did. When he did speak to them in that voice, they knew they had to mind. It was not a loud voice or a rough one, but it was strict, and they did not know of any way that they could have disobeyed it.

"It will be good for them to be with you all summer, Tomás," Mother said. "They mind you better than they do me."

That hurt María worse than if Mother had scolded them herself. She hung her head so as not to cry and went to work mixing meal with water to make *tortillas*.

Then Ana came in with mud all over her moccasins, from taking the horses to the ditch for water.

"There is my hard-working farmer," Father said, smiling at her, and María felt worse than ever for a minute.

But Mother said, "We have two good housewives in the family, too," and that made María feel a little better.

The next day, as soon as Mass was over, the family all hurried home to get some breakfast and get ready to start. Mother gave them *tortillas* and milk, and put oven-baked bread and *frijoles* and dried meat and more milk in a basket to take with them. When the lunch was ready, they all got into the wagon, and Father brought the lines down over the horses' backs to start them.

The road was the same one they had taken when they started to Chimayó. It went along the river under the trees, and wound up and down the little hills in a slow kind of way. It was a road that was going somewhere, but was in no particular hurry to get there. The family felt the same way. They wanted to go and they wanted to be in the new place, but they did not want to hurry about any of it. María and Desidéria took their strings from around their necks and started making pictures again. María found that she could make the two women walking and the shooting arrow even in the moving wagon, but Desidéria had to stop with the rope corral and the turkey claw.

So the wagon went along the road, and the road went along the valley. The children tired of their strings after a while, and turned around in the wagon, so they could see what they were coming to, instead of watching things they had not seen before leave them. Ahead of them the valley opened out, and the road crossed a wide arroyo. On the right bank of the arroyo were little twin cottonwood trees growing side by side.

"Look at the trees," María said. "Mother, look at the trees. They're growing there as if they were sisters."

"I think they are sister trees," said Father, laughing. "That is our land, and I found the two little trees growing there when I bought it."

"They're nice little trees," said Desidéria. "I like them."

"Well, I don't, much," said Ana. "I wish they were apple trees. Cottonwood trees aren't much good except to chop down for firewood."

"Oh, don't chop them down," María exclaimed. "Please, Father, don't chop them down."

"Well, we won't," said Father. "We'll leave them. If you and Desidéria like them so much, they can be your trees, and you can take care of them."

"Oh, thank you," cried María. "Listen, Desidéria, they are our trees, our two little trees. Which one do you choose?"

"Can I choose first?" asked Desidéria. "I choose the one on the right, then. That will be my tree."

"The one on the left is mine," said María. "I like it best anyway."

"There isn't much to choose between them, as far as I can see," said Father, "but that makes a good name for the place. We'll call it 'The Little Trees,' and you and the trees can grow up together. We'll plant an apple tree for Ana, and she can raise that."

"Can I have all the apples from it?" Ana demanded.

"You can have all of them," said Mother, "but I hope you will share with your sisters and me, because we don't have any fruit trees. I haven't any tree at all," she added, smiling.

"But you have the whole house at home," Ana reminded her.

"Yes, and I share it with all of you," said Mother.

"All sisters share with each other," said Father, and Ana nodded, and said, "I'll share my apples if they'll share their firewood when the cottonwood trees blow down."

"We will," said María, and Desidéria added, "We surely will."

"Can we eat lunch under our trees, Mother?" asked María.

"Well," said Mother doubtfully, "they don't make much shade."

"They make all the shade there is," Father said. "We can eat there. Then we'll pick out a place to build the house."

The little trees made more shade than anyone had expected. After the family had eaten their lunch, Mother said, looking around her, "I think this would be a good place for the house. It's near the road and easy to get to, and the water in the arroyo is near. This ought to be all right."

"If María and Desidéria think so," said their father, looking at them sidewise. "These are their trees, remember."

"Will it hurt the trees, Father?" María asked.

"I don't think so," answered Father. "We'll build carefully, so that the trees will shade the yard around the house, and I don't think it will hurt them at all."

"Will it be a regular house, like the one at home?" Desidéria inquired.

"No," said Father. "It won't be an adobe house. Look, I'll show you how we're going to do it. Come here."

They all got up from the ground and followed him, back a little way from the trees. Father looked around until he found a long stick. He began to draw lines on the ground with it, marking out a square.

"This is where the house will be," he said. "The walls will go on these lines."

"They aren't very straight," María objected.

"We'll straighten them out later," said Father.

"When you're doing that," Mother suggested, "I think you ought to make them longer, too. That doesn't look like a very big room to me."

"It will look bigger when the walls are up," said Father. "We can always add another room, too." Then he looked at Mother, and shook his head. "All right," he said. "We'll make it bigger. You'll be in the house all day, while I'm outdoors."

"Thank you," said Mother. "I'll need the room to cook in."

"What kind of walls, Father?" asked María. "If they aren't adobe, what kind are they?"

"We'll use cedar posts at the corners," Father said, "and then set willow posts in the ground along the sides."

"Is that all the walls there'll be?" Ana questioned. "Won't they leak if it rains?"

"We'll fasten the willows together by weaving other willows through between them, along the sides," Father went on. "Then we'll cover them all over with cottonwood branches, lapping them over each other, so that the rain will run off."

"Not branches off our trees, will they be?" Desidéria asked anxiously.

"No, not off your trees," her father answered patiently. "They aren't big enough. Now, I can't tell you about the house unless you let me talk."

"No, Father," said María politely. "Excuse us for being rude."

"I excuse you," said her father. "Now," he went on, "the willows that are set in the ground will go high enough up in the air to make a shade over the roof. I think we'll use big *vigas,* Reyes," he said, turning to Mother, "and make a very solid roof, so we can all sleep up there."

"That will be nice," said Mother. "Can we have that door open to the east, so that the house will be cool inside in the afternoon?"

"That's the way I had planned it," her husband answered. "Is there anything else you want built specially?"

"Well," said Mother, "I remember my father used to have a summerhouse up on the mesa south of the village. It was fun to go there and we all liked it, but my mother didn't have an oven, and she always missed that. I'd like you to build an oven, please."

"We'll build an oven the first thing," said Father. "Where would you like to have it?"

"Well," replied Mother, "I like to do my cooking right inside the door on the south side of the room, so that I can get the breeze and still be shady. So I think the oven should be a little way from the house but on the south side, where it will be easy to reach."

"That's a good place to put it," said Father.

"That's all I can think of now," said Mother. "If I do think of anything else, I'll let you know."

"All right," said Father. "I want this house to be nice for everybody."

"Thank you," said Mother.

"When are we going to move here?" Ana asked. "We'll have to come pretty soon, won't we, to take care of the corn?"

"I'm going to start work tomorrow," said Father. "We ought to be living here now, but we'll wait till school's out next month."

"Oh," said Ana. She looked disappointed. "I thought the corn was more important than school."

"It is for grown people," Father said. "Corn is their work, and it is everyone's life. But not for children. School is their work. You must stay in the pueblo with your work until you finish and your harvest is in for the year."

"Yes, Father," said Ana. She looked less disappointed now. "I never thought of it like that before."

"I went to school and finished, and I know I'm right," said Father. "You'll find out later how right I am."

None of them said anything more. Father had the stern, kind sound in his voice again, so there was nothing more to be said. The family got in the wagon and got ready to go home.

"Have a good time with your strings, girls," said Mother over her shoulder. "When the building and moving start, you won't have much time for playing."

"Are we going to move everything, Mother?" María asked. Her fingers were moving fast, making the walking figures. She didn't have to watch her hands now; she was so sure of what they were doing.

"Not everything," said Mother thoughtfully. "Just what we need. I'll need the *metates*, of course, and the cooking pots—"

"And the coffee pot," her husband put in.

"And the coffee pot," Mother went on, "and the bedding and mattresses, and our clothes—"

The Little Trees

"Can we take our toys?" Desidéria asked, "Our dolls and things?"

"Don't interrupt," said her mother. "You can take one doll apiece. That's all you'll have time for."

"Can we build playhouses here?" María wanted to know.

"The summerhouse will be a playhouse for all of us," said Mother. "You won't need pretend playhouses when we're here."

"All right," said María, but she wondered if it really would be a very happy summer for her and Desidéria without the things that they were used to for playing.

There was no playing about the moving. Mother began getting ready as soon as they got back to the village. Every now and then she would stop what she was doing, and say, "I think that's everything we need. We mustn't take too much. This is to be like a picnic." Then she would start gathering up more articles and piling them together to take along. She had a whole room full of things ready to go, when the time came to move.

They left on the day after school closed. All of the week before, Father and the Spanish boy named Juan whom he had hired had been putting Mother's things in the wagon and carrying them to the summerhouse. On the last night, when he came home late, Father said, "I think we've moved everything, and we've tried to put it in the house just the way you wanted it. Things may not be quite right, but we did the best we knew how."

"Thank you," said Mother. "I'm sure everything will be all right."

"Well," said Ana, "I'm not sure. I don't think that Juan knows much. I don't like the way he hoes corn."

"He's a good boy," said Father, "and I was right there myself to help him with everything."

"We'll wait and see," said Mother. "Myself, I believe it will be all right."

Going to the summerhouse in the wagon was so exciting that the children could hardly sit still. María and Desidéria stood up in the wagon, facing forward, and four different times one or the other cried out, "There they are! I see them! I see our trees!"

And each time Father said, "Sit down and be quiet, girls. Those aren't your trees yet."

There was no place for the children to sit except on top of the blankets, for the wagon was piled full of things Mother had used at home until the last moment. When they sat on the blankets, the girls slid downhill every time the wagon went over a bump, and since the road was made of bumps, they were sliding most of the time. It was fun at first, but after a while María grew tired of it. It was really more comfortable for her to stand up.

Then the family saw something ahead of them that was green, with a square, greenish-brown block under it, and Father said, "All right, you two. There are your trees."

He stopped the wagon under the little trees, where he had stopped it on the first day. They all got down in front of their summerhouse. The willow branches in the walls were already turning yellow-brown, but the cottonwood leaves kept most of their green, though it was a different green from that of the little growing trees. Mother looked at the summerhouse, and said, "It's certainly a fine one, Tomás. I'm sure it will be big enough."

"I think so," said Father. "Come inside and see what we've done."

They all went inside. There was a questioning look on Mother's face, behind Father's back, but she did not say anything until she was inside the house. Then she said, "It's beautiful, Tomás. It's just the way I wanted it."

"I tried to remember where you said you wanted things," said Father. "Juan and I tried to be careful where we put them."

"You certainly were," said Mother. "Why, if we hadn't brought a cold supper with us, I could start cooking now."

"Good," said Father. He looked pleased and happy. "I'll go out and see to the horses, then."

When he had gone out, Mother stood looking at the room and shaking her head.

"Every single thing is backwards from the way I wanted it," she said, "but we'll leave it the way it is for a few days. Then he won't notice when we change it. María, you and Desidéria can start getting the supper basket from the wagon, and don't ever tell your father what I just said."

Part II: The Bowl Is Polished

9. The Schools
(1887–1898

Like all the children they knew and with whom they grew up, María and her sisters first went to school in the pueblo. There was a government school there, and when the two girls started, the teacher was a white man who had married a Santa Clara woman. They had a large family of half-Indian children, who went to the school, too. The teacher had learned Tewa from his wife, and he often used it in speaking to the school children.

At the end of the year, the school had exercises. All the parents were there. Some of the children did arithmetic sums on the blackboard, and others sang songs or recited pieces. After the exercises were over, Juan Gonzales, who was an important man in the pueblo, said to Father, "Tomás, what do you think?"

"I don't know," said Father slowly. "I've always believed that the one thing that couldn't be taken away from you was your education. Houses can burn, and crops can fail, and money can be lost or stolen, but what's in your head is yours."

"That's what I think," said Juan Gonzales. "I don't believe these children are getting much more in their minds at school than they would at home."

"No," replied Father, "they don't seem to be. When I went to the priests' school in Santa Fé, they made us practice reading and writing and speaking Spanish until we thought in that language instead of in our own. But these children are still speaking and thinking in Tewa. They don't make good figures on the blackboard, and when they try to write, it looks like a lot of chickens scratching."

"That's what I think," said Juan Gonzales again. "I believe if this teacher doesn't go away pretty soon, you'll have to write a letter to the government about him."

"I'd be ashamed," said Father. "I'd have to write the letter in Spanish, because I don't know any English."

"They can get somebody to translate it," said Juan.

Father did not have to write the letter, as it turned out. Soon afterwards the teacher's wife got homesick for her family at Santa Clara, and they moved back there. Then there was a time in the summer when people wondered if the school would open at all. In the fall, when everybody was really beginning to think about it, a wagon drove up to the schoolhouse, and the new teacher got out.

The new teacher was Miss Grimes. She had a young face, but her hair was white. Soon everybody in the pueblo could guess why that had happened to her, for after Miss Grimes had been there a week and had settled into the teacher's house by the school, her sister came to stay with her. The sister was older than Miss Grimes, and she was sick; you could tell that by looking at her. In fact, Miss Grimes said that one reason why they had come to San Ildefonso was so that her sister could live outdoors and get well. There was a porch on their house, and Miss Grimes put a bed out there so her sister could sleep out of doors. Even in winter the sick woman slept there, with sheets hung up around her bed to keep the worst of the cold away. The children called her "The Snow Ghost," because she was thin and white and lived wrapped up in white sheets.

Right from the beginning, María loved Miss Grimes. Miss Grimes told the children, on the day that school opened, that she did not know any Tewa. "I'd like to learn it, of course," she said, "but until I do, you'll have to help me out by speaking English." The children all agreed that they would try. It was odd, but as long as Miss Grimes, who was a smart woman in every other way, stayed in San Ildefonso, she never did learn to speak Tewa. People had to go on helping her by speaking English all the years that she lived there.

Everybody was willing to help, because Miss Grimes was nice and friendly. She visited all the houses, and she knew everybody in the pueblo by name. If she went to a house at mealtime, she sat down and ate with the family, and afterwards she helped wash the dishes. She was never cross, and she never refused to help people who were in trouble.

Once María spoke to Miss Grimes about it. "My mother says that you aren't like other white women," she said. "Nobody else we ever knew was as easy to be with as you are."

"Your mother is easy to be with, too," Miss Grimes answered. "She is a real lady."

"Is a lady a grownup?" María wanted to know.

"A lady is a person who is friendly and helpful and kind, and who treats people nicely, so that they will like to have her around," answered Miss Grimes.

"Can a little girl be a lady?" María demanded.

"She can be if she wants to be," Miss Grimes assured her. "You are only a little girl yourself, now, but you are a lot like your mother. Already you are a real lady in your own way."

"Thank you," said María. She felt shy about being a lady, and she could not look at Miss Grimes at all for a few minutes.

"You have to keep trying, you know," Miss Grimes went on. "You have to keep thinking and trying, and not ever stop, if you truly want to be a lady."

"Thank you," said María again. Then she raised her eyes, and looked directly at Miss Grimes. "I'm going to keep trying and trying to be a lady like my mother and you."

She did keep trying, and so did Desidéria. They learned a lot of things by watching and listening, and they must have learned more than they realized. On the last day of school, the third year Miss Grimes was in the pueblo, Juan Gonzales said to Father, "That was better than a few years ago, wasn't it?"

"It certainly was," Father agreed, "I could tell all the letters and figures they put on the blackboard, but most of the time I couldn't understand a word they said!"

"That's right," said Juan. "I think those girls of yours were the best of them all, too."

"Oh," said Father, trying to be honest and modest at the same time, "I don't believe they were. I think all the students were just about the same."

Nobody said anything at all to María and Desidéria. They had good marks, and Mother told them she was glad they had worked and studied hard, and that was all. But one day during the summer the governor and two of the councilmen of the pueblo came to see Father. They all sat and talked for a long time under the apple trees by the *acequia*. The girls went away from their playhouses to sit in the kitchen, because they did not want to disturb the men. When the visitors had left, Father came into the house.

"Well, Reyes," he said to Mother, "I have a surprise for you."

"What's that?" asked Mother, looking up at him. Her fingers kept right on stringing beans for dinner, even when her eyes were on Father's face.

"The council has had a meeting," Father said, "and they chose the students they want to send away to school next fall. They want both our girls to go to St. Catherine's Indian School in Santa Fé."

Mother sat with her hands still, staring at him. "Both our girls!" she repeated. "We have three who are old enough to go."

"Yes," said Father. "They wanted all three to go, but I told them we needed one girl here to help us. Ana is growing up and pretty soon she will be thinking about marrying, so they decided that just the two younger ones should go."

"I see," said Mother slowly. "Well, that's all right. We will need one of them at home, as you say. Ana has never cared as much about school as the others anyway. She will be happier at home, I think."

María and Desidéria had sat still without speaking as long as they could. Now they began to ask questions.

"When will we go?" María asked, and, in the same breath, "How long will we stay?" queried Desidéria.

"One at a time," said Father, holding up his hand. "You'll go in the fall, when school opens. If you are good girls, and the Sisters like you and want to keep you, you can stay all year. Maybe the next fall you can go back again. That depends on how you behave and how much you learn."

"I never went to the Sisters' school," said María. "I never knew anyone who went there. Did you, Mother?"

"Did I know anybody who went, or did I go myself?" asked her mother, smiling. "Yes, to both questions. I went for three years, when I was about your age. My parents sent me."

"Why did you stay so long, Mother?" Desidéria asked.

"I liked it there," her mother said quietly. "I wanted to stay all my life, and be a nun."

"Why didn't you?" María questioned.

"My parents sent for me," her mother replied. "They had picked out a young man for me to marry, so I came home like a good daughter, and married him." She looked up at Father, and smiled. "I've never been sorry," she added.

"That's good, Reyes," Father said. "I didn't want you to be sorry."

They were silent for a moment, all of them, and then Father put his hand on María's head and broke the stillness. "We'll have a lot to do to get them ready for school," he said, and Mother agreed, "Yes, they'll need new clothes, and shoes, and all sorts of things."

From then on, although it was almost two months before school opened, everybody was busy getting María and Desidéria ready to go. Mother had decided that they needed a new kind of clothes. They had always dressed like all the other women and girls in the pueblo—with flowered or striped blouses and plain-colored dresses that fastened over one shoulder and under the other arm. The girls wore moccasins without stockings, and in warm weather they often went barefooted. Their hair was cut in straight bangs across their foreheads, and made into braids that were tied up at the napes of their necks with strips of hand-woven cloth. The girls wore hand-woven belts, too, and bead necklaces, and on Sundays they wore earrings.

Mother thought that these clothes would not do. She went to talk with Miss Grimes about it. María went with her to interpret, but the two women seemed to understand each other before she could translate what they had been saying.

"I want them dressed like white girls," Mother said. "I don't want them to look old-fashioned and backward in that school."

"I think you're right," Miss Grimes agreed. "I'll tell you what we'll do. I'm going away for two weeks. I'm leaving Monday. If you would like me to, I'll get patterns and materials for the new dresses, and send them back right away so you can start making them."

That was the plan, and within ten days the patterns and materials had come, and Mother and the girls were making dresses. They had to sew everything by hand, but they all worked together, and the work was quickly finished. As soon as Miss Grimes returned from her vacation, María and Desidéria went down to show her their new clothes.

"They look very nice," Miss Grimes said, "just like the pictures on the patterns."

"Do we look like ladies in them?" María inquired. She had been wondering about that. Miss Grimes had not sent the kind of bright-colored materials the girls usually wore, but what they called Spanish colors: browns and grays and dark blues.

"Yes, you do," Miss Grimes assured María now. "You both look like real, grown-up ladies. Wait a minute, now. I have a present for each of you." She went into the next room, and came back carrying two carefully wrapped tissue-paper packages, just alike. "There you are," she said, handing one to each of the girls.

There were three hair ribbons in each package; plaid ribbons with different-colored backgrounds. The girls stared at them. They had never seen such ribbons before.

"Oh, thank you," said María, at last. She got up. "I guess we'd better go home now. We want to show these to Mother."

"You're welcome," said Miss Grimes. "Wear them and be happy with them."

The night before the girls left the pueblo, Mother came in and sat down on the edge of the bed after they had undressed.

"There's something I want to tell you," she began slowly. "It's about your confirmation. Most girls are confirmed before they're as old as you are, but you haven't been. The Bishop just hasn't been here,

is all. So I am going to tell the Mother Superior at the school about that, and that I think you both ought to be confirmed this year. Remember that and think about it. That's an important thing."

"Yes, Mother," said María solemnly. "We will." She and Desidéria did not talk about their confirmation after Mother had left them, but they both lay and thought about it until sleep wiped all thinking from their minds.

Mother and Father took the girls to Santa Fé in the wagon the next day. María and Desidéria wore their new dresses, and Mother made them ride on the seat of the wagon so that the dresses would not get mussed. She herself sat, wrapped in her blanket, in the wagon box. The girls' bundles of clothes and books were beside her, and once

María turned around and saw her mother sitting with one hand resting on a bundle of dresses, patting it a little as if it were a child. Tears came into María's eyes, and she turned around again quickly, and looked straight at a tree beside the road until it had gone by and her tears had stayed behind with it.

That was a long day's ride. Late in the evening, when the family was all tired, they came over the crest of a big hill. On its long downward slope before them, they saw little shiny lights, dotted through the piñones and junipers, and growing brighter as the dusk grew darker.

"This is Tesuque Hill," said Father, answering the question María had not yet asked. "Most travelers rest here for the night, and go on to Santa Fé in the morning, when they're fresh."

But he shook the reins over the horses' backs, and the family kept on traveling down the hill, until lights grew up around them, framed with the darkness of houses, and they were in the town. Then there was a gate, with a bell that Father rang, and one of the Sisters opened the gate for them when she heard the ringing. Then there were lights and corridors and people talking, and then Mother and Father were kissing their children good-bye, and then, at last, there was bed. When the girls wakened in the morning, the school was all around them, and they were starting in as pupils.

The classes in the Santa Fé school were harder than those Miss Grimes taught. Most of the Sisters were strict with the girls, and they did not laugh much. Only Sister Brigita, the sewing teacher, did not mind if the girls talked and laughed quietly as they worked. María liked sewing anyway. It was the pleasantest part of school to her. She did well at it.

"You are good with your hands, María," Sister Brigita said once, and María went around feeling good about it until late that afternoon. Then she went to confirmation class, and Father Antonio talked to the girls about the sin of pride and how it was one of the seven deadly sins and sent by the devil. So María went to bed much ashamed of herself, thinking of all the things she did poorly, instead of sewing, which she did well.

One of the things that María did not do well was letter writing. As it was easy for Desidéria, they worked out a plan about it. María darned Desidéria's stockings, and in return Desidéria wrote María's letters home. Each of the girls had to write a letter a week, and sometimes Desidéria had a hard time thinking of enough to tell to make two letters. Usually she managed to. Then María would copy her letter, so that the Mother Superior would see that they were in different handwritings when she opened and inspected them before they were mailed.

All through the year everything the two girls did was pointed towards their confirmation. This was to come at the end of May, at the time when school closed. Late in April, the Mother Superior instructed the girls to write letters to their parents, inviting them to come for the closing exercises and the confirmation service. All the girls did as they were instructed, and then talked and talked about whether their parents would be able to come. Two weeks after the invitations had been sent, the Mother Superior called María and Desidéria into her office.

"I have a letter for you, girls," she said, and smiled a little when she saw how carefully they opened it.

The letter was from Father, written in the fine hand that he had learned at the Priests' school when he was a boy.

"*Señoritas, mias Hermosas,*" the letter began, and it went on to say that he and Mother would plan to attend the closing exercises, and the confirmation, and then take the girls home the following day. "*Con felicitationes,*" the letter ended. María thought that she had never seen a finer way of signing a letter.

The next day the girls had another surprise. When they went into the sewing room, there were eight new white dresses, with veils to match, laid out on the work tables—one for each member of the confirmation class. Sister Brigita and the other girls stood by and smiled, and Sister Brigita said, "The dresses are presents from all of us. The Sisters gave the materials, and the other girls gave the work. Come and let us try them on you, so we can be sure they fit."

The white dresses were all made differently, and each of the veils had a wreath of a different kind of white flowers to go around the wearer's head. María's dress was made with a long, full skirt, to make her look taller, Sister Brigita said; and her flowers were white sweet peas. Desidéria's flowers were daisies, and her dress had puffed shoulders, so that she would not look so thin. The girls had never seen such beautiful dresses in their lives, and they had never dreamed of owning any like these.

"Now we'll have to be ladies," said María to her sister when they were back in their own cubicle in the dormitory. "Only ladies have the right to wear dresses like those."

88

The Schools

The next event came at the end of the week, on Saturday morning. Confirmation was to be at noon on Sunday, and First Communion on Saturday evening. The Mother Superior sent for María and Desidéria to come to see her.

"She has a surprise for you," Sister Brigita told them.

The surprise was their parents. Somehow the girls had not expected to see them until the next day, but there they were. Mother Superior let the family have a bread-and-milk lunch together at one end of the refectory table, before the closing exercises started that afternoon.

Everybody had worked hard getting ready for the exercises, and many Santa Fé people, as well as the pupils' parents, had come to see the performance. The little girls sang, and some of the big girls recited pieces. Desidéria had an arithmetic problem to do on the blackboard, and María was one of the girls who wrote out sentences, to show how much their writing had improved.

Then the Mother Superior awarded the prizes for the year. "For proficiency in composition," she read out, "Desidéria Montoya. Desidéria has done better in English than any other girl in school in her grade." They all clapped when Desidéria went forward to take the little figure of the Sacred Heart that was her prize. María was proud of her sister. She thought of all the letters Desidéria had written for her, and wondered if they had helped win the prize without anybody's even knowing about them. She thought she had a right to be proud of Desidéria, and not feel sinful about it, since this was not her own achievement.

Then the Mother Superior read, "For proficiency in sewing, María Montoya. María is the best seamstress the school has had for a long time," and María felt herself going up the aisle, walking carefully in order not to trip before she got to the front of the room. The Mother Superior handed her a big picture of Saint Joseph, and María clutched it carefully and forgot about her feet, as she went back to her chair. Mother and Father leaned over and looked at the picture and admired it, as they had Desidéria's statue.

"We'll put them both in the living room at home," Mother whispered. "You ought to keep them always."

After the exercises, the girls seemed to spend most of their time in the Cathedral. There were many children from all over Santa Fé who were to be confirmed, and the services took a long time. It all happened in a dream, the lights of the candles and the music and the Bishop, tall in his white robes. The Cathedral itself was beautiful with flowers, but it seemed far away from María even when she knelt in it. She kept remembering the little church in the pueblo, that she was used to, and from it her mind went on to the Sanctuario at Chimayó. Those were churches where you could reach out and touch God. Here, in this big cathedral, He was lost, in some way, and far from her, yet frighteningly real.

When the *"Te Deum"* had been sung at the end of the Sunday service, and it was all over, María drew a deep breath. Now they were going home. She and Desidéria looked for their parents but could not find them.

"We can go up to our room and pack," María said practically. "They can find us there."

They took off their new white dresses and veils, and hung them up carefully, to pack last of all. Then they put on school dresses and got busy. Just as they were finishing, Mother came in. "Don't pack too much, girls," she said. "Mother Superior wants us all to stay until tomorrow, so they can have a picture taken of the confirmation class. We'll start home right away afterwards, and spend the night with our friends in Tesuque Pueblo."

As the girls had never had their pictures taken, the next morning was the most exciting time of all. If they had known beforehand what was going to happen, it might have been too much for them to bear. After breakfast, Sister Brigita and Mother got the whole class together in the dormitory, and made sure that the girls looked just right. Then they marched in a procession, two and two, down the street and around the plaza to the photographer's. Mother walked at the head of the line, with her back looking very straight, and Sister Brigita walked last to make sure everyone behaved. She need not have bothered. The girls were all too much impressed with what was happening to be naughty.

"I never saw nicer girls, Sister," said the photographer when the picture had been taken. "They all acted like ladies." Sister Brigita and Mother beamed, but they made sure that the girls kept right on behaving themselves on the way back to school.

When the bundles were in the wagon and they were ready to start, with the girls sitting in the wagon bed because now they were going home and could wash and iron their dresses when they got there, Sister Brigita came out to say good-bye. "But we'll be looking for you next year," she said, as she shook hands with María.

The Schools

"I don't know whether we'll be back, though," María said.

Father turned around on the wagon seat and smiled at her. "I was saving it, to tell you on the way home," he said. "The council decided that you were such good girls, and wrote such nice letters home, that they would send you back for another year."

"Oh," said María, in a small voice. She felt ashamed. "I guess only Desidéria can go, though. She wrote all the letters."

"All of them?" demanded Mother.

"All of them," María whispered. She felt worse and worse, with Sister Brigita looking at her.

All of a sudden Sister Brigita laughed. "Well," she said, comfortingly, "you admitted it honestly, like a lady. And after all, who won the sewing prize? You had to do that yourself. I can't get along without my prize sewing pupil, Reyes," she said to Mother, "so be sure you send her back. Let's just regard this as a confession, and keep it secret, shall we, all of us?" She leaned over the side of the wagon and kissed each of the girls lightly on the cheek. "Go with God," she said, in Spanish, "and come back to us soon."

The next day, after she got home, María went to see Miss Grimes to tell her everything that had happened. Even though Sister Brigita had said it was a confession and a secret, she added the part about the letters, too. "What do you think?" she asked anxiously, when she had finished. "Was that unladylike?"

Miss Grimes sat quiet, thinking, for a long time. "To let Desidéria write the letters was unladylike," she said. "But to own up to it when you could have profited by it was right. Don't do wrong things if you can help it, ever, but if you have done something wrong, don't be afraid to say so." She smiled a little. "It takes a long time to be a real lady, you know," she continued. "Your mother is a grown woman, remember. But still, I think for a little girl, you are a real lady, too, María."

10. The Meeting
(1899

María and Desidéria stayed at the Sisters' school their full two years. Then they went home, back to the pueblo. Things there had changed in some ways and had stood still in others. The houses and the fields and the cottonwood tree in the plaza were the same as they had always been, but there were changes in the people. Some of them looked older and weaker, and some of the younger ones looked stronger, as if they were making themselves ready, without knowing it, to take the older peoples' places.

It was strange about this strengthening change. Suddenly you be- gan to see people whom you had never noticed before. Where there had been someone whom you took for granted as you would a cow or a dog, now there was a surprisingly familiar strange person. And what was most surprising of all was that the new person—or his new personality—seemed to feel the same way about you.

María felt the strangeness of getting older most strongly with her teacher whom she loved. After she had slept at home in her own bed and before she saw even Grandmother, María went down to the village to see Miss Grimes. The teacher was at home, with her sick sister, and they must have been waiting for María for Miss Grimes opened the door as soon as she knocked.

"Come in," she said. Behind her, her sister, too, said, "Come in," in the tired voice of one who has been ill for a long time.

María came into the warm room, and when her teacher asked her to, she sat down. There were many questions to be asked about the school in Santa Fé, and the things that María had learned there. There were plans to be made about what she should do next.

"What do you want to do with your life, María?" Miss Grimes asked her.

"Why, I don't know," María said. "Just what most ladies do, I guess. Get married and have a house and take care of babies."

The Meeting

"That's a fine life if it's what you want," said Miss Grimes slowly, "but you don't have to live it if you don't want to. You are a bright girl, and you work and study hard. If you wanted to, you could go to school and college and learn to be a teacher yourself. Then you could come back here and teach other children in your own pueblo. There should be many more Indian teachers teaching Indian children."

"That would be good," answered María thoughtfully. "It would be helping, wouldn't it?"

"It would be helping in a very important way," said Miss Grimes. "And it would be interesting for you, too. You would get to travel a great deal, and to see many things."

"Travel beyond Santa Fé?" María questioned.

"Travel as far as you like," said Miss Grimes smiling. "You could travel to New York, if you wanted to. I went to school there myself. That is a great city, and a wonderful one. You should certainly see it for yourself."

"What is it like, being a teacher?" María asked. "Is it happy?"

"In some ways it is very happy," Miss Grimes told her.

Suddenly the sick sister, who was so quiet they had forgotten she was in the room, spoke from her corner by the fireplace. "It's a lonely life for a woman," she said quickly and sharply. "Your first choice is the best one, María. Live like other ladies."

"I don't know," said Miss Grimes, speaking more to herself than to the others. "I don't regret teaching. You see something grow when you are with children. And, as María says, it's helping." She turned briskly back to the girl. "I'll tell you what," she said. "If you want to go ahead studying and learning while you think about being a teacher, I'll help you and you can help me. You can be the schoolhouse housekeeper, if you like, and help with the sweeping and cleaning up, and I'll give you lessons in return. Would you like that?"

"Yes," said María. She drew a deep breath, and stood up. There was a lot to think about, all of a sudden. "I think I'd better go home now, please," she said.

"That's right," said Miss Grimes, standing up herself like one lady saying good-bye to another. "You go home and tell your parents about it, and talk it over with them. Then, if they give you permission, we'll do it."

"Good-bye, then," said María.

"Good-bye," answered Miss Grimes.

On her way up the hill to the house, María met her father.

"How is Miss Grimes?" he asked.

"She's all right," said María. "She told me something, Father."

"Is it something serious?" Father asked, looking at her sober face.

"I guess it is," María replied. "I want to tell you and Mother about it."

"All right," said Father. "Come home, now, and tell us. You can go to see your relatives this afternoon."

Mother was grinding corn meal when they went into the kitchen. "Come and help me, please," she said to María. "I've had to do all the grinding by myself since you and Desidéria went away and Ana got married. You can break up the corn on the coarse *metate.*"

"I wanted to talk to you," said María, kneeling down by the *metate.*

"Well, we can talk and work at the same time," said Mother. "What have you to tell us?"

"Miss Grimes was talking to me," María began. It was hard, suddenly, to find the right words for what she had to say. "She was talking about what I was going to do when I grew up."

"Yes?" said Father. "What does she think you should do?"

"She said I could be a teacher," said María in a rush. "She said I should go away, maybe even to New York, and study and learn and everything. Then I could come back here and teach in the school. She said Indian teachers should be teaching Indian children."

"That's a good idea," Father agreed. "The more Indians are with Indians, the better off they all are."

"But the government would have to hire you to be a teacher," said Mother. "I would like it if they hired you to teach here. That would be all right. What would happen, though, if they hired you to teach somewhere else?"

"I don't know," said María. "We didn't talk about that."

"You have to think about it," her mother reminded her. "It's something that could happen, and if it did, you would have to change your planning, you know."

"Well," said María, "maybe I could ask them to send me here."

"Yes," said Father, "you could do that. And the council could ask to have you sent. That would be all right. What else did Miss Grimes say?" he demanded.

"She said I could be a kind of housekeeper at the schoolhouse and help her this winter," answered María. "She said she would give me special lessons in return for the work, and in that way I could be studying and learning for a while before I went away."

The Meeting

"That would be good," said Father. "Do you want to do it?"

"I guess so," said María. "I want to stay home for a while, anyway. I don't want to go off and start learning to be a teacher right away."

"Well," said Mother, "I don't think you ought to go. You've just got back from doing a lot of studying, and you don't know what you want to do, really." She sat back from the *metate* on her heels, and looked straight ahead of her at the kitchen wall. "It's like my wanting to be a nun, when I was your age. Now I'm glad that my parents made me change my mind about it. It's the right life for a woman, to have her own house and her own children and her own man. It's right to be at home, in your own pueblo with your own people."

She looked across at her husband, and smiled, and he smiled back at her. It was a special kind of smile, one that they seemed to keep for each other.

"Being a teacher is a little like being a nun," said Mother, briskly, bending forward over the *metate* again. "You have to be very strong inside yourself and very sure about what you want to do, if you start in on it. You don't have other people to help you. Except for God and the saints, you have to stand by yourself in that kind of life."

"It takes strength to be a mother, too," said Father gently.

"Yes," agreed Mother, "that takes strength. A different kind of strength. But you have somebody helping you, and you are in your own pueblo and with your own relatives all the time, and that helps you, too. Every woman has her own strength to do what she needs to do. You have to know what kind of strength you have and how to use it."

"Well," said Father, thoughtfully, "María is lucky. She has a chance now to find out if she has the kind of strength she needs to be a teacher, before she makes up her mind. Let her help Miss Grimes this winter. If she learns a lot and is happy learning, we can begin making plans for her to go away if she wants to."

"That's all right," Mother agreed. "We can see, too, if she has the kind of strength she needs for planning things for herself. It takes strength to make your own plans and not to have somebody else make them for you all your life."

It was a strange conversation, to María. Her parents were talking about her as if she were not there, and yet she felt as if every word they spoke was being said directly to her.

"I'll tell Miss Grimes," she said, with a funny feeling, as if she were interrupting.

"You can tell her," said Mother. "You can tell her this afternoon, after you have seen your relatives and greeted them."

Desidéria came in then. She had been down to see Ana and her new baby. Ana had married while they were at home the summer before, and the baby was only two weeks old and was Desidéria's god-daughter. Ana and her husband had been at the house to greet the girls when they reached home the night before, so María felt that she had already seen her sister. Desidéria, though, could not seem to get enough of the baby.

That afternoon María and Desidéria went together to visit their other relatives. They started at Grandmother's house and then went on to see their aunts and uncles. It was like a party, all the way around the plaza. Everyone hugged them, and cried with joy to see them again. Everyone gave them coffee or milk to drink, and *biscochitos* and *empanadas* to eat. There was excitement around them all the time, and the girls began to feel that going away was an adventure; everyone was so glad to have them back. All the relatives asked the same question, "Now you really are home to stay? Aren't you?"

And every time the girls gave the same answers. Desidéria said, "We never want to go away again," and María said, "We really are home."

Last of all, they went by Miss Grimes' house, on their way home to supper. Miss Grimes was in the kitchen, cooking, but she heard their knock at the front door, and came to let them in.

María said, "I talked to my parents, the way you told me."

"What did they say?" Miss Grimes asked.

"They said for me to help you," answered María. "They said I would be at home for a year, that way, and still I would be learning about what I wanted to do."

North Plaza, Looking South

"That's good," said Miss Grimes. "You can start in the fall, when we get back from our vacation."

"All right," said María. "Thank you." And she and Desidéria, who had not said a word to the teacher during the whole time, went back up the hill in the twilight, to their mother's house. María felt funny about not having told Desidéria all about the plan right away. It was strange not to tell her sister, the first one, so now she said, "Miss Grimes wants me to work as a schoolhouse housekeeper for her. She'll give me lessons, so maybe I can learn to be a teacher."

Desidéria turned and stared at her. "What do you want with more lessons?" she demanded. "Haven't you had enough of them? First we went to school here, and then we went to Santa Fé for two years more school, and now that we're home, you want to go on having more lessons."

"Well," María protested, "you can't be a teacher unless you study a lot yourself first."

"Why do you want to be a teacher?" asked Desidéria disgustedly. "That's all right for white people. But Indian girls don't have to be teachers. They have houses and babies to take care of."

It was all the same thing. Everybody thought the same way. Even Miss Grimes' sick sister had said just what Desidéria did. It was puzzling.

"Well," said María, stopping by the irrigation ditch and kicking little loose gravel stones into it with her toe, "you don't get to have a house and babies of your own just by wanting them. You have to know how to do things, and you have to get a husband. It takes time, too, like learning to be a teacher."

"Ana didn't know how to do things except farm," objected Desidéria. "She manages her house and the baby all right."

"Well, she still had to get married first," said María firmly. "I don't know anybody to marry, and I'm not planning to get married."

"It doesn't have anything to do with you," snapped Desidéria. "It's up to our parents to find somebody for us to marry, and to get everything ready for us."

"Maybe it is," said María, "but I don't know that I'll like the one they pick out for me. I might want to marry somebody else."

"If they pick him out, you've got to marry him," said Desidéria, and she turned and went into the house. María followed her.

The family went to The Little Trees for the summer, and it was the best summer there that María ever remembered. Looking back at it when she was older, she could not remember anything special that happened; they were just together and happy. Ana and her husband came, too, so that Ana's husband Cresencio could help Father on the farm, and the family all ate a lot and laughed a lot. Even though María and Desidéria were almost grown up, it was like the summers there that they remembered from the time when they were little girls. Then it was fall, and time to go back to the pueblo again.

Miss Grimes and her sister had gone away for their summer vacation, to visit their relatives in Boston, but they returned about the same time that the family did. Miss Grimes got ready right away to start school, and María began to work helping her.

The schoolhouse had been closed all summer, of course, and the first thing they had to do was scrub and clean it and calsomine the walls, in order to have everything ready for the children. Miss Grimes had brought a lot of magazines back with her, and she set María to work cutting colored pictures out of them, to be pasted along the walls. The cutting was easy and fun, for María could sit and look at the magazines and read the stories in them while she worked. Pasting was harder, but it was fun, too, to match the edges of the pictures to each other and make them go neat and smooth around the room. Scrubbing the blackboards was not fun. It was just plain hard work. While they worked, Miss Grimes told María about things that had happened to her in the East, during the summer.

"I went to New York for a week," she said. "My sister stayed in Boston and rested, but I went there. It is a wonderful city, María. You must go there some day when you are older."

"Yes," said María, scrubbing away at the blackboard.

Later in the day, Miss Grimes gave María some books to take home with her. There were a geography, a history, and a spelling book.

"You don't have to start studying now," Miss Grimes said. "Wait till we finish the cleaning and you aren't so tired. But since these are the books I want you to use, you might as well take them."

María was too tired to study that evening, but she sat down and looked through the books. The history book had pictures in it, and she read what it said under the pictures. There was Columbus on a ship, sailing to discover America, and Columbus getting off the ship and meeting the Indians. There was a picture, too, of William Penn signing a treaty with the Indians. María decided that the men who painted them had never been in a pueblo. The Indians certainly did not look like anybody she had ever seen. The books looked interesting but hard. They were certainly harder than any books she had ever studied before. María decided that studying did not get any easier as you went on with it. A teacher had to do an awful lot of work before she even began teaching.

Later, María said something like that to Miss Grimes. Miss Grimes, who was grading spelling papers, nodded. "That's true," she said. "And a good teacher never stops working and studying and learning. That's part of her life. But don't forget, María, that the same thing is true of any way of living. There's always something more to learn about whatever you do."

María had never thought about life in that way. That evening she spoke to her mother about what Miss Grimes had said.

"Do you have to keep on learning?" she inquired.

"Yes," said Mother, "I do."

"But what?" María pressed her. "You know everything there is about cooking and housework and taking care of children."

"No, I don't," replied her mother. "I've never been able to make good *empanadas* in my life. Grandmother makes fine ones, and she has shown me how she does it lots of times, but mine never turn out quite the same way as hers. I don't know whether I'll ever learn to make good *empanadas,* but I'm keeping on trying."

"Oh," said María.

"Another thing," Mother went on. "I brought you and your sisters up all right, but I lost three babies. I still might have another baby, and it would live or die, as things happened. I'd like to know how to keep all the babies alive. That's something nobody knows, I guess."

"I see," María said.

The weather was beginning to get cool now, and the mornings were cold. Miss Grimes had to work harder than she had before to keep her house warm and comfortable. María helped her as well as she could, but it was too much of a job, even for both of them. The worst task was chopping wood for the fireplace and the stove. Neither Miss Grimes nor María was a very good chopper.

"Juan Gonzales helped me with this work last winter," Miss Grimes said. "He's too busy with fall plowing now to do much else, though. I'll have to try to find somebody else."

That night María asked her father if he knew of anybody who could chop wood for Miss Grimes.

"Julián Martínez might," said Father. "That family doesn't farm much. The father makes flour sifters and saddles, and Julián helps him sometimes, but that's about all. The old mother takes care of the garden. Why doesn't Miss Grimes get Julián?"

"I'll tell her," promised María, and went on with her studying. She had got up to reading about William Penn in the history book. Except for the fact that he was a good man who liked the Indians, there did not seem to be much to remember about him. He was more interesting than Julián Martínez, though, whom she remembered as a bad boy who ran away from school and would not study when he did go to class. There was not as much about him to remember as there was about William Penn. Still, when she was reciting the William Penn lesson to Miss Grimes the next day, she was reminded of what her father had said and repeated his words to the teacher.

"Father says that maybe Julián will help you with the wood," she finished.

Miss Grimes looked doubtful. "I don't know whether he wants even that much to do with school," she said. "Still, it won't hurt to ask him. I'll have to pay him money to get him to work. He won't do it for lessons, like you." She and María both laughed a little, and then they went on with William Penn.

The Meeting

The next day was Saturday and the day after that was Sunday. María stayed at home and helped her mother on both days. She did not go back to the schoolhouse until late Monday afternoon. When she got there, the blackboards were all covered with writing and would have to be scrubbed. Miss Grimes had gone home, for she was not at the school; but she must have been planning on coming back, for the door of the schoolhouse stood open.

María was scrubbing the blackboard, when she heard the door, which she had closed, open behind her. She thought it was Miss Grimes, and without looking around she said, "It sure is hard, but I'm getting it clean."

"That's good," said a voice behind her in Tewa. A strange voice, a man's voice.

María turned quickly from the blackboard, to face the man who had come in. At first she did not recognize him, he was so tall and straight; then she knew by his face that he was Julián.

"Hello," he said, when María just looked at him.

"Hello," she answered finally.

"Where's Miss Grimes?" Julián asked. He had a nice voice, a good, deep voice of a man.

"She isn't here," María said. "I guess she's at home."

"I guess so," said Julián.

"Did you come to chop wood for her?" María asked then. And when she had asked the direct question, which might have been impolite, she felt so shy that she stood and looked at the floor.

"I came to chop wood," said Julián. He, too, looked at the floor as carefully as if he had lost something there and was trying to find it. Then he said. "I guess I'd better go, now. I'll go to her house for Miss Grimes."

María heard his feet go off across the floor even in the soft moccasins he wore. She turned back to the blackboard and began to scrub. All of a sudden it was the most important thing in her life to get that blackboard clean.

11. Time Together
(1899–1903

It was never clear, in their own minds or in anyone else's, how María and Julián began seeing so much of one another. There was a day when they were almost strangers, although they had been seeing one another all their lives. Then, the next day almost, they were not strangers at all; and they were seeing each other almost daily.

Without their planning it so, most of the meetings took place at the schoolhouse in the late afternoon. María would be cleaning the room—scrubbing the blackboards, and sweeping, or washing windows, just doing whatever there was to be done. Julián would come to the schoolhouse to chop Miss Grimes' wood for the next day. Somehow or other, they would get to talking, and their talk would go on until María had the schoolroom cleaned and was ready to start home. Then Julián would walk up the hill with her and come back to the schoolhouse to chop the wood.

Miss Grimes was the first person who noticed anything. She could not help noticing, because the woodpile by her kitchen door kept getting higher and higher, and still there were new pieces added to it daily. At last she spoke to Julián about it. "I think we have all the wood we'll need for a while," she told him. "You won't have to chop any more for a few days."

Julián did not speak a great deal of English, but he did know some words. So he smiled amiably at Miss Grimes, and the next day he came back and chopped more wood. Miss Grimes spoke to him about it again; this time Julián turned to María and asked her, in Tewa, what the teacher had said.

"You know just as well as I do," María said, giggling.

"Sure I do," replied Julián, "but I want to be sure I understand just exactly what she said."

"Well," María informed him, "she said just exactly what you think she said. She said for you not to chop any more wood for three or four days."

"Do you want me not to chop wood?" asked Julián.

María swept the floor more intently than she ever had before.

"I don't care what you do," she answered. "If you want to chop wood and Miss Grimes wants you to chop wood, it's all right. If you don't want to chop wood and Miss Grimes doesn't want you to chop wood, it's all right, too. It's up to you both. You've got to make your own decisions."

Miss Grimes had been waiting patiently and silently while all this talking was going on. Now she asked, "What did Julián say, María?"

"He said he'll do what you want him to," María answered. "He won't chop any wood till you tell him to."

Julián understood everything they were saying to each other, but he did not say anything himself. He just smiled at María out of the corners of his eyes, and went out. When María started to go home, later, Julián was waiting for her by the door of the schoolhouse, and he walked up the hill with her as usual. Neither of them said anything about what had happened.

The next afternoon Julián came to the schoolhouse as usual.

"I thought you weren't going to chop any more wood," said María.

"I'm not," Julián said. "Not till Miss Grimes tells me to. I thought I'd help you with the sweeping. That way you'll get through sooner, and I haven't much else to do. Nobody wants any saddles right now."

So Julián helped her with the sweeping, and after that he walked home with her.

That night Mother spoke to María about Julián. "You see a lot of him," she said.

María had not thought about the matter in that way, but now she realized that she had been seeing Julián every day for a long time.

"I guess I do," she agreed.

"When a young man and a girl see so much of one another," her mother went on soberly, "it usually means something to them. Do you think it means anything to you?"

María hung her head and didn't answer.

"Well, then," her mother asked her, "do you think it means something to Julián?"

María still hung her head, but this time she said something. "I guess it does," she replied.

"I don't want to worry you," said Mother, "but I think you ought to know something. Your father and I have been thinking a lot about this lately."

"Yes, Mother," María said.

"You have always been a good child," Mother went on, "and we want you to be happy. You thought you might be happy if you studied and learned to be a school teacher, and that was all right. Whatever you do, we want it to be the right thing for you."

"Yes, Mother," María repeated.

"If you want to get married, we want you to be happy about that, too," continued her mother. "You ought to think a lot about the young man you're going to marry, before you make up your mind."

"I wasn't thinking about marrying Julián," María protested.

"Then you shouldn't see so much of him," her mother pointed out. "If you keep on seeing him every day, people will expect you to marry him."

"That isn't any of their business," said María. It made her angry all of a sudden to have people thinking about her, and about the things she did.

"Everything that happens in the pueblo, and to the people who belong to the pueblo, is a little bit everybody's business," her mother told her. "Now we want you to be happy, as I said. The best way to be happy is to marry a good man, who will make a good life with you."

"Julián is good," María said.

"Julián isn't bad," her mother corrected her. "He doesn't farm much, but he helps his father make flour sifters and saddles. That kind of work is all right when people need sifters and saddles. When they don't it isn't such a good way of living. I can use up a sifter about every two years, and most of the other women do the same thing. A saddle lasts ten or twenty years, depending on how you take care of it. Even if Julián and his father make all the sifters and all the saddles for four pueblos at once, it just will bring in enough for them to live on without adding anyone else to their family."

"Maybe Julián could learn to farm," María suggested.

"Maybe he could," Mother agreed. "If he does, then he will have something to live on and his wife will have something to live on. That would be all right. Then there's something else," she added. "If Julián really wants to marry you, he ought to send his parents to talk to us. That shows that a boy is really serious about how he feels about a young woman. Felipe Gonzales' parents have already been here to talk to us about you, for him."

"I don't want to marry Felipe," said María.

Time Together

"Maybe you don't right now," said her mother reasonably. "He went at it the right way, though, and your father and I would like to see you marry a man who did things right. And Felipe has his own land already and is a good farmer."

"I don't want to marry Felipe," said María, starting to cry.

"Think it all over," said Mother, getting up. "It's your life, and the decision is up to you. But we have to tell Felipe's parents about it pretty soon, so you'd better do your thinking quickly." She shut the door behind her, and left María alone to think things over.

María was still thinking the next year. She could not quite make up her mind yet what she wanted to do. One afternoon Julián came to the schoolhouse, as usual, to help her with the cleaning. He had something on his mind, too; she could tell that without his saying anything. When they had finished washing the blackboards and sweeping the floor, Julián sat down at one of the children's desks, and look up at María. He looked funny, sitting there with his long legs stretched out on either side of the desk, looking up at her with steady eyes.

"My uncle came to see me last night," he said.

María knew about Julián's uncle, Juan. He was a good singer and drummer who went to all the pueblos on their feast days, and sang and drummed as hard as he did when he was at a dance at home. She nodded her head, and waited for Julián to go on.

"The Indian Agency was talking to my uncle," said Julián. "They want him to get some Indians to go to St. Louis. They're having a world's fair in that place, and they want some Indians to go there and stay, and dance and sing. All kinds of Indians: San Juans and Tesuques and Santa Claras, and San Ildefonsos—everybody."

"How long are they going to stay?" María asked.

"A long time," said Julián. "Four or five months anyway." He began to pat the palm of his hand on the desk before him, as if he were beating a drum. "They have a place for the Indians to live, and they'll give them food, and they'll pay for the traveling, and they'll pay money for dancing and singing."

"Much money?" María asked.

"Lots of money," said Julián. "Fifty dollars a month, maybe."

"When do they start?" questioned María.

"In May," said Julián. "That's about four months from now."

María said nothing. She was thinking that four months was a long time or a short time, as you thought about it.

"Would you like to go?" Julián asked her suddenly.

Still María sat and said nothing. Then she raised her head, and drew a deep breath. "Felipe Gonzales," she began.

"What about Felipe?" Julián demanded.

"His parents came to see my mother and father a long time ago," answered María.

Julián grinned widely. "Trust Felipe," he said. "He always had to do things the right way." Then he sat up quickly. "What did your parents tell his?" he asked.

"Nothing, yet," María said. "They're still waiting on me."

"What are you going to tell them?" Julián wanted to know.

"I don't know yet," said María.

"Who are you waiting on?" asked Julián. "Me?"

"I guess so," said María. She felt as if she wanted to cry.

"Maybe my parents are waiting on me, too," said Julián, slowly. He grinned again. "I know my uncle is waiting on me, and I've been waiting on you." He got up, swinging one leg over the top of the desk. "I guess I'd better go home and talk to my mother and father," he said. "Can you walk up the hill alone all right?"

Time Together

María had to laugh at that question. "I've been walking up that hill alone all my life until the last year," she said. "I can still do it without you."

"All right," Julián said. "Good-bye."

They went out of the schoolhouse together, but as soon as they were outside, they parted. Julián went walking very fast, down to the village, and María went almost running, up the hill to home.

When she got into the house, she put her shawl away and began to help her mother with the supper. It was *atole* and milk and *frijoles,* as their winter suppers often were. María wished a little that they were having better food. This looked so plain, in case anyone came in and saw them eating it. No one came in during supper. No one came in while María and Desidéria washed the dishes. María began to think that perhaps no one would ever come; and she was so tired from the thought that all she wanted to do was to go to bed and cover her head. She felt as if some one had shamed her. She was glad that no one knew about her shame but herself, but not glad enough to feel better. Then there came a knock at the door.

"There are neighbors," said Father, getting up and going to open it.

"Probably Mrs. Gonzales," said Mother.

She gave María a straight look. "You'd better go to your room," she said sternly.

María did not say anything. She took a long time getting up and leaving the room. By the time she was halfway across the floor, Father had the door open. María saw that it was Julián's parents who had come in, not Felipe's. Then she hurried away as if there were a bear in the living room and it might catch her.

After what seemed to her as long a time as four full months, her bedroom door opened, and her mother came in.

"That was Julián's parents," Mother said abruptly.

"Yes," answered María, "I know."

"Well," said Mother, "do you know what you want to do? Both families are waiting now for you to make up your mind."

"I know," said María.

"Well," asked her mother, "what is it?"

"I want to marry Julián," said María.

"Have you thought it over carefully?" her mother questioned. "If you marry Felipe, you know what's ahead of you. It will be a sure life. But if you marry Julián, you don't know. Nobody can know now what life with him will be like. Remember, he isn't doing any steady work like farming. Maybe the life will be good, but maybe it will be bad. How can you be sure?"

"I can't be sure about that," María answered. "You never can be sure about everything in this life, it seems to me. I can try to make it a good life, though. I can work hard to make it good. I know that I can do that. I know that the time I spent with Julián this winter has been good. I know he was nice and kind and fun to be with."

"Life isn't all fun," said her mother, sadly, "Even being happy with somebody isn't all fun."

"I guess not," said María. "I'd still rather be with Julian than with anybody else."

"If that's the way you feel about it, that's the way you feel," her mother agreed. "All right. I'll tell your father. You've made your decision. Just remember that when you make this kind of decision, you have to stay by it all your life. The church says so and the council says so. This choice is what you're going to live by from now on."

"All right," said María. "I'll remember that. I think we'll all be happy now I've made it. Julián's smart. He can learn to farm when we get back from St. Louis."

Mother stopped at the door, and turned to look at her. "That's another thing," she said. "Are you sure you're not marrying Julián just to get a trip to St. Louis?"

"I'm sure," replied María. "I'd want to marry him anyway. I want to come back from St. Louis and live here in the pueblo, and never go away from home again, ever."

"Not even to study and be a teacher?" her mother asked.

"Not even for that," said María, "just to stay here and be at home."

"All right," said Mother. "If you feel that way, it will be good."

She went away, to tell her husband what María had decided.

12. The Wedding

(1904

A wedding was a time for happiness, María knew. There was gayness and good feeling all through the pueblo when two people were getting married, and she had often watched the happiness growing for others. But that there could or would be excitement, too, she had never guessed.

The excitement began for her when Julián's parents came to bring her the bethrothal present. It was the same present that every young man gave to the girl he married, and María gave him the same thing in return. They called the gifts Indian *rosarios,* because each was a string of beads. The Indian *rosarios* were not like church rosaries. The Indian ones were made of all different-colored kinds of beads: red and blue and yellow and white and mixed colors, strung on fine sinew or cotton threads. The mothers of the young people strung the beads. Sometimes they put a holy medal or a silver cross on as a pendant, but the beads were not made into decades for praying.

Reyes hunted a long time through all the beads in the trading post, to find just the right ones for María to give Julián. When she had chosen them, most of the beads were small blue and white ones, but there were a few large round ones, like balls, with flowers on them. They were very beautiful. The pendant was a little, old silver cross.

After the beads were strung and ready, Julián and his parents came to the house to bring María her *rosario.* They wore their best clothes, and they came and knocked at the front door, and waited for Reyes to open it. When she did so, and asked them to come in, they all bowed their heads to her. When they were inside the living room, they stood and waited to be asked before they sat down.

María sat by the fire. She felt a little bit the way she had when she was meeting Julián at the schoolhouse, glad and natural. Then she glanced up and saw that he was looking at her, and her head dropped forward of itself. She was ashamed to have his eyes on her when all the parents were there with them.

Julián's mother said to Reyes, "We have brought a gift from our son to your daughter. Here it is."

She held out a small package, wrapped in a silk handkerchief. Mother took it, and replied, "My daughter has a gift for your son, too. Here it is," and she handed Julián's mother another small silk package. Then each of the mothers unwrapped the gift she held, and looked at it and admired it. After that, they exchanged the beads again. Julián's mother hung his *rosario* around María's neck, and Reyes hung María's around Julián's neck.

"Kneel down," said Father then. It was the first time he had spoken, except when he greeted the guests.

The two young people knelt before him, and he laid a hand on each head. He prayed a long time in Tewa, asking that their life together be good and happy; that they have good health and many children, and work hard. Then Julián's father prayed in the same way; and after he had finished, the two mothers made their prayers for success and joy for their children.

But that was not the end of the ceremony. Julián's mother went to the door and brought in some bundles that she had set down outside when she came in.

"We have brought the bride's clothes," she said. "We want her to be our daughter soon."

"That is good," said Mother. "They won't have to wear the *rosarios* long, to show that they are engaged."

Everyone smiled at that. They could all remember couples who had worn their *rosarios* a long time, because they wanted to have the fun of being engaged without the worry of being married.

Julián's mother began unwrapping the packages. The bride's dress was two mantas, the best, dark blue kind. There was a flowered blouse to wear under them. The upper part of the blouse sleeves was made of blue silk, and the lower part and the ruffles at the wrists were of pink. Then there was a pink scarf for María's head, and an orange shawl that was embroidered with many-colored flowers. The man at the trading post said there were very few shawls like that. They came from over the sea and cost a lot of money. The best part of the outfit, María thought, was the moccasins. They were beautifully made, with hard black soles that turned up all around the feet. The moccasin uppers were of white-tanned deerhide, and were made to wrap like smooth, thick bandages, around and around her legs. María had always had nice moccasins, but never any as fine as these.

The Wedding

When all the clothes had been unwrapped and admired, Julián's mother said, "We have been thinking about when to have the wedding. I think it will have to be two weeks from Monday, and then that night they can leave for St. Louis."

"That's very soon," said Reyes regretfully.

"If they don't get married then, they'll miss the trip," Julián's mother reminded her.

"Yes, that's right," Reyes agreed. "Well, we'll get ready, then. We've decided to give them the little house in the village that belonged to my husband's mother. We'd rather live here, because we are nearer to our lands. While they're away, we'll get the house in the village ready for them to come back to."

"Thank you, Mother," said María. She was so surprised that she could hardly speak. Her grandmother had had a nice little house, and María had always liked it.

"There's something I want to say," Julián said. His voice was steady and quiet, not gay and running up and down as María was used to hearing it. "You all know I never have farmed much. But I think a man ought to farm and take care of his family, if he has one. I want to ask my father-in-law to let me work with him when we get back. That way I'll be helping him and learning about farming at the same time. I think that's a good plan for us."

"It is a good plan," said Tomás. He sounded pleased. "I'm getting older, and I have to hire somebody to help me with my land. If I can hire my son-in-law, that's better than hiring somebody from outside. Everybody will be getting ahead. I'll be glad to teach you and to have your help."

"Thank you," said Julián, still with his voice quiet and steady. "I'll be as good help as I can, and try not to be slow about learning."

After that, Julián and his parents got up and said good-bye and went away. Reyes turned to María and smiled. "This is going to be better than I expected," she said. "I was afraid Julián would want you to live on sifters and saddles. That's good work, but it doesn't put beans in the pot."

María laughed with the happiness that was coming up inside her, like a spring out of the ground. "I must get Tía Nicolasa to help me make pots to put the beans in," she said. "We have to get everything ready and all gathered together, to start in with our own house."

"You won't have much time for that," said her mother. "I don't want you to start making pottery and get your hands all rough just before you get married. Let that wait till you get back. I'll lend you the few little things you'll need to get started with."

"All right," María agreed. She would have liked to start right from the first with everything all her own. She was too happy to argue with anybody, though, least of all with her mother.

The first thing that had to be done was to get the parents' house ready for the wedding and the party. It was up to the bride's parents to hold the first part of the wedding. Mother was always very particular about her house, and nobody had ever seen it dirty or untidy, but she wanted it extra nice for the wedding. She and María scrubbed everything with sand, to get the whole house clean. Then they washed things with water, to take off every bit of the sand. Then they whitewashed all the walls, even though the house had had its spring cleaning about a month before. Every night her mother made María rub her hands with tallow so that they would be soft and not rough from all the house cleaning. Between times María had to pack her clothes in shawls and blankets, to take with her.

María wondered a little sometimes about the furniture for her new house. She knew that there were some things in the house already. Of course there was a fireplace, and the *metates* were still set in place in the kitchen floor. She could be sure of things to cook with, anyway. But she would have liked to have some extra things, to make the house look pretty.

It was at the end of the first week of house cleaning that María saw a wagon driving up the hill to her mother's house. She knew it was not an Indian wagon, for the driver was walking, not trotting, his horse uphill. She did not recognize the driver. He stopped in front of the house and tied his horse to a sapling. When she opened the door in answer to his knock, María saw that the man was Spanish.

"Good morning," he said. "Does Tomás Montoya live here?"

"Yes, he does," said María. "Will you come in?"

The man pulled off his wide hat as he stepped into the living room. "I'm looking for Tomás' daughter, María," he said.

"I'm María. What do you want to say to me?"

"I come from Chimayó," the man answered. "A long time ago, when you and your sisters were little girls, you went there to visit my parents. Do you remember?"

"Yes," said María. "It was in Holy Week."

"That's right," the man agreed. "When you were there, you saw a painted chest my mother had. Do you remember the chest?"

The Wedding

"Of course I do."

"My mother said she promised that when she died, she would leave the chest to you," the man went on. "She is very old now, but I don't think she will die for a long time. She got to thinking about the chest and her promise to you when she heard that you were getting married. So she sent me to bring you the chest as a bride's gift."

"That's very good of your mother," María said. "How did she know that I was getting married?"

"Oh, somebody told her," said the man. "You know how things get told." Then he smiled. "I was coming to Santa Fé anyway, on business. I have the chest here in my wagon. Where would you like me to put it?"

María had been so interested in what the man was saying that she had forgotten everything else. Now she was startled.

"Wait a minute," she said. "I'll call my mother."

Reyes recognized the man as soon as she saw him and spoke to him by his name. The man explained again about the chest.

"Well, there's one thing for your house," said Reyes, smiling at María. "Your first wedding present, outside the family, too." She turned to the man. "You can bring it in here for now," she said, "and then, later, we'll put it in María's house. It's too late for you to go on to Santa Fé today. We want you to have dinner and spend the night with us. My husband will be in from the fields soon, and we both want you to stay here."

"Thank you," said their Spanish friend. "I'd like to do that."

"Come and drink some coffee," said Reyes, "and when Tomás gets here he'll help you carry the chest into the house. It must be heavy."

"Not very heavy," said the man from Chimayó. "My mother only left two blankets in it. She spun the wool for the thread and my father wove the cloth, long ago when they were first married. She said there was no sense in sending María an empty chest."

That night, when Julián came to the house as he always did after supper, María showed him the chest. Julián got down on his knees beside it, where the chest was set by the fireplace, and looked at it carefully.

"It's beautiful," he said. "All those flowers and designs. I'd like to paint things like that."

"Why don't you?" asked the man from Chimayó.

"Maybe I will someday," Julián said. "I'll have to learn how to make the chests first, though."

After that so many things happened that it seemed as if nothing happened. People came and went all over the house. Ana brought her baby and came to help. Desidéria was there all the time, of course, but they were sisters and did not count as company. Tía Nicolasa and Tía Juanita came, to help get the wedding feast ready, and they stayed right in the house instead of going home at night. Other women came, too, until there were so many of them grinding meal in the kitchen that María hardly had a chance to get ready her basket of fine-ground meal to take to Julián's parents.

She ground a big basketful; she filled the biggest basket she could find. Taking the meal was supposed to show that she was a good worker and not lazy, and she wanted Julián's parents to be sure about that. She ground the meal until it was as fine as the wheat flour at the store, and then she sifted it through an old, clean apron. When she had finished, you could hardly tell that it was corn meal.

On Saturday evening María and her sisters, with Tomás and

The Wedding

Reyes, put on the best clothes that they had. María wrapped the basket of fine meal in a piece of clean, freshly tanned white buckskin her uncle Juan had given her, and set the bundle on her head. Then the family all walked down the hill to the house of Julián's parents, through the warm pink spring dusk.

Julián and his family were waiting, with the door open, ready to welcome their visitors. María entered the room first, with her family following her. Slowly she walked across to where Julián's mother sat by the fireplace.

"Here," María said, lifting the wrapped basket of corn meal from her head and setting it on the floor before the older woman. "This is what I have brought you to prove that I am ready to be married to your son."

"Thank you for your gift," said Julián's mother. She unwrapped the basket and folded the buckskin on the floor beside her. When she saw the meal, she sat perfectly still for a moment, looking at it. Then she put out her hand and let the meal run through her fingers, and all of a sudden she smiled.

"This is the finest meal I ever saw," Julián's mother said. "I thought for a moment you were bringing me wheat flour from the store."

Then everybody laughed, and María looked up and met Julián's eyes. Her own eyes and her head dropped with shyness, and yet all of a sudden she felt something big and happy growing up inside her, and she realized that she was excited. She was so excited for a few minutes that she could hardly breathe.

When they got home, Tía Nicolasa was sitting by the fire, waiting for them. "Was it all right?" she asked.

"It was all right," María said.

"Good, then," said Tía Nicolasa. "Now that it's all right and we know you really are going to get married, I'll give you my present." She picked up a bundle from the floor beside her. "Here it is," she told María.

María took the package and unwrapped it. Tía Nicolasa's present was a double-spouted wedding jar. Her aunt must have worked very hard to make the jar, because it was the most beautiful piece of pottery María had ever seen. The background was cream-colored, and there were designs of flowers and water snakes painted on it in red and black. Around the lips of the spouts were designs of little squares linked together at their corners.

"Those stand for your house," said Tía Nicolasa. "The water snake is to bring you luck and happiness, and so are the flowers. I put the best designs on it that I knew."

"Thank you," said María. "Thank you. I like this better than any pottery I've seen."

They all laughed at that, and then Reyes scolded them, and told them all that it was time to go to bed. They all needed a lot of sleep because there was work ahead of them.

The next day, Sunday, was the day for the Indian part of the wedding. It was to be at noon, after everybody had got home from Mass. Reyes had a hard time making up her mind about things. She thought they all ought to go to Mass, just as they usually did, but she was afraid the feast would not be ready if all the women left the house. She gave up thinking about it finally. Tomás went to Mass, and the rest of them stayed at home, so it was really all right.

It was right at noon when the family saw the procession coming up the hill. First walked Julián and his uncle Juan, who was Julián's own age. They were finely dressed. Julián was wearing a silk shirt, with pink and blue sleeves, just like the one his family had given María, and a striped blanket. His hair was braided, and the braids were wrapped with red silk handkerchiefs. On Julián's feet were beaded moccasins and on his legs were beaded white buckskin leggings with long fringes. The leggings and moccasins belonged to his uncle Juan, and had come to Juan, through a friend at Taos, from the Cheyenne Indians. Juan was very proud of them, but he had lent Julián his leggings and moccasins to get married in, and just wore trousers and high-heeled cowboy boots himself.

Behind the two young men walked Julián's parents, and behind them came the rest of their family. Then there were all the rest of the people in the village, with the oldest men walking first. Everybody in San Ildefonso had been invited. It was a big crowd. María wondered for a moment how they were going to get eighty people into the house.

Tomás opened the door for his guests and welcomed them. Then María came from her bedroom, with one of her girl cousins walking beside her. She went over to Julián's parents, and they bowed to her, stiffly, as if they had never seen her before. Twice to the right and twice to the left they bowed, with their arms opened wide, before they embraced her. Then her parents greeted Julián in the same way. That was so each family could show its respect and love for its new member.

María and Julián knelt, then, before their parents. María's mother

The Wedding

took the *rosario* from María's neck and put it on Julián's, and his mother gave María the necklace he had been wearing. Then their parents put their hands on the young people's heads and blessed them.

After the blessing from the parents, the old man who was the religious head of the pueblo came to the young people. He took the wedding jar from Reyes, who had already put a little water into it. The old man added a tiny pinch of medicine, and gave the jar to each of them in turn to drink. When he put the spout of the jar to María's lips, and she tasted the water, she thought he must have added an herb, but she never knew what plant it was.

When María and Julián had drunk from the jar, the old man talked to them. Part of the time he prayed, and part of the time he spoke directly to them. He told them that marriage was important and serious, and that they must not be foolish and hard on one another, but get along nicely together, so that the people who loved them would be proud of them. Then he put his hands on their heads and blessed them. He walked to the door and poured what was left of the water on the ground, then gave the jar back to María.

"Keep this carefully," he told her. "May your marriage last as well as a good jar."

Then the serious part of the wedding was over. Julián and María got up from their knees, and the people gathered around to congratulate and embrace them, and to wish them happiness. Then Reyes said, "We want you all to stay for our wedding feast."

Nobody had expected to go home, but they all thanked her politely, and the women started bringing in the food. There were tamales and *frijoles* and stew and *atole,* and milk and coffee to drink, with lots of sugar in the coffee. There were little cakes with sugar sprinkled on top of them and roast goat meat. It was a big feast, but it still was only half of the food the women of the family had cooked during the week. Everyone ate and talked, after María and Julián had been served, and had taken their first bites of beans and *tortillas* from the same plate and their first sips from the same cup of coffee.

The feasting lasted all afternoon, and then it was time for the bridegroom and his parents to go home. Reyes made María go to bed right away. For a long time María lay quietly, listening to the other women in the kitchen washing the dishes and laughing and talking. She felt a little lonely and a little scared, but still the big excitement was welling up inside her, and she had to swallow it before she could breathe.

María

Then on Monday came the church wedding. The priest had come back, all the way from Santa Cruz, especially to marry them. Julián had planned it that way, so that they could do everything just right.

María and her cousin and the parents went to the church for the wedding, by themselves, and the rest of the family stayed at home to get the second feast ready. It was very quiet in the church, and the Mass and the ceremony took only a little while. It was easier to get married in the church than in the Indian way, María decided.

They all went back to the house together. It had been decided to have the fun part of the wedding all in one house, instead of each family's giving a party, so that everybody could be together. The people were all at the house, waiting for them, and as soon as the crowd saw the wedding party they began to laugh and joke, to wish them luck and much happiness, as they had done the day before. Then everybody started in feasting, without waiting for the bride and groom to eat first this time.

After the food was cleared away, the fun dancing began. It was what they called a *panshari,* with dancing in two lines, one for the men and one for the women. Juan had his drum, and he and some of the other men played and sang for the dancing. Everyone was having such a good time that they forgot about time. Suddenly they heard somebody knocking at the door. María looked around and could miss nobody. The whole pueblo still seemed to be there in the room. Tomás went to the door and opened it. A white man stood there. He looked impatient.

"I came for Julián and María Martínez," he said. "It's time for us to start, if we're going to catch the train to St. Louis."

María had forgotten that she was going away, and now she had to leave without even changing out of her wedding clothes. It seemed as if she did not really get to say good-bye to her family.

Julián called across the room to Juan, "Come on. I'll give you back your leggings on the train," and then they were all out of the house and in the white man's wagon, leaving their people laughing and dancing and singing and crying behind them.

13. The Return
(1904

Spring had been making way for summer when María and Julián left the pueblo. Summer was making way for fall when they came back. It had been a long time in months, and a longer one in the things that had happened. María knew in her own mind that she was the same person who went away, but she could not make herself feel the same way.

In the first place, there was just the fact of being married. Married women did not change the style of wearing their hair any more, as they used to in the old days. There was a difference after marriage, though, that did not have to show in your looks. People spoke differently to married women; they were more respectful and did not joke as much. A married woman herself was supposed to speak more formally, and to make jokes only with her sisters, and maybe with their husbands.

Then there was the fact that María had almost stopped speaking English. She and Julián had spoken Tewa together, and in St. Louis they spoke it with the other Indians. The language seemed to set them all apart, in something that was left of their own world, and to separate them from the life of the white people who came to the World's Fair to look on, just as their Indian clothes did. The white people asked many questions, and they said a great deal about the Indians that would have been rude from people who knew better. As long as those white people thought the Indians did not know any English, they kept right on saying funny things out loud. The Indians pretended they did not understand what was said, and then they had something to laugh about when the white people had gone home and the Indians were alone on the fair grounds.

It was a man's place to talk to outsiders anyway. Julián had begun to learn a little English, and when they left St. Louis, he could say "hello," and "good-bye," and "six bits," and "My wife made this bowl," as well as anybody. All María had to do was to sit and make pottery, and sometimes dance. She made little bowls and ollas, not anything big and fancy, and she left the pieces plain, without designs on them, because the white people seemed to like plain polished red bowls.

Things were different in the pueblo when they got back, too. There had been a dry spring, with the crops making slowly, or burning up in the fields when the hot winds struck them. Up in the mountains a timber company had begun cutting off the big trees. When the late summer rains came, there was nothing on the mountains to stop the water, and it came right down into the river and the ditches. The streams overflowed their banks, and carried away hunks of good farmland. The people's fields were pushed back, away from the land that had been farmed along the stream banks.

With the high water had come big trees, for the timber company had floated logs down the stream to get them to the sawmills at Bernalillo and Albuquerque. The trees tore at the banks, and helped the water cut away the land. It was a bad time for everybody. Men like Tomás, who were good farmers to begin with, had saved some of their crops, but others had lost all that they had planted. It looked as if men like Julián's father would have to get help from others to carry their families through the winter.

When María and Julián came back to the house, riding in one of the government wagons that had met the travelers at the railroad station in Santa Fé, Reyes and Tomás came running out to meet them. Their arms were open to greet their children, and the tears were streaming down their faces from joy. It embarrassed María to see her father cry, and it made her cry, too. Or maybe it was just being home and going into her mother's house that brought tears to her eyes. All she knew was that she was too happy to laugh.

"Your own house is ready for you," Reyes said when they had all quieted down a little. "We moved your things into it a week ago. Desidéria and I have cleaned and swept it every day since then, to have it ready for you. As soon as we take these bundles down there, you'll be moved in."

Julián smiled. "There isn't much in these bundles to move," he said. "Most of these things are presents that we brought for our families."

That reminded Reyes. "Oh," she said, putting her hand over her mouth. "Your family, Julián. We forgot about them! Juanita, run fast and tell Julián's family he's here, and tell Ana and Desidéria they're back. We'll get dinner here for everybody, and then we can all hear about the trip."

But when the others were there, and they had all eaten and sat back to rest after eating, there were so many things to tell that María and Julián could not find words for them. Instead, they unwrapped their bundles and unpacked the presents they had bought with the money from pottery-making. They had bought a new cardboard suitcase to hold the things they had bought for themselves; but the presents were in bundles, wrapped up the way Indians always wrap their good things.

They had brought dress goods for all the women and shirtings for all the men. Julián had brought a pound package of tobacco for each of the fathers. They had thought a long time about special presents for the mothers, and finally decided to give them candy. There was a big two-pound box for each mother. On the lids of the boxes were pictures of beautiful ladies, sitting in the curves of crescent moons. The lady on Reyes' box had blonde hair that spilled over the edge of the moon and down around her feet; and the lady on Julián's mother's box had dark hair arranged the same way. Neither of the ladies had on very many clothes, but at that they were better covered than some of the ladies María and Julián had seen on candy boxes.

"Thank you for the presents," everybody said, and they passed the gifts from hand to hand for all to see and admire. Reyes opened her box of candy and Tomás his tobacco, because they were the hosts. Everybody ate one piece of candy, and each of the men rolled and smoked a cigarette, to show how much they appreciated the hospitality of their friends.

"We're glad you're back," said Tomás, when his cigarette was drawing right. "Not just because of the presents, but because we need you. I need Julián's help in the fields right now, to get ready for spring. It's going to take lots of hard work to make crops for next year."

"Maybe I won't be very good help," said Julián doubtfully. "I still don't know much about farming."

"You'll learn," Tomás assured him. "I'll teach you. You ought to learn pretty soon, because the next thing you know you'll have a family to take care of."

Nobody else said anything about that until just before they were ready to start for home. Then Reyes spoke to María, as they were together tying up some bundles of food for breakfast.

"I can tell," Mother said. "There's going to be a baby. That's good. You'll have to take care of yourself, though. Don't work too hard in the house, and let Julián help you. There isn't so much to do in the fields that he can't help you as much as he does your father."

It did not take them long to get settled down in the house, with everything ready for them beforehand. María used most of the money that was left from the trip to St. Louis to buy corn, and dried squash and beans. The rest of the money she spent on sugar and coffee and lard. Reyes gave her some articles for her storeroom, but María wanted to feel that what she had in her house was her own, that she had got it for herself.

Theirs was a small house on the north side of the plaza. There were really only two rooms; one for cooking and one for sitting and sleeping, but Tomás had added a third room at the end of the kitchen to be used as a storeroom. The new room stuck out beyond the level of the other house walls on that side of the village. Tomás laughed when he showed it to them.

"In the old days the council wouldn't have let you do that," he told them. "An enemy could have hidden in the angle of the wall and killed everybody in the village some night when they were all asleep. Even nowadays it was hard for the council to decide. They had to talk it over for a long time."

The Return

Julián laughed. He was always laughing in those days. "The only enemy that could hide there now is a horse," he said. "If we had a horse, I'd put up a brush shelter there for him."

"On the north side of the house!" said Tomás. "That wouldn't do your horse any good. We'll have to teach you to do better than that, if you're going to make a farmer."

María laughed, too. "I guess all Julián knows about horses is how to make saddles for them," she said.

Tomás turned and looked at his daughter, hard. "Every horse needs a saddle and Julián makes good ones," he told her. "Never make fun of your husband where anyone can hear you, not even your own family, María. If you want to say something like that, say it to him when you're alone."

María hung her head and turned and went into the house. It was so seldom that her father scolded anybody that sometimes she forgot that he could. He was right about this, she knew, and it was something that she would have to learn and remember.

She was busy learning a great many things those days, as it was. Mother came almost every day, to show her and tell her what to do. María had thought that she knew a lot about housekeeping and cooking, because she had grown up doing them, but having her own house made everything different, even though it was a little house. María wanted the house to be nice. She was proud of it, and proud of herself for having it.

Reyes taught her, first of all, to work slowly and steadily. "If you get tired out doing the first thing there is to be done, then the other things don't get finished," she said once; and later she added, "A baby is a heavy weight to carry even before it's born. That work you must do. What strength is left you can use for your other jobs." Then she said, "No baby is proud of a lazy mother. Just because this one is coming, you mustn't stop doing things that are to be done. I'll tell you what my mother told me. As long as you are active, your baby will be the same way. If you sit down or lie down all the time, the baby will get fat and lazy, and maybe the cord will get twisted around its neck and choke it to death while it is being born. So you must keep on working."

It wasn't hard for María to keep on. She felt well, and she wanted to work. She would have liked to make some more pottery, now that she was back and could work with Tía Nicolasa, but the winter weather was too cold and damp for that. The clay would not dry

123

properly at this time of year. Instead of making pottery, María pieced quilts out of the scraps of her old dresses, and carded the wool to fill them, and then tacked the covers and fillings together. She wanted to have a quantity of bed clothes to fill her wedding chest.

Julián was working and learning that winter, too. He would come home in the evening, tired and smelling of cold wind and horses, to sit by the fire and tell María things she had known all her life. He would tell her how the earth curled away from the plow blade and how the furrows curved with the borders of the fields. Julián was always fascinated by the patterns of things. He liked best that part of farming where he could see the earth and the things that grew out of it making designs before his eyes.

"I think I'll learn to like farming after while," he said once. Then he laughed. "I'd like it better if I could do it sitting down and looking," he added.

But Tomás said that Julián worked hard and was getting to be a good plowman. The only trouble with Julián's plowing was that sometimes he got impatient and tried to hurry his horses. When he planted winter wheat, it was the same way. His hand went too deeply into the sack, and he threw the wheat too far on either side. But still he was learning. Sometime he would make a good farmer.

Winter had always been the time in the pueblo for learning, for sitting by the fire in the evening and hearing the old people tell stories. It was a time for growing underground for people as well as for plants. María was glad that they had returned home at the beginning of that time, and that she and Julián and the baby's new life all were growing together.

Part III: The Bowl Is Fired

14. The Toilsome Spring
(1907

The third spring after María was married came on very slowly. Easter was late, way up in April, but even after Easter there was a snow that caught the fruit trees when they had just finished blooming, and froze the small, unprotected fruits into solid balls of ice. The furrows that had been plowed in the fall were set and frozen into the ground, with no green between them to blur and then obliterate their ridges. The sky was gray-blue instead of blue-blue. It seemed as if spring and summer had been unhappy there before and did not want to come back to be unhappy again.

Then the weather turned hot overnight, and with one rush everything gave way. All the things that had been frozen were melted, at once and without gradual softening. This melting was a breaking down and a falling in. The frost that had held things together was gone; and without the frost to bind its particles, the earth itself collapsed. Again the water came down the streams and the rivers, bringing the big trees with it, and water and trees tore at the banks and cut gashes in the fields. The earth was stripped and torn, and it seemed that there would never be anything worth having again.

That was a time when all the men worked harder than they had known that they could work. There was just one thought in all their minds: to save the stream banks and so save their fields. No matter what else happened, and no matter what else there was to hold them from their work, the saving of the lands came first. The men left the care of the gardens and the animals to the women, and went out into the ditches and worked there.

Since Tomás was on the ditch committee that year, he had to work harder than anyone else, to set an example. Because Julián was Tomás' son-in-law who was working with him in his fields, he had to work with the older man and keep up with him. They went out to the fields early in the morning. Often they did not come back until after dark, and there were nights when the men did not come in at all. Those were the nights when small fires burned along the edges of the ditches, and some of the women got up in the middle of the night to boil pots of coffee and to carry them out, with baskets of food, to the workers.

Desidéria, as well as Ana and María, was married now, and Juanita stayed a good deal of the time with one of her sisters. Reyes came down to the village herself, and stayed with María.

"You are the daughter who needs me right now," she said. "You are the one I have to look out for and think about, with the second baby coming. Besides, your man is helping mine with the fields and the work."

It seemed strange to María that her mother should talk to her about "your man and my man," but it was a pleasant strangeness. In this spring that was like no season she had ever known before, one more thing that was strange could hardly surprise María. She accepted what Mother said without questioning.

They cooked together a lot that spring. It seemed to María sometimes that they were always lifting pots on or off the cooking fire. It had to be good, solid food, to build back the strength that the men lost in their working. *Frijoles* and *posole,* with meat, most often. Big, solid *tortillas.* Reyes tried making wheat-flour *tortillas* for a time, because they seemed to fill the men up quickest, but she went back to using corn meal, because those were the *tortillas* that kept the workers going longest. Milk and fruit were always in the house, but the men paid little attention to them. They wanted heavy food, and with it they wanted plenty of coffee.

Spring was the time for cleaning and mending and replastering the houses, for making adobes for the summer sun to season, and for repairing the damage that winter had done to the pueblo. This year the houses had to go unmended except for the work that the women could do. The men were all too busy trying to save enough of their fields to make a crop to take care of the houses. Women could plaster and do small jobs with adobes; they could mend the roofs and clean the houses and the plaza; but women could not make bricks or do the big repair jobs. They could only replaster the outside of the kiva. For the first time the village began to look as if it were not taken care of as it should be.

María's second baby was going to be born in this hard time. The thought that a baby was coming when things were not going right made her unhappy, although she wanted the baby very much and

The Toilsome Spring

was glad that she was going to have it. Babies made a good life. They rounded out a family and completed it. Every home should have babies, lots of them.

"There's just one good thing about it," Reyes said one day. "We won't have to send the men away from home while this baby is being born. They'll be gone already."

"Yes," María agreed. She had been wondering a little about how they were going to manage that part of it and explain it to Julián. When he was at home, he wanted to be with her; and she had been afraid that she might hurt his feelings again when she had to tell him that he must go away for the time that this baby was being born, too.

The night of the baby's birth was one of high, wild wind. The little fires along the ditch banks were bending themselves down to the earth, as if they would reach out and snatch for themselves the fuel that the men fed to them sparingly. The wind tore at the roofs and chimneys of the village, and blew down some of the pots that people had put on top of the chimneys to make them draw better. It was a hard night to sleep in. Reyes went out to get Ana and Desidéria as soon as María's pains started.

When she came back, Mother was laughing a little. "You might as well go ahead and have that baby now," she said. "Nobody can sleep on a night like this anyhow."

It was broad daylight when the baby got there. Reyes took it and bathed it in warm water; then she wrapped the child in a square of clean, soft cloth she had torn from the back of one of Julián's old shirts. Cloth like that had been softened and bleached by the sun, and was the best thing there could be to wrap a baby in. Reyes brought the baby, fresh and round and red, to show to María.

"Here's your daughter," she said. "Now Ana can take her up on the roof and introduce her to the world by her Indian name."

María looked and looked at the baby. She had waited a long time for this, but the baby girl was worth waiting for.

"What's her name, sister?" she asked Ana.

"Yellow Pond Lily, like yours," Ana answered. "I always thought that was one of the nicest women's names I ever heard."

Julián and Tomás came home that noon, and Ana met them at the door of the little house.

"No men can come in here," she told them. "Wait a minute, and I'll show you why."

She went back into the house and took the baby from its blanket

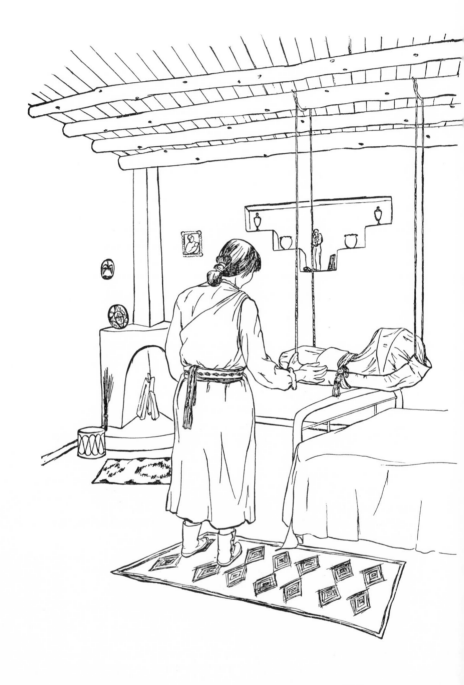

swing-cradle beside María's bed. When Julián saw his daughter, and heard her name, he threw back his head and laughed.

"Yellow Pond Lily!" he said. "Why, you ought to name her Pottery Colored Pond Lily! She's so red she looks like a bowl that's just been fired."

"You stop making fun of her," Ana said bossily. "She's a beautiful baby. Now you wait here, and I'll bring you some dinner. You can eat supper and sleep at my house, both of you. Mother will have to stay here and take care of María for the four days before you can see her."

"I'd like to see her for a minute," Julián said. "Just to tell her we're back from the ditch and that it's going to hold."

"I'll tell her all that," Ana said. "You know it's the rule that she can't see any men for four days now."

Tomás put his hand on Julián's arm. "It's all right," he said. "The women make rules like that so they can talk things over any way they like, and sleep and eat a lot. It's hard on a man to know his wife's having a good time when he can't have any of the fun, but that's the way women are. They like to have good times by themselves."

Julián nodded seriously. "I guess so," he answered. "There are a lot of things about women I don't know yet."

"There are a lot of things about women you never will know," Tomás assured him, "but when you're as old as I am and have seen as much of women as I have, you'll know it's no use trying to understand them."

So the men sat down on the doorstep in the blustering wind and ate their beans and meat out of the pot that Ana brought them, and finished their meal with *tortillas* and coffee, as if they were eating in the kitchen as usual.

At the end of four days, they had the public naming ceremony, Julián could come into the room for that, with everybody else. Women had been coming to the house all during the four days, and the front room was full of the gifts they had brought for the baby and her mother: corn meal, and dress goods, and torn-up old shirts, and buckskins, and all sorts of other things.

"Well," said Julián, looking around, "it looks as if our neighbors wanted to make our daughter rich."

"Maybe she will be," said María.

Julián shook his head. "I don't believe she will be," he answered.

"After all, her father's just a farmer. He doesn't own a timber company. And he's just a beginning farmer, at that, not like her grandfather. He's a good farmer and knows how, that one."

Tomás, who was sitting beside the fireplace, laughed when he heard that. "Any man who wants to can learn to farm," he said. "It just takes learning, and the sooner you start learning anything, the better you know it and the better you can do it. The trouble is that all the water came at once this spring. Now it's dry weather and it seems to be staying that way. The farmers are going to be out of luck after all, and the men who know trades will be able to earn the best livings."

"Nobody buys saddles when the horses are dying of drought," said Julián, gloomily. It was the first time María had ever heard him say anything really sad.

On the eighth day, though, when María got up and began to help Reyes a little with the housework, Julián came home in the evening laughing and excited. "Something new is happening," he said. "Some white men came to see the governor today."

"Who are they?" Reyes asked, stirring the *posole* over the fire. "More timber men?"

"No," replied Julián, sitting down in the warmest corner, by the fire. "They come from a long way away, from Washington."

"Government men," said Reyes, and she shut her mouth as if she were setting a mouse trap.

"Not government men," said Julián. "They say they're teachers who want to study."

"Teachers study at colleges, not in pueblos," said María. She remembered all that Miss Grimes had told her about it.

"These men don't want to study in the pueblo," Julián answered. "They want to study up on the Pajarito Plateau. They want to go to that old village at Puyé Canyon where San Ildefonso came from, and study there."

"Why don't they go ahead and do it then?" demanded Reyes. She did not like Anglos much at any time, and this was all strange to her.

"They want to dig up that old village," Julian said. "That's why they have to come here and see the governor. They have to get permission from him and the council before they can work there."

"Will the council give them permission?" María asked, absently. She had just found out that when she slipped her finger into the baby's fist, its tiny hand closed around hers. The feeling the child's grasp gave her was a warm one that she loved.

The Toilsome Spring

"Maybe they will," said Julián. "The Anglos say that they'll hire some of the men to dig for them, if they get the permission."

"It all sounds silly to me," Reyes said. "First they want to dig, and then they want to hire men to do the digging. Why don't they make up their minds what they want to do, before they come and talk about doing it?"

"There are just four of them," Julián told her. "That old village is big, big. Four men couldn't dig up one corner of it, not if they worked all summer. Besides, without crops, the men here are going to have to do what they can to earn money. This way they can do something and not go far away from home."

"It's another change," said Reyes, setting the pot off the fire. "Everything these years is changing. When I was a young woman, just starting out, people stayed at home and took care of their farms, and the water stayed in the ditches and helped them, instead of running all over the place the way it does now. I don't like all this changing."

"Maybe it's good," said María. "Maybe there have to be changes. Anyway, changes that happen so people can stay near home aren't bad. I don't want to go away from home again, ever."

"You don't have to go," said Julián. "If I can get a job at the digging, I may go, but you can stay at home here with your Yellow Pond Lily if you want to." He looked hurt, and María smiled at him.

"I'll go if I can," she said. "It might be better for the baby, though, if she and her brother and I stayed here."

"Wait till you see whether they're going to dig and if they want to hire you for the work," said Reyes. "You don't know anything about it yet."

15. The Job
(1907

As it turned out, Julián was one of the first men that the Anglos hired. They wanted young men, who could work hard and steadily, and were not tied down to watching and caring for big fields. Julián was just right for what they needed, and they asked him to go to work as soon as the council gave permission for the work to be done. There was to be a camp up in the Puyé Canyon for all the workers, because the old village was too far from the pueblo for the men to go back and forth. Julián still wanted María to go up to the plateau with him, but she held back.

"There are too many strangers there and the baby's too little," she said. "I'd rather stay at home here, where I know how things are going to be. Besides, if I stay here, Mother and I can dry a little fruit together."

"I wish you'd come," Julián said again, but that was all.

They had to do some planning, to get ready the things for Julián to take. This was not like going to St. Louis; it was not the kind of trip for packing all his best and newest things. This time he was going to do plain hard work, with all sorts of digging and climbing, so what he needed were old, heavy clothes. They packed the old things, carefully, in bundles, and María packed the bundles in a gunnysack. The workmen were going to take their own beans and corn meal and all cook together, and the plan was for the Anglos to add other foods, and everybody eat in one group. That made it easy to plan about food, anyway.

"What will it be like, eating with white men?" María wondered, and Julián answered her, "You ought to know. Didn't you eat with white girls when you were at school?"

"Well, but they were just school girls," María said.

The packing, and sacking up beans, and generally getting things ready, only took them four days. If they had just been getting Julián's belongings packed, it might not have taken so long, but at the last minute Reyes had decided that she wanted María to close the house in the village and come to stay with her.

"It's too lonely for you, staying in a house by yourself," Reyes said, "and besides, I need some help with the housework."

So María packed up clothes for herself and the children, and they went back up the hill to the old home. She did not have to do much packing or planning for that trip; it was just a little move, and she could always go back to the house in the village for anything that she needed. Still, it was a move, and she had to do some thinking about it.

Telling Julián good-bye was the hardest thing that María had to do. They did not want to fuss or cry over the separation, because they would not be apart very long, just for the three months of the summer. But it was a good-bye, and María found that there were tears in her eyes and on Julián's cheeks when the time came for his going. In order that her parents should not notice how distressed she was, María turned around and picked up the baby. She held the child up against Julián's face, pressing her first to one of his cheeks and then to the other.

"Tell your father good-bye," she said. "You'll be a big girl when you see him again."

Julián smiled a little. "Don't grow up too fast," he said to the baby, "I want to be able to recognize you when I get home."

After Julián was gone, home seemed very quiet to María. She had her parents and her sisters, and they had always been enough for her before. Now she missed having someone to talk to who could understand things before she said them. Even to her mother, she found that she had to say things right out, in full words, to explain what she meant.

So many of the young men were gone that the pueblo as a whole seemed quiet. The dances that were given during that summer were mostly women's dances, with the older men helping out with the drumming and singing. They were pretty dances, and everybody who was there enjoyed them, but women's dances did not have the same feeling as the dances in which everybody took part. Then there was a lift and a sweep to the dancing and the singing, as if the voices and movements of the people made a strong wind that swept bad things away and brought good ones in. The women's dances were gentler and quieter, as if they were coaxing the wrong things to go away, and beseeching the good ones to come to the pueblo.

María did not take part in the dances herself. Always before she had loved to dance, and she was a good dancer. This summer, however, the thought of being away from the baby for so long at a time seemed to worry her. She wanted to be with the small Pond Lily and to watch her grow and get strong. Four nights getting ready for a dance, and a whole day while the dancing was going on, was too much time for her to be away from the child. María went down to the village and watched the other women dancing, but that was all.

The baby was growing steadily but, it seemed to María, slowly. When she spoke to her mother about it, Reyes laughed at her. "All babies grow that way," she said. "You don't want her to grow up like a weed and then turn brown and stop, do you?"

María was satisfied. Her mother had had many babies and had reared four of them, so María was sure that Reyes knew how babies grew and the best ways for them to be. María stopped worrying and went on working at the fruit-drying and pottery-making. She had decided to make herself a whole set of storage and cooking pots during the summer, so that her house would be well equipped when the winter came and Julián was back.

Summer was a hard time for babies in the village. Those children who were sickly seemed to get worse with the coming of the hot weather. Maybe it was because she had a baby of her own to think about, but María thought that she had never heard of so many babies' being sick and dying as she did that summer. Nearly every family seemed to lose a child. It was bad. It was part of all the bad things that were happening in the pueblo.

When the day came for the Corn Dance, María was really worried. Everybody who could was supposed to take part, because that was the most important dance of the whole year. She had been excused from dancing, because she had a little baby to take care of, but she knew that she had to go to watch the dance. That in itself was a kind of taking part. Three babies had died in the village during the previous week. María was afraid to take her baby down to the pueblo, but there was nothing else for her to do. They all had to be there and watch the dance, even if María did not take active part.

It was a hot, long, slow day. Usually María felt that Corn Dance days went quickly, but this one seemed to her to drag. That was because the young men were away, everyone said. If the men had been there, the dance day would have gone by quickly. That night, when María put the baby to bed, she noticed that its forehead was hot and that its little hands felt hot and dry. During the night María awakened suddenly. There was not a sound in the room, but she knew that something was wrong. When she lighted a lamp and bent over the cradle, the baby began to cry, a little, fretful, whining whimper. The child's forehead was hotter than ever, and she moved herself restlessly from side to side of the hammock cradle. The baby was very sick.

Reyes came at María's call, and together they did all that they could. They bathed the baby with cool water, and made up the cradle with clean blankets, and gave the child first cold water and then hot Romero-weed tea to drink.

"We've got to get the fever down," Reyes kept saying. "That's what makes her so sick. We've got to do everything we know to get rid of the fever."

"She just gets hotter and hotter," María answered. "Isn't there anybody who knows what to do?"

"Nobody knows much about it," Reyes said. "If God wants the

baby to get well, she will. We can try to make her comfortable and not so hot. That's all."

"Maybe we should send for Julián," María suggested. "He could help us lift and carry, and he might know what to do."

"There isn't anything he could do," Reyes told her. "That's just silly. Men aren't any help at times like this. Get me another basin of cold water and a clean cloth, so I can bathe her again."

Summer nights are short, María thought as she went for the water. Summer nights are always short. Why does this one stay so long? Has a winter night mixed itself up with the middle of summer? She came back with the water, cool from the well and the night air, and watched Reyes bathe the baby another time.

"It might help to smoke her with cedar," Reyes said suddenly. "Build a fire on the hearth, a little one, so that the cedar twigs will smoke well."

Tomás was awake by this time, and he helped María with the fire. While he was building it, María went out to the cedar tree behind the corral and pulled off twigs and branches, as many as she could, to make a fresh, strong smoke. She fed the green bits to the fire slowly, until the room was filled with their perfume, like incense in Mass. Reyes brought the baby in from the bedroom, and passed her four times through the smoke, as near to the fire as she dared.

"I think she's better," Reyes said then. "She's cooling."

"Let me hold her," María begged, and held out her arms. Reyes laid the baby in them, and María sat close by the fireplace, where the last of the cedar smoke could cover her and the baby.

She was still sitting by the fireplace when night went away and dawn came. Reyes came over, and touched first the baby and then María's shoulder.

"Give her to me," Reyes said. "It's time I held her now."

María laid her hand on the baby's forehead. "She's all right, isn't she?" she asked. "The hotness is gone. She's very cool."

"She's all right," said Reyes, with tears pouring down her face, and María understood what her mother meant.

"She's dead!" she cried. "She's dead, and you didn't tell me!"

"She's all right," Reyes insisted. "She's with God, in His Heaven. Nothing is ever going to hurt her again. Give her to me now."

She took the baby from María, and Tomás came and took his daughter away into the next room. Then he went down to the village to get the priest. After that, he went for Desidéria.

The Job

María lay quietly on her bed, looking at the ceiling, until her sister came into the room. It was not until Desidéria sat down beside her and touched her hand that María moved or spoke. Then, when she tried to tell Desidéria what had happened, she began to cry.

In the old days, when a little baby died, its family buried it under the floor of their storeroom at once. That way the baby was at home, with its own family. Somehow, thinking about that hurt María as badly as thinking about the baby's death. The thought that she might accidentally step on her own child made her shiver. She asked her mother if the baby could be buried in the churchyard.

"Your father thought about that," Reyes told her. "He asked the priest, and it will be all right. We'll have the funeral in the church, and bury the baby there. Then when Julián gets home, you can show him the place."

"He won't want to see it," María said through her tears. "He wanted the baby to be well. He wanted to be able to hold her and talk to her again. Now he won't ever see her."

"Hush," Reyes said, sternly but quietly. "Suppose he had seen her when she was sick. Suppose he had seen her suffering. Would you want that? This way he will remember her well and happy. That's better for him."

"Why did I have to see her sick?" María demanded. "I didn't want to see her suffer. Why did anybody have to? Why didn't she get well?"

"Nobody knows those things," her mother answered. "One thing we do know. Women can stand some things better than men can. Women are strong inside their hearts. They can endure what they have to. It's harder in some ways for men. That's why they have women, to share their troubles."

"Women should have someone to share their troubles, too, it seems to me," María said.

"They have each other," Reyes assured her. "That's why women are mothers. They know how to take their own troubles and those of others, too. Men can't do that, unless they're priests and have nothing but other people's troubles to think about."

"I want to send word to Julián, though," María insisted. "I don't want him to come home expecting to see the baby and have to tell him that she's gone."

"That we can do," said her mother. "Your father can go. That will be all right."

"I'd like for him to," María answered.

"One thing you will have to remember, though," Reyes went on. "When Julián comes home, you'll have to comfort him anyway. You can't go back to living together as if this hadn't happened. His work is to go out and earn money for you this summer. Your work is to make his life right and good. That's going to be your job. It's your job for all your life."

María nodded. "I can do it, I think," she said. "I can do it, if I have help from you and Father this one time."

"That's our job," said Reyes. "We have to help our children, and make things better for them. Living is like that. We have our jobs of work to do, and our jobs of helping. As we get older, we have more of them, because as we get older, we get stronger and able to do more things. Always remember that."

The days that followed were days of waiting. Tomás went to the mountains and came back in three days. When he reached home, Tomás reported that Julián had wanted to return with him. "He said that married people should be together in their time of trouble," Tomás said. "He told me that he didn't want to be married just for the good-times part of it, but to share whatever came to you, even if it were bad. I told him to stay there, though. You don't need as much helping now as you may need later. And you both need the money. We all, everybody in the village, need money if the working men can earn it."

"That's right," agreed Reyes. "It isn't just their own families those young men are helping and working for. If one family can get ahead, then it can help other families that don't have any working members. In that way, the whole village is better because a few men can get work."

"That's right," Tomás agreed. "We have to think about that part of it as much as about our own part. The village belongs to everybody, and we're all part of it. If one family suffers, the whole pueblo suffers; if one family does well and is happy, then the whole pueblo should be doing better, too. We all have to think about the others and about how to help them."

"I know that," said María, slowly. "You and Mother have been teaching me those things ever since I was a little girl. We all belong together, just the way sisters belong together. It all makes one family."

After that there was another time of waiting. They all knew and understood and agreed that it was necessary for Julián to be away just then, that he was doing his share in something that was bigger than any one man or any one family. Still the time seemed to María to go slowly. She would catch herself watching the shadow of the big cottonwood tree in the plaza almost every afternoon. It seemed to her on some days that the shadow did not move an inch away from the trunk of the tree for hours at a time.

Then there came a day when the people in the village could see first blue clouds and then black ones over the Sangre de Cristo Mountains. Tomás came in to supper that night with a smile on his face. "There's rain to the east," he said. "Now, when we get rain to the west, we'll know that summer is over."

It was another two days before the clouds began to gather and darken above the Pajarito. Everyone had been watching for the cloud shadows, without saying anything. Now, when the shadows had begun to form and to darken along the river valley, the words that had been held back could be spoken.

"Now the men will be coming back," said María relievedly, at evening.

"Now they will be home soon," said Reyes. "No more digging and work up there once the rains come. Nobody can make deep holes in the ground when it's wet."

Tomás laughed. "You women!" he said. "You talk about doing good for the pueblo, and how willing you are to help, but the minute you see a chance of getting your own men back, you forget about everything but having your family together."

María did not answer him. Her family would not be together, even when Julián came back, but there was no use in talking about it.

The big rains had really come at last, and the men were back in the plaza in another two days. Their families had seen the wagons and horses a long way down the road and were waiting for them under the cottonwood tree. As soon as the wagons stopped, the men got down and went over to their mothers and sisters and wives, and greeted them. After the first excitement was over, the head man called the men back together into a group by the big tree.

"Now we're going to pay you off," he said. "All the men who went have worked hard and well, and have earned their money. This is where they get their reward, right here, so their wives will know about it." He smiled a little. "This way, the wives can get their shares of the money," he said. Then he began to call out the names of the workingmen, one at a time. As each man heard his name called, he came forward to get his pile of silver dollars, one for each day that he had worked. Some of the piles were smaller than others, because some of the men had taken time off to go hunting or fishing. One of the biggest piles the head man gave to Julián.

"There you are," he said. "Good pay for a good worker."

Julián made his mark on a piece of paper, as the other men had done, to show that he had received his money and was satisfied with what he had been paid. Then he tied the silver dollars in his neckerchief and brought the money over to María.

"You'd better keep them for me," he said. "Keep them until we decide what to do with them, anyway."

"All right," said María. "We can make a plan when we get home, I guess."

They stood and waited with the rest of the group until all the men had been paid off. Then the head man turned to Juan Gonzales, who was now the religious head of the pueblo.

"All these men are tired," the head man said. "Everybody needs a rest. The Indian men can go home to their families, so they'll be all right. But the rest of us have a long way to go before we can see our families. Is it all right if we camp over on the north side of the pueblo, behind the houses there, for a few days?"

Juan looked around and found the governor and the councilmen of the pueblo in the crowd, with his eyes. He looked at them and they looked at him, and then Juan turned back to the head man.

"Go ahead and camp," he said. "It's better if you don't camp on the north side of the pueblo, though. It's kind of low there. Go up on the little hills behind Tomás Montoya's house, where you can keep dry if it rains. Do you need any men to help you?"

"We can make our own camp," the head man said. "If we have the permission of the pueblo, everything is all right."

"You have the permission," said Juan. "That's all right. You go ahead."

As soon as the white men moved off to make their own camp, the rest of the group began to break up. All the men were anxious to get to their homes, and their families were just as anxious to have them there. The little family groups split off from the main group, a few people at a time, and soon there was only the big cottonwood tree left standing in the middle of the plaza, alone.

María and Julián went right across the plaza to their own house. They wanted to be alone together at first, and to talk things over a little before they saw other people. María opened the door, and they went into their sitting room. It was strange to them, and cold, as closed rooms in adobe houses often are, even in summer.

"Now we are in our house," said Julián, and María answered, "Now we are in our own house again."

"It's not right," said Julián. "It doesn't feel the way it should. Something is lacking that it will take a long time to replace."

"That thing we can never replace," said María. "We can try, but the new lives will always be somehow different. That one is gone, and we can't bring it back."

"That's true," said Julián. "We'd better not talk about it, I guess. Better not think about it, even."

"We can't not think about it," María said. "All we can do is to think about other things too. The other things that are going on around us all the time. We need to think about them, anyway."

"That's right," agreed Julián. "We can start thinking about them now. First I think we ought to think about dividing our money. How are we going to do that?"

"Some for your family and some for my family and some for ourselves," answered María promptly.

"You must have been planning that," Julián guessed.

"Yes, I have," said María. "That's the woman's part of it, to make that kind of plan."

"Well, it's a good thing that's up to you," said Julián thoughtfully. "I guess I just don't do much of that kind of planning myself. How do you want to share the money, now? Have you planned about that?"

"Well, yes, I have," María answered. "I made a plan about that a while ago. Because there are three families, most people would say we ought to divide the money three ways. I don't think it will go like that. Ana's husband and Desidéria's husband were both working this summer, and they'll give some of their money to my parents. That means my father and mother will be sharing three ways, so they won't need so much money from anyone. But you are the only son in your family who was working, so you are the only one to help your parents. And I'm the only wife you have, so you have to help me. I think we ought to divide the money in fifths. Then we can give one to my parents and two to your parents and keep two ourselves. My father was farming this summer, and he'll divide his crop with us and with your parents, so that will be fair for him. Then, if any of us need sifters or saddles or any of those things, your father will make them for us. So that is fair for him."

Julián grinned. "You have it all planned out, don't you?" he asked. "You do a good job of planning, it seems to me."

"Well, if that's part of my job, I ought to do it right, it seems to me," María told him. "Does that plan satisfy you?"

Julián grinned again. "Well," he said, "it's all fair and right for the families, but where do I come in? I earned that money, you know. Don't I get any share in it?"

"I guess so," said María, smiling. "I guess you ought to have part of it for yourself. I tell you what. We'll take out one dollar now, before we divide the rest of it, and that will be yours. Here it is."

"Thank you," said Julián. He spoke solemnly, but there was a small smile behind his eyes. "This is my own dollar to carry in my pocket."

"To carry in your pocket or to spend," said María. She turned away to the fireplace, to get ready to start dinner.

"I tell you what," Julián said behind her, "while you're cooking, I'll go across to my mother's house and see them. Then I'll come back here to eat."

"Do you want to take them their money?" María asked.

"No, I guess not," said Julián. "We can go there together after supper and take them theirs, and then take the other share to your mother and father."

"All right," said María. "You go on now, and come back as soon as you tell them 'hello.' By that time I'll have something ready for us to eat."

She turned back to the fireplace, and behind her she heard the house door close as Julián went out.

It was an easy supper to get. María had brought the beans from her mother's that morning, ready cooked, and she had only to heat them and add a little more chile to the pot for Julián. *Tortillas* she patted out and cooked easily and quickly. There was milk to be poured into the cups when Julián got back. After she had everything ready, María found that she was still waiting. More to have something to do than because it was necessary, she decided that this was a good time to hide their share of the money. She cut a hole high up in the wall of the living room, using a hatchet to hack away the adobe plaster. Then she went out into the yard behind the house and mixed clay and water to make a stiff new plaster. She put the money in the hole and smoothed the plaster over it; then she hung the picture of St. Joseph that had been her sewing prize over the cache. Now she knew where the money was, but no one else would know, not even Julián until she told him.

Then she realized that the room was getting dark and the sun was low, and the day was almost gone. Supper was ready and more than ready. The food would be spoiled if she tried to keep it much longer, but still Julián had not come home. María went to the window and looked out across the plaza towards his mother's house. A storm was coming with the sunset, and the light that lay now flat across the plaza was gray-yellow and frightening. This was not a good light. It did not make colors on the cottonwood tree or the houses; it threw its own color against solid objects, washing them with dirty yellow-gray on one side, turning them solidly black on the other.

Everybody was indoors eating supper, and the plaza at first looked deserted. Then María saw a man's figure move away from the cotton-wood tree and begin weaving towards her across the open space. She knew him at once. There was no other man in San Ildefonso who walked in just that way, or who had those same long, thin legs. It was Julián. Something was wrong with his walking; it was unsteady, and he seemed to lean first to one side and then to the other. He walked as if he had lost the power to guide himself.

Still María watched him as he came unsteadily closer. She knew that he might be sick, that she ought to run from the house and help him. Yet, to her eyes, his was not the walk of a sick person. Something was wrong, but not with his body alone. A man with a sick mind would walk that way, she thought. Julián had always been happy and laughing before. Surely his mind could not have become so suddenly sick as this.

When he stood before the house and she saw his face, then María knew that something had happened to the mind inside him. His face had fallen to pieces. The features were all there; he was not hurt or bloody; but those features were not connected with one another. His eyes seemed to look in different directions. There were shadows on his cheeks, cutting into and sharpening his nose; and his mouth was loose, as if he could not hold his lips together. It was Julián's face still, but it was not his face as she had always known it.

Fear took hold of her and shook her, so that she could hardly hold herself standing by the window, so that her own face felt as if it were falling away from its bones. Without a word, shawlless, she ran from the house, past Julián. He put out a hand to stop her, but she did not stop; and as she passed him, she saw him waver and fall. Still she ran, across the plaza, through the passageway between two houses on the south side of the square, and to Juan Gonzales' house in the fields below her father's. She was ashamed, ashamed to tell her family what had happened, ashamed to ask help of others. But Juan Gonzales was the religious head of the pueblo. Surely, if anyone knew what to do, it was he.

Juan's fat, comfortable wife came to the door when María knocked. She asked no questions of the younger woman. Juan himself got up from the supper table and came over to where María stood by the door. "What is it?" he asked.

"It's Julián. Something's wrong with him. I never saw him like this before. Maybe he's drunk." She knew as she spoke that there was no maybe about it.

"I'll come with you," said Juan. The sky was black when they came out of the house, and thunder roared and muttered over the Pajarito.

Julián lay where he had fallen, before the door of María's house.

"Help me with him," said Juan. "Pick up his feet, and help me carry him. Quickly!" Together they lifted Julián into the house and laid him on his own bed. "Let him lie there," said Juan. "Now that he's sleeping, let him sleep. Later I can talk to him."

"Can I take off his shoes?" María asked. Julián's feet looked uncomfortable, sticking straight up in the air in his heavy working shoes.

"If you want to," Juan said. "He won't know. He might get the covers dirty, though. Here, I'll help you."

Together they took off Julián's shoes and loosened his collar and belt. Juan stepped back and looked at the unconscious man. "This is a bad thing," he said. "How did it happen?"

"I don't know," María answered. "He went to see his mother. He had a dollar from the money he had earned. That was his share. The rest we were going to divide with our families. He earned all the money, and it seemed like right to let him keep a little of it."

"He must have gone to Spanish Pete's," said Juan slowly. "That's the only place around here where he could get *vino*."

"But it's against the law to sell it to Indians," María protested. She had heard her father say that.

"Spanish Pete doesn't care much for the law, I guess," said Juan. "This has happened before to other men. Sometimes it's an accident. They don't know what they're drinking or what it can do to them."

The Job

"This is an accident," María said. "Julián was never drunk before. It has to be an accident."

Juan shook his head slowly, from side to side. "The first time always is an accident," he said. "It's when they get to craving drink more than anything else in the world that it stops being accidental."

"Why does Spanish Pete stay here?" María demanded. "Why doesn't the council make him move away? You're the head of things. You could make him go."

Again Juan shook his head, more slowly than before. "We can make people move out of the pueblo if they do things that are bad," he said. "If Spanish Pete lived in the pueblo, it would be easy. We could get rid of him then. But he's smart. He doesn't live here. He's across the road on Spanish land and our rules can't touch him. We can punish the men he makes drunk, and if he got drunk himself and came into the pueblo we could punish him. He doesn't drink, though. That's the worst part of it. He poisons other people but not himself."

"What can we do?" María asked, beginning to cry. "What can I do?"

"You'll have to help Julián not to let it happen again," Juan told her kindly. "All of us have that work to do. I have young sons, and I have my part in not letting them learn about drinking. Julián has learned about it. Your job now is to help him forget about everything except the sickness and the shameful part of it."

"What else is there to forget?" María questioned.

"I never was drunk myself," said Juan quietly. "Your father and I, the men our age, never had a chance to drink or wanted to do it. So we don't know of ourselves. Men who do drink tell us that the *vino* tastes good and that for a while, right after they drink it, it makes them feel good inside. I don't know. Then, for another while, when they sleep like this, they forget the bad things that have happened to them. That's the big thing some of them want; the forgetting. I don't know. Wait till Julián wakes up and ask him, if you want to."

"No, I won't," María answered. "I don't want to know. I don't want to talk about it. This is an accident, this first time, just as you say. I'll wait and see if it happens again. If it does, and I know it isn't an accident, then I'll ask him and try to find out why he does it. This is bad enough now. Maybe it will be the only time, though, and I don't want to make him unhappy about it if I don't have to."

Juan smiled at her, a little sadly. "You talk like a good wife," he said. "You know your job, and I think you want to do it the right way. Wait and see. You may be right. Forgetting all about it unless it happens again will be part of your job, too."

"Being a wife sounds like the biggest job there is, sometimes," said María soberly.

"It's next to the biggest," Juan reminded her. "Being a mother is bigger. You have to be strong inside yourself for both those jobs. No one is going to be able to help you except God and the saints and our own old ones. They can give you help when you need it, if you learn to ask them for it in the right way."

"That's what my aunt said, when she was teaching us to make pottery," said María. "Is all of life working?" she asked Juan suddenly.

"All of life is working in some way or another," he assured her. "We work at happiness and being well. That's part of the job of being a whole person. Becoming a grown man or woman depends on learning that and knowing and remembering it. If you learn that part of the job, then you can do the rest with your own strength."

16. The Potsherd
(1908

The summers after the baby's death the archaeologists returned to San Ildefonso. The white men were going up on the Pajarito again, to dig out some more of the old houses there. It surprised Juan Gonzales to see them come back into the plaza.

"What do they want to start all over again for?" he asked Julián, who answered, "They say that that was a big town once, up there on the Rito de los Frijoles. They want to know all about it and the people who lived there."

"Well," said Juan Gonzales, "the people who lived there were our ancestors. Why don't they ask us about them? We can tell them things."

"Would you tell them everything?" asked Julián. "Would you tell them about the ceremonies and the songs and things like that?"

"No," answered Juan slowly, "not those things, of course. I'd tell them the things I thought they ought to know."

"Well, that's it," Julián said. "They say they can learn about some of the other things by looking at the old houses."

"They can't learn the songs and they can't learn the ceremonies," Juan said. "Those things they have to be taught, and nobody here will teach them or tell them."

Later in the day, Tomás came to María's house, and came out in the kitchen, where she was getting dinner. "Is Julián going with the white men, up on the Pajarito?" he asked her.

"I don't know," said María. "If they want him to work up there, he'll probably want to go."

"If he goes, you'd better go with him," said Tomás.

"Why?" asked María. "If I stay here, I can help Mother with the fruit again this summer."

"You'd better go," Tomás repeated. "Then you can watch Julián, in case those men offer him liquor."

"That was an accident last summer, when he got drunk after the baby died," said María. It was the first time any of them had spoken directly of the one time that Julián had been drunk.

"We think it was an accident," said Tomás. "Spanish Pete said it was an accident, when I talked to him. But you ought to be there, to make sure another accident doesn't happen."

"It might be better anyway," said María slowly. "Babies always die in the village during the summer. Maybe my first one will be all right if I go up there now. Maybe they're catching some germs here, the way Miss Grimes used to tell us."

"Maybe it's germs, whatever they are, and maybe it's bad spirits," said Tomás. "I don't know. If the bad spirits start walking through the village and touching the children, they die just the same as if the germs had caught them. The children who are away from the pueblo will be safer then."

"Yes," said María. "All right. If Julián goes this time, I'll go too."

"That's right," her father agreed. "A wife promises to leave her family and go with her husband when she marries him in church, remember." He laughed a little. "It's hard to choose, isn't it? Well, you go on up there with Julián, and don't think about us. Mother can dry fruit without you, if she has to."

Still later that day Julián came in with one of the white men. María was sitting in the kitchen, shaping a meal bowl. She had little time for making pottery these days; just when something in the house was broken and had to be replaced, did she do any pottery-making. The rest of the time she was too busy with the house and with taking care of their little son to think about handwork. She missed working at pottery, in a funny kind of way. It was quieting to sit on the floor like this and to feel a bowl or jar growing under her fingers.

The white man sat down on the kitchen stool, when María offered it to him, and watched her fingers. It made her nervous to feel the stranger's eyes against her hands. Her fingers slipped, and the coil of clay with them, so that she made a mistake in shaping the bowl. She dipped her fingers into the bowl of water on the floor beside her and repaired the error.

"His name is Jack," said Julián in Tewa. "He was working last summer. I like him. He wants me to go back with them."

"All right," said María, her eyes on the bowl and her moving fingers. "If you go, I want to go with you. Then maybe whatever it

Tyuonyi Village on the Rito de los Frijoles

is that makes the children die in the village in the summer won't get my little boy."

"Well, all right," said Julián. "I guess that's all right. I'll ask him." He turned to the white man. "My wife wants to come with me," he said in halting English. "Can she go?"

"I guess so," said Jack. "We'll ask the head man about it. Will she cook?"

"She's got to cook," replied Julián. "I got to eat."

"That's a nice bowl you have there," Jack said to María. "Do you make many of them?"

María looked at Julián, and he interpreted. She did not want to speak English to this stranger white man, now that she was out of practice with the words.

"You tell him," she said to Julián, when he had repeated the question to her in Tewa.

"I will," said Julián, and he turned around again to Jack. "She makes a little pottery," he said. "What she needs to cook with."

"Does she decorate it?" Jack asked. "Put designs on it, to make it look pretty?"

"No," said Julián, "she just makes it plain, to cook with. We have some of that old pottery, like you talk about. It sure is pretty. But she don't make it like that. Takes too much time."

"I didn't know there was anybody left here who made pottery at all," Jack said.

"Lots of ladies still make pottery," answered Julián. "They just make it for what they need and to give for presents, though."

"I should think they'd make it for sale," said Jack thoughtfully. "Anybody would like to buy the old, fine kind of pottery."

"Nobody wants to buy it," said Julián. "Just Indians buys Indian pottery from each other."

"That's too bad," said Jack. "Well, get your things ready, Julián. We'll start for Frijoles day after tomorrow, the head man says."

Two days was not very much time to get ready to move up into the mountains for the summer. It was not like getting ready to go to The Little Trees when they were all children, María thought. Now she had to choose and sort and pack things all at the same time, instead of taking days and weeks to do the work. She had no chance to put articles aside in a separate packing room. Julián tried to help her, but she had to tell him to go and choose his own things and get them ready, while she made up the bundles for herself and the cooking.

Even after that Julián was not any help. He kept coming and asking
her whether he should pack this or that, and if she thought he had
taken enough shirts. Finally María told him that however many
shirts he had taken would have to be enough. She was too busy with
the blankets and the cooking dishes to worry about shirts.

There was no time for her to fire the pottery she had been working on. She put it out in the sun to dry and harden as much as it
would and decided to fire her bowls after she got back. Jack came by
on the evening of the second packing day, with another white man,
and they stood outside the house and looked at the pottery for a long
time before they knocked at the door. María was alone in the house,
but she let the strangers come in.

"*Hablar Español?*" asked the second man. He was smaller than
Jack, and thin and wiry. He looked older, too.

"*Poquito,*" María whispered.

"*Muy bien,*" said the man, and he went on talking to her in Spanish. He explained that he directed the work on the Pajarito and was
in charge of the other white men and of the Indians who were going
to work there. Jack had told him that María made pottery, and he
had come to see her work.

"There it is," said María, gesturing towards the door. "You saw
it when you came in."

"Yes, I saw it," said the head man. "However, I'd like to have you
show it to me."

"All right," said María, and led the way outside the house. There
was not much for her to show. The pottery consisted entirely of meal
bowls and yeast bowls, which were easy to make. The meal bowls
were larger than the yeast bowls and were more open at the top, but
that was about the only difference in them. María had smoothed the
bowls down as much as she could and had made them as neat as
possible. That was all—just plain, smooth pottery bowls of different
sizes. They were all made of hard, rough clay, like that in Nambé
and Taos pottery, and were polished and smooth inside.

"You shape it well," said the man.

"It isn't hard to shape," María said.

"Do you ever put designs on it?" the head man asked, as Jack
had done.

"No," said María, "I'm no good at decorating things. I never tried
anything like that. We just make it to use, and it doesn't need to be
pretty for that."

"When we get up to Pajarito," said the head man, "you ought to try making pottery there."

"I don't think I can," said María. "I need tools and things to work with, and they'd be too much bother to carry. Besides, I'll be busy with the cooking and my little boy."

"Well, you can try if you want to," said Jack, and the two men went away.

In spite of the fact that it had been so hard to get started, living up on the Pajarito was rather like living in the summerhouse at The Little Trees. The white men had brought tents for everybody, including the Indians. Three of the other San Ildefonso men had brought their wives with them, and each Indian family had a small separate tent. The other Indian men lived together in two big tents. The white men had small tents like those they had brought for the Indian families, and two of them lived in each tent. They pitched the tents in the bottom of the canyon, beside the Rito de los Frijoles, and it looked as if there were a little new town down there.

The big, main, old town of Tyuonyi was built at the bottom of the cliff, a little away from the stream. Above it, in the cliff itself, some of the houses of the old town had been built; and part way up the cliff were houses made by building stone walls in front of the caves to enclose them. The top houses of all were just caves, without any walls at all. These caves were the places where most of the work was being done that summer.

María and her son stayed at the bottom of the cliff with the other women and children. She had thought that it would be harder to take care of Julián and the boy and to do the cooking in a tent than it was at home in the pueblo, but she found out that it was easier. Her tent was so small that when she had made the bed and put the clothes away after breakfast, her housework was finished. She found that she had time to sit and talk with the other women, to do some sewing, and even to go walking along the Rito, looking for wild plums. The life was all easy and pleasant and quiet. If María had brought her tools and some clay, there would have been plenty of time for her to make some pottery.

María did find a clay bed on one of her walks up the Rito, but she did not try to bring any clay back to camp with her. She remembered that if she made any pottery now, she would have to figure out some way to take it home with her at the end of the summer, and she did not want to worry about that.

The Potsherd

Julián was the one who was doing art work. Jack had found a painting of a water snake in one of the caves, and he asked Julián to copy it. Julián did such a good copying job that Jack and the head man found him a supply of drawing paper and colored pencils and started him to drawing all sorts of pictures. Julián copied the designs on the cave walls; and sometimes he drew pictures of dancing people; but most times he painted pictures of skunks. He had the right to paint pictures of skunks. The white men did not know that was the reason, and they just thought the skunks were funny. They said it was just like Julián to paint those pictures. He was always making jokes.

One evening Julián and Jack came back from the caves with a handful of stones.

"You look at these," Jack said to María, holding them out to her. "You tell me what they are."

The stones were very beautiful. They were of different shapes and sizes and colors, but they were all hard and highly polished. Some of the stones were polished only on one side, and some were polished all over. The smooth sides were almost as shiny as mirrors. María took one of the stones in her hand, and it fitted the curve of her thumb and fingers as if it had grown there.

"These are polishing stones," María said. She had got over the worst shyness; she could talk to Jack a little now.

"For pottery?" Jack asked her.

"Yes, for pottery," María said. "For rubbing smooth that red paint they put on the pots. Look. You can see. Here are little cracks in this stone, and the red paint is still there, in the cracks."

"Oh," said Jack, looking closely, "I see. Then this one was used for white paint, I guess. There's white along its cracks."

"That's right," María agreed. "These are good stones. She must have liked them a lot, that woman who used them. What are you going to do with them?"

"Take them to the museum in Santa Fé," Jack said. "All these things we find here are going to the museum."

"All right," said María.

That night she did not sleep a great deal. She kept thinking about the beautiful old polishing stones Jack had. It would be nice to have stones like that and to work with them. Jack had found a lot of stones, but maybe he had not found all of them.

In the morning, after her work was finished, María went along the cliff to a place where no one had ever dug. She looked all over the ground, but there was no trace of pottery to be seen. When she saw by the sun that it was almost noon, she went home and cooked *atole* for Julián's lunch. He did not like *atole* much, even with honey, but it was quick and easy to fix, so she let him eat it.

In the afternoon, she went back to her hunting. This time she climbed the cliff and looked into one of the caves. It was a shallow cave, but the old people must have lived there at some time, for there were smoke smudges on the back wall. María scratched in the earth of the cave floor, and there she found what she was looking for. Four smooth, polished stones. Three of them were black and shiny, and the fourth was white and shiny, but the red paint that had rubbed into it had stained it pink. The stones were very hard, and they fitted her fingers the way the others had done. María tied the stones in a handkerchief and put the bundle in the front of her dress to take home with her. That night she showed the stones to Julián.

"I don't know," he said doubtfully, looking at them. "I don't think you have the right to keep those. The museum men want these things."

"I'm going to keep them," said María. "I need them. It isn't stealing. I just found them, and those men couldn't use them."

At the end of the summer the head man came to their tent. Everyone was packing and getting ready to go, and María's things were all tied in bundles on the floor.

"María," the head man said in Spanish, "I want to talk to you."

María's stomach turned over inside her. Julián must have told him about the stones. The man had come to take them away from her.

"It's about your pottery," the head man went on.

María put her hand over her mouth and stared at him above it.

"I didn't mean any harm," she said. "I thought you didn't need those old stones. You had so many of them."

"I don't know what you mean," said the head man. "What old stones?"

"Those old pottery stones I picked up," María said.

"I didn't know you had any."

"Just four," she told him. "I wasn't stealing them. You had a lot, and I needed some good polishing stones like my aunt's."

"That's all right," said the head man. "Show them to me, if you please. Then you may keep them and use them."

María reached into the front of her dress and brought out the handkerchief in which she had tied the stones. She had kept them with her all the time, ever since she had found them.

"Here they are," she said when she had untied the handkerchief.

The head man looked at the stones and felt them in his fingers, as if he were making pottery, but he did not say anything for a long while. Then he laughed.

"I came to ask you if you would make some pottery in the old way, using the old stones," he said. "I have a piece of that pottery here, with a design on it. I wondered if you would copy it."

"Let me see," said María.

The piece of pottery was thin and hard, almost like stone itself. It was a dark, shiny gray, with a design drawn on it in fine black lines. María had never seen any pottery like it before. It was beautiful.

"I can try," she said, when she had looked at the potsherd carefully. "I never saw this kind of pottery made, but I can try. I can't make the design, though."

"Why not?" asked the head man.

"I never made any designs," María said. "I don't know how to draw."

"Maybe Julián can do it," the head man suggested.

"Men don't very often decorate pottery," said María, laughing.

"Well," said the head man, "I don't see why he shouldn't do it. He likes to draw, and he is good at it. You like to make pottery, but you say you can't draw. So that ought to make it easy for you both to work together. You make me a bowl this winter, with this kind of finish, and Julián can decorate it with the same kind of design. Then when I get back in the summer you can give it to me. I'll pay you for your work."

"All right," said María. "We can try, I guess."

"Take the piece of pottery home with you," said the head man. "That way you can look at it and see what you're doing. And take the stones and use them. That will make it nice, if you make the old kind of pottery with the old tools."

"All right," María said again. She tied the potsherd in a separate piece of cloth, carefully, so that it would not get broken, and put the little package in the front of her dress with the handkerchief that held the stones. She had them all together, then, but the stones could not bump into the sherd and break it. She felt safer about everything.

"We'll try," she said, and laughed a little again. "I don't know if you'll like it, but maybe you will. Anyway, we'll try."

When they got home from Frijoles in the fall, María found that there were many things she had to do. She wanted the house clean and neat for the winter, so the first few weeks she spent in cleaning and plastering and calsomining the rooms. When that work was finished, she cleaned out her storeroom and put away the vegetables and fruit and corn that Tomás had harvested and divided with María and Julián. Then she had to make new clothes for the little boy to wear, and after all that she made herself two new dresses.

All the time the old potsherd was in the back of her mind. She was thinking about it as much as she was about her other work. Every time that she was conscious of thinking about the pottery, she put the thought away. It was like fruit ripening on a tree. You could go out a few times in the season and look at it on the branches, but you could not do anything until the fruit was really ripe. María let the thought of the potsherd ripen slowly in her mind. When the time came and she and the thought had ripened, she would be ready to work.

Once or twice Julián spoke about the sherd to María. He asked her once where it was, and if she would mind letting him see and handle it. Another time he asked her when she was going to start making the pot.

"When the time comes," she told him.

"It's a long time coming," said Julián.

"I'll be ready for it," María answered, and that was all that either of them said.

Soon after that, the first boy was named in English. Julián wanted to name him Adam, and María asked if it were because Adam was the first man.

"No," Julián said, "it's for Adams, that worked on the job last summer. I like that Adams, and he's got a good name. I'd like to call my boy for him."

The Whole Pot

"Why don't you call him Adams?" Tomás asked when he heard this.

"Because everybody always forgets about that extra 's' anyway," said Julián. "If we call him Adam to start with, they won't have to forget."

So there was the first new man of the family. Somehow, when she looked at him now, María knew that she was never again going to have to worry about this child. He ate and slept, and when he waked, he laughed. He needed hardly any care.

So, one morning, María awoke with all her other jobs finished and was ready to begin on the pottery. After breakfast she got out the potsherd and sat down by the fire with the fragment in her hand. She sat and looked at the sherd for a long time. The clay was so thin and hard that she had to study the broken edge for a long while to find out whether anything had been mixed with the paste. She wished that she had a little glass that folded out of a case, like one the head man had, to make small things look larger. At last, by tipping the broken edge of the sherd towards the firelight, she caught a small, bright shine on one spot in the sherd. That was it, then. There was fine sand mixed with the clay.

María went out to the storeroom and looked at her own supply of clay and sand carefully. She had good, fine clay, but no sand that was hard and small enough. She wrapped her shawl around her and went over to Tía Nicolasa's house, taking the piece of pottery with her.

When María showed her the sherd, Tía Nicolasa grew most excited.

"This is beautiful," she kept saying. "I never saw pottery like this before. It's very beautiful."

"The sand is so fine," said María. "I don't know where to get fine sand like that."

"The blue sand bed on the way to Española has fine sand in it," Tía Nicolasa answered. "Not everywhere, but in some places. That's where you should go to get your fine sand."

"I could sift it and get out the finest part," said María thoughtfully.

"That would be a good thing to do," Tía Nicolasa agreed. "You ought to do the same thing with the clay, too. Then that will be fine and hard and right."

Since it was winter and most of the work in the fields was finished, Julián could take María to get the sand. The trip was not long; about two hours each way in the wagon was all. One day would do it. They left Adam with Desidéria, who promised to take good care of him. María packed *tortillas* and beans and milk for lunch, and she and Julián started out.

It was the first time they had been away from the pueblo and alone together since they had gone to St. Louis. At first María felt shy and almost as if she were traveling with someone she did not know well. Then Julián began to sing, drumming with his hand on the wagon seat beside him, and the horses started to trot uphill, and she was happy. It was a warm day for December, with lots of sun and a little wind that picked heavy thoughts from your heart and carried them away. Riding together and being together was good, and it seemed a short trip to the sand bed.

María remembered what Tía Nicolasa had told her.

"The finest sand is just in certain places," she told Julián.

"We'd better hunt for a place, then," he said.

They separated, and went back and forth across the surface of the sand dune, looking for the best place to dig. At last María called, "Here it is. I think this is a good place to start."

"All right," said Julián. "I can't seem to find anything special. It all just looks like sand to me."

He brought the shovel from the wagon and peered doubtfully down at the place where María was standing.

"It doesn't look much different from the rest," he said.

"It is, though," María insisted. "It's finer. I can feel it with my fingers. You can dig here."

"Well," said Julián, "all right." He still looked doubtful.

María brought the two flour sacks she had packed in the wagon, and Julián began to dig up sand to fill them. María watched him closely, and when she thought he was getting near the coarser sand, she warned him about it.

"I still don't see any difference," Julián protested. "You must have good eyes to be able to tell."

"I'm watching," said María, and Julián laughed.

"You must be," he said, and finished filling the sacks, taking the sand only from the places where she told him to dig.

When they lifted the filled sacks into the wagon, though, they could both tell the difference in the sand. The sacks were heavier than they would usually be and little rings of sand sifted out through the cloth onto the floor of the wagon. These were good, new flour sacks that María had bought at the store for just this trip. There were no holes in the bags, but the sand came through the cloth as if they had been coarse bran sacks.

"That sand is the right kind," said María contentedly.

They rested and ate their lunch on the sunny side of the sand dune, where the wind could just touch the tops of their heads but not get down around their shoulders or blow sand at them to make them uncomfortable. When they had finished eating, they sat on, looking out across the valley to the river and to the rim of Pajarito Plateau beyond.

"This is good country," said Julián, and María agreed, "I never want to live anywhere else in all my life."

Julián laughed at her a little, nicely. "You won't," he said. "Pueblo Indians belong here. This is their country. They'd better like it, because it's all they have."

Going back to the pueblo, María thought about what Julián had just said. He was a man who liked to be going, to be seeing new places and meeting new people. He was a man who had a need for that in his life. She liked doing that herself; but if she knew that she would never go anywhere again, she could be happy still, with Julián and Adam and her father and mother.

Anyway, just this little trip was like going through new country, from the first time she remembered. Things had changed. There were houses where once there had been fields, and fields where once there had been marshlands along the river. Most of all, there were bare spots on the mountains, where there had once been dense, heavy coverings of big trees. That was the biggest change; it was because that change had taken place that the others had come about. Maybe if there were some way to stop the timber companies from cutting off the big trees, the other changes would stop of themselves. That would hold back time, so that they would all be young a long time together, and babies would be little and soft. Then she shook her head.

"What are you thinking about?" Julián asked.

"That maybe there might be a way to stop changes."

"There isn't any way," said Julián. "That's the way things are. That's part of living."

"That's what I thought, too," María said.

They went along towards home then, and when they had almost reached the pueblo, Julián said, "I want to stop here. I need some of that yucca."

"To wash your hair? We have plenty for that at home. This kind doesn't make very good suds."

"To wash the pot's hair," said Julián, handing her the reins. He climbed down from the wagon, and went over to the yucca plant. It was one of the long, tall, spindly kind with leaves like narrow knives. Julián did not dig up the whole plant but just cut the main stem through above the root and brought the top of the plant back to the wagon.

"There," he said, "that ought to make me some good paint brushes."

The next morning María had Julián bring one of the new sacks of sand into the storeroom, where she could get at it easily. She thought for a while, as she washed the dishes, about how she was going to sift the sand. The flour sifter was the only real sifter that she had, and it was too coarse to use. Then she remembered how the sand had worked its way through the sacks, and she decided to use a cloth for a sifter. She stretched a piece of an old shirt over a bowl, and poured the sand on the cloth. Gently, she worked the sand back and forth with her fingers and watched the pile on the cloth grow smaller as she worked. The sand was sifting through, steadily and slowly.

The Whole Pot

After that, María started in to sift the clay. It was finer than the sand to begin with, so she began by sifting it through a piece of flour sack. She needed much more clay than sand and it went through the cloth very slowly, but by noon she had a pile in the bottom of a dishpan. She thought it would be enough. Julián came in for dinner, and found her cooking and smiling.

"What's the joke?" he asked her. He was a man who always loved jokes.

"I was remembering," María replied. "I was remembering when Desidéria and I were little girls and made ourselves toy dishes. Tía Nicolasa made us sift the clay and sand for them then. I wouldn't think anything about it any more, but then it was just as hard work as sifting these things was this morning."

"Well," said Julián, helping himself to the beans, "if you keep on making fine pottery, maybe you'll get so this won't be anything to think about, either."

"Maybe," said María, and sat down beside him to eat her own lunch.

After they had eaten, Julián got out his new clump of yucca. He sat and looked at it for quite a while. Then he cut off a piece about six inches long from one of the heaviest leaves. He trimmed the blade of the leaf back to the stem, so that all that was left was a narrow, three-sided little stick.

"It looks like the quill of a feather," Julián said, holding the stick out on the palm of his hand, and studying it.

"Miss Grimes told us once that the white people used to write letters with feather quills," said María. She was sitting on the opposite side of the fireplace, mixing sand and clay together, getting ready to add the water to them.

"Maybe they were smart," said Julián. "I'll have to try a feather quill for this some time." He put the yucca quill in his mouth, and began to chew its thicker end, so that bits of the hard, stiff part came away from the long fibres. When he had his mouth full of the scraps he looked at María suddenly, startled.

"Spit it in the fireplace," she said. "You can't go running to the door every time you get a mouthful. Next time you'd better do it outdoors, where you can spit as much as you like."

"Thanks," said Julián, when his mouth was empty and he could speak. "I'll remember about that," he went on. "This stuff doesn't have much taste, but it's puckery."

María brought some water and began to mix it with her clay and sand. The stuff was so fine that it made only a small ball in the bottom of the mixing pan, instead of the big pile she had expected.

"I can make just one pot this time," she said, looking at the mixture.

"That's all they want of this kind," said Julián. "They didn't tell you to go on making a lot of these pots. Just one was all."

"Well," said María, "I thought as long as we were at it we could make four or five. Then maybe they could sell the extra ones, the way they said."

"Maybe," said Julián. "I think we ought to wait and see how the first one turns out. Are you going to start now?"

"Not this afternoon," María answered. "Good clay is better if it rests overnight. I'll start in the morning, and then the pot will have all day to dry."

She went ahead with the work that she had to do in the house, while Julián sat and looked at the potsherd and tried to draw its designs on a clean board with his new brush. Finally he put the brush away and shook his head. "I can't make it come out right," he said. "Besides, how can I know what kind of design to make till I see the pot?"

María started in shaping the pot the next morning. From the way that the sherd curved, she thought it must have come from a big bowl, although she could not be sure. Besides, she did not have enough fine clay ready to make a very big piece of pottery. She patted out a clay *tortilla* for the base, and then pinched off a small piece of the clay, punched it thoroughly to get out the air bubbles, and began rolling it between her hands to make the first coil.

The fine mixture rolled and worked more easily than any clay she ever remembered handling. She was surprised at how quickly she could build the bowl, and how thin she could make it. Before noon the shaping and polishing were finished, and she set the bowl on the kitchen table to dry. It was round and firm and lighter than any piece of pottery she had seen made in San Ildefonso.

When Julián came in, he stood and looked at the bowl for a long time. "Is it dry enough to paint?" he asked.

"I don't think so," María answered. "It ought to dry overnight, I believe."

"That's all right anyway," Julián said. "I've got to figure out what to paint it with."

"What did they use on the old pots?" María inquired.

The Whole Pot

"Jack said probably guaco," answered Julián. "He said they made a syrup out of guaco, like sugar syrup, and boiled it down till it got thick. Then when the pot was fired, the guaco burned and made a black design."

"We haven't got any guaco," María said.

"I guess I'll have to go out and look for some this afternoon," replied Julián.

"It's pretty late in the year to find any growing," María reminded him. "It all dries up in the fall."

"Well, I'll ask around," said Julián. "Maybe somebody will have some syrup made up to use for tea, or something."

When he came back late in the afternoon, he had a little jar in his hand.

"Where did you get it?" María demanded.

"Your Tía Nicolasa had it," Julián answered with a grin. "When you want to know anything about pottery, you go to your Tía Nicolasa. So did I. She said she made it up a long time ago, to decorate a storage jar. Then she put it away and forgot about it, so it dried out. She says if we grind the dry syrup up fine and boil it down again with lots of water, it will be just as good as ever."

"Well, we can try," said María. She put the hard little black cake that she found in the bottom of the jar on the fine *metate,* and ground it until it was a powder she could have sifted through a cloth like the clay. Then she put the powder, mixed with water, in a bowl by the fireplace, and let it cook slowly. There was a faint, plantlike smell all through the house in a little while and by bedtime they could smell nothing else.

While María ground and cooked the guaco, Julián sat by the fire. Sometimes he looked at the bowl, and sometimes he looked at the potsherd in his hand. He was studying them both together, one with the other, and he never moved or spoke until María gave him a bowl of *atole* for supper. Then he ate it, and said, "That was good. What was it?"

"Coffee," María told him.

"I'd like another cup, please," said Julián. This time she did give him coffee, and he drank it and never knew the difference. At bedtime he got up, stretched, and said, "It will fit," and they went to bed without another word.

The next morning Julián took his bowl of guaco and his yucca brush into the living room as soon as he had finished his outdoor work.

Then he took the new bowl from the kitchen table. Last of all, he got the potsherd and set it beside the bowl on a stool. Then he sat down on the floor, with the pot of guaco beside him, dipped the brush into the paint, and went to work. María went away and left him. She wanted to sift some more sand and clay and get ready to begin another bowl.

When María went to call him to lunch, Julián had finished his part of the work. He was still sitting on the floor in front of the stool, and before him was the bowl, covered with fine gray lines. They made a pattern of a water snake, with square, even designs for the pueblo and the fields around it. María had never seen a bowl like this before.

"It's beautiful," she said, when she had looked and looked.

"It's all right," said Julián. "It came out all right. The lines matched."

"It looks as if the design grew on the bowl," María said.

"It's all right," Julián repeated. "I like it. I like this sort of work. It's like making saddles. You think what you're doing, and that makes your hands do it. It's good. Everything goes with you. Not like plowing, when everything can go against you."

María laughed. "You'd better be a potter," she said. "It's better to do something you like than something you don't like."

"Men aren't potters," said Julián, putting his brush down on the floor beside the pot of guaco, carelessly. "Is lunch ready?"

18. The Firing
(1909

Tía Nicolasa had always said that firing was careful but easy, and with the plain, undecorated wares María had found it so. You had to be careful to get the pots evenly stacked with the wood and the dung cakes, and you had to be careful to get the fire hot and to keep it that way. Otherwise, it was easy enough to light the fire and to let it burn. Tía Nicolasa, though, seldom made painted wares.

María asked her aunt to come help with the firing of the special bowl, and when Tía Nicolasa heard that she was planning to fire just the one piece she laughed and said that she would come. Then she thought the matter over for a few minutes, and added, "I believe I'd better bring over some pieces to be fired, too."

"Why?" María asked her.

"Why," Tía Nicolasa said, "it isn't easy to fire just a few pieces, and I don't see how you're going to manage one all by itself. What you'd better do is make a few more, and I'll bring mine, and we'll fire them all together."

"All right," said María. When she got home she told Julián about the plan.

"I think we'd better make some more of the new kind of bowls," she said at the end.

"You mean the old kind," Julián said, smiling a little.

"The new old kind," put in Tomás from the corner of the fireplace, where he sat holding Adam and visiting.

"The kind the white people want," María said impatiently. "We have all the cooking pots we need right now, and if we can sell some of these, I think we ought to make them."

"I don't know whether they'll sell or not," Julián said in a stiff kind of voice. "I don't think you ought to work so hard at something when you don't know what's going to happen about it."

"I can always use some bowls," María informed him, "or, if I can't, my sisters can. I think we ought to make some more."

"You're the one who makes them," Julián reminded her. "Women are potters. Men aren't supposed to be."

"I don't think you ought to make them," María persisted. "But you can decorate them in your spare time. You do a lot of painting, anyway. Men are the painters, not women."

"Well, all right," said Julián slowly. "I can do the painting, I guess. That's a man's work."

"Don't paint any skunks," said Tomás, and Julián said, "I don't think skunks would look nice on pottery. I'll just paint the kind of designs they put on those old pieces."

It was a pleasure for María to have the painting for Julián to do. He worked at it in the evenings, when his other jobs were out of the way. Finally he could work in the kitchen with the family all around him. The boy could play, or sometimes cry, and the rest of the family could come in to visit, but the activity did not seem to disturb Julián at all. Only if outsiders came in, would he put his work away, and then he was impatient to get back to it as soon as the visitors were gone. One reason that María was glad to see him painting, although she did not say so even to her mother or father, was that it kept Julián at home. That way she knew he was not going off to Spanish Pete's, where he might buy wine.

They made four more pots, and then the fine sand was all used up. Tía Nicolasa had her pottery ready by that time, and they waited for a good day for the firing. Even in winter there were still, windless days sometimes, and they had to have a day when the wind was not blowing, so that the smoke would go straight up in the air instead of settling on the pottery.

María had Julián build a firing place behind the house and lay the fire, so that everything would be there ready when the right day came. Julián made a hole in the ground first. He put down cedar bark and then a layer of broken pots and whatever scraps of metal they could find on the dump. Then he put a big pile of cedar wood, chopped and ready, beside the fireplace. Even when the firewood in the house ran low while she was waiting, María would not use the cedar from that pile. That was for the pottery, and she wanted to keep every bit of it.

Then one morning in early February, they wakened to find that the sun was coming up clear over the edge of the hills and that the air was not stirring at all. Tía Nicolasa was knocking at the door before they had finished breakfast. She had some of her bowls with her, and she asked Julián to go down to her house and bring back the rest.

"I just kept on making and making while I was waiting," she said. "I didn't know I had made so many until I got them out and tried to carry them."

Julián went for the bowls while María and Tía Nicolasa carried the first pottery out to the fireplace. They put Tía Nicolasa's pots down on the firebed of broken pottery and scrap metal, and built a shelter over them with the first of the cedar sticks.

"Now yours come next," Tía Nicolasa said. "They're least likely to be smoked up if they're in the middle of the pile."

María set her painted bowls carefully down on the firewood and placed another rack of cedar over them. By that time Julián was back with Tía Nicolasa's pottery, and they made a top layer of that. They covered the pottery with more cedar, and then Tía Nicolasa took a little buckskin bag from the front of her dress and sprinkled corn meal over the whole pile, while she said a prayer for the pottery to be good. Then all together they heaped on more cedar and covered the whole pile, sides and top, with cakes of dried cow dung.

"Now," said Tía Nicolasa, and she lighted the pile, at the bottom, with a brand from the kitchen fire. Then they all stood by and waited for the pottery to cook.

The cedar and dung burned fiercely, with a clean, hot flame. It was too hot for anyone to get close to the fire, but Tía Nicolasa watched it carefully. When the flames died down and she could see that there was more heat in one place than in another, she hurried up to the fire and added fuel to the spot that was not hot enough. That kept the flames burning evenly. When the fire began to die down all around the pile and there were only embers left on the ground, Tía Nicolasa said, "Now we can let it go out."

The heat from the embers was still strong and clear, and as the flames died away, a little wind came up. The last of the smoke flickered and wavered in the air, and what had been a straight line of smoke reaching up towards the sky bent in the middle like a tree, and like a tree stooped as if to touch the ground.

"Oh," María cried, "my pots! My painted pots! They'll be all smoked!"

"Maybe not," said Tía Nicolasa comfortingly. "Maybe some of them will have a little smoke cloud on one side, but I think that's all that will happen."

"We wanted them to be perfect," said Julián. "We wanted them to come out just right, the way they went in."

"There doesn't seem to be any way to make all the pottery you fire come out right, every time," said Tía Nicolasa slowly. "I wish there were. I never fired pottery yet without losing a few pieces. Potters expect to have some spoiled, that's all."

"It doesn't seem right to me," insisted Julián, thoughtfully. "There ought to be some way to make it all come out right every time."

"Well, looking at it now won't help it any," Tía Nicolasa said. "We might as well go on in the house and wait for it to cool so we can handle it without spoiling it any more than we have to."

María glanced up at the sun. "We can eat dinner while we're waiting," she said. "It's nearly noon, and we're all hungry."

"That's a good idea," Julián agreed, and they all went in to dinner. As María had left a stew and some beans cooking near the fire, the food was ready for them. Tía Nicolasa stirred and tasted the stew while María made *tortillas*.

"I'm going to put some more chile and a little *orégano* in this," Tía Nicolasa said. "That always brings out the flavor."

María laughed, as she spread the *tortillas* down on the hot stone griddle to bake. "I used to think you didn't care whether food had any taste or not," she said. "You never seemed to pay any attention to it when we were children."

"I still think there are other things that are just as important," answered Tía Nicolasa, "and there are other things I'd rather do than cook. But when you have to wait for the other things to work out and there isn't anything but cooking for you to do, you might as well do it the best way you can. A woman's a woman, with a family to feed, even if she makes pottery, too."

"I'll remember that," said María.

Tía Nicolasa laughed again. "I must be getting to be a pretty old woman," she said, "when I start giving advice to the younger ones. Young women are still learning, and they have to learn from the ones who went first; but I never thought of myself as one of the first ones before."

"That's funny," said María, "I've always thought of you that way. All my life I've been learning from you, just the way I learned from Mother and Grandmother. It seems natural for you to be teaching me."

"I suppose," said Tía Nicolasa, "that you'll find out, as you get

older, too, that there really isn't any difference between your sisters' children and your own. You'll love them all about equally, I expect. I know my sisters and I always have."

"Maybe," said María, slowly. She looked across the room, at the little boy hanging in his cradle from the *vigas*. She felt sure that she would not mix her feeling about her children and Desidéria's. Adam was her own son, and she would only feel this way about a brother or sister, if he had one.

After dinner was eaten, Julián went out and looked at the pottery fire, and then he came back to the kitchen where the two women were washing the dishes.

"I think it's ready," he said. "The smoke and flame were gone before we ate, and now there isn't even any red in the embers. All I can see is a pile of white ashes."

"I'll come and take a look at it," said Tía Nicolasa, drying the last dish. "Throw out the dirty water, María, and come on. You can sweep the kitchen later. This is the important thing now."

There were only the white ashes left, as Julián had said, and Tía Nicolasa looked at them and nodded. "It's all right," she said. "Look out, Julián! Don't put your hand in it. The ashes are still hot, even if you can't see the heat. Here, let me lift the pottery out with a stick."

The pots at the top of the pile were hard and dull when Tía Nicolasa lifted them out by putting the end of the stick inside their rims and swinging them free of the heap of ashes. There were little smoke clouds and smudges on the sides of the vessels, but Tía Nicolasa didn't seem worried about them.

"It doesn't make any difference with these," she said, blowing the ashes away from the pottery in order to see what had happened. "One of them's cracked down the side. Too bad. I'll have to throw that one out. I tell you, María, we'll break it up and leave it here, to add to the pottery in your firebed."

"Thank you," María said. She reached for the stick in her aunt's hand. She could hardly wait to see the pots, while all this talking was going on. "Here, I can take out the next layer."

"Gently, gently," cautioned Tía Nicolasa. "You can't hurry pottery. Let it cool a little minute longer, and then you can take it out. The wind can't break it then."

María bent forward and blew the ashes away from her pottery. She did not want to reach into the fire with the stick until she could see every piece and know just what she was doing. She might break a bowl, and she did not want to do that through carelessness. Julián bent over beside her and blew, too.

"Now," he said excitedly, "I can see the shape of every piece."

Gently and carefully María lifted out the first vessel. It was a jar with a narrow mouth, and she could catch the stick inside the rim and hold it firmly there until she set the piece on the ground. The jar rang a little as it touched the hard earth, and Tía Nicolasa nodded.

"That's a good one, I can tell," she said. "Hard and perfect, or it wouldn't make that noise. Not a crack in it."

Julián reached for the stick without speaking, and lifted out the next piece. It, too, was a jar, and it, too, rang as it touched the ground.

"Another perfect one," said Tía Nicolasa. "María, run and get a cloth from the house to lift the bowls. We should have brought one with us."

When María got back, her aunt and Julián were still standing by the pile of ashes, looking down at the bowls. The jars stood beside them, coated with ashes, and María laughed at the sight.

"I thought you'd be cleaning them by this time," she said, and Julián shook his head.

"We can do that all at once," he said. "Here, let me have that cloth. I'll get the bowls out."

Quickly and lightly, one at a time, he lifted the three bowls free and set them down on the ground. María was not sure that he did it purposely, but she noticed that every bowl rang as he let go of it.

"Every one perfect," said Tía Nicolasa. "I wish I could say as much for mine. Now we'll wipe them off."

Julián still held the cloth, and it was he who dusted the ashes from the sides of the vessels. Then he stood back, and they all looked at the new old pots.

Three of the pieces, a jar and two bowls, were almost perfect. There were faint fire clouds near the bases of the three vessels, but the upper parts of their sides, near the rims, were unmarked by anything but the fine, clear black lines that Julián had painted on them. Those three were just the way María had known that they would be.

Something had happened to the other two, however. Instead of being light gray with fine black lines on them, they were an even black all over. They looked like pottery from Santa Clara Pueblo, except that they were not polished and shiny like Santa Clara pottery.

"Something happened to them," said Julián, his face settling with disappointment.

"They were too near the edge of the fire," Tía Nicolasa told him. "The smoke from the dung cakes got on them and turned them black. That's what must have happened."

"It's too bad," said María. "I wanted every one of them to be perfect."

"They're good pots," Tía Nicolasa reassured her. "You can use them for a long time."

"They aren't the pretty kind that will sell," María protested.

"Get some fat and polish them before they get cold. Then they'll look better," Tía Nicolasa suggested. "You can do that while I take out the rest of mine."

"Oh, don't bother," said Julián. "I don't even want to look at them. They've spoiled all my painting, those old dungs."

"They won't be good cooking pots unless you grease them," insisted Tía Nicolasa. "You don't want to just throw them away, do you?"

"No," said María. She brought some lard from the house, and smoothed it on the warm sides of the pots, on Tía Nicolasa's as well as her own. The fat made the black pieces shiny, and they were hard and thin and fine in every other way. It was just that they stood for carelessness in careful work that made them ugly, María thought.

"Well," said Julián when Tía Nicolasa had taken her good pottery and gone home, "that's that. We've made them their pottery, and I hope they like it."

"One thing about it," said María thoughtfully, "we got the pottery all out whole. None of it broke."

"That's because your aunt put them in the best part of the fire," Julián reminded her.

"I don't believe it is," said María, "not all of it. That's only part of the reason. I think some of it is because the clay and sand were so fine and good, and I worked them so carefully. I want to make some more pottery, and work the stuff for them that same way."

"We can try," said Julián slowly. "This time we'll make a lot of pieces, and see if it makes any difference where they are in the fire. We'll make enough for a whole firing of our own pottery. Then we'll know for sure which is the reason that yours turned out this way."

María started to remind him that men were not potters and that she had made the pots. Then she changed her mind and went quietly to put the black pieces away out of sight, in the storeroom.

19. The Selling
(1909

From February to May was the busiest time of the year in the pueblo. All the heaviest work came then, with the plowing and planting of the fields and the cleaning and opening of the ditches. Especially in the years after the big trees had been cut and the mountains let the water pour down their sides, there was a great deal of irrigation work to do.

Ditches were men's work. Women had no part in the job, except to see that the men were fed. Early each February the council of the pueblo met to plan the work for that year. Then the councilmen sent out the crier, to stand on the roof of the governor's house and tell the men of the village what each of them was supposed to do. Everyone waited for the caller to come out and make his announcement about the work. Until they knew what was planned for the community, the people were slow to plan their own work. When each man knew his part in the general scheme, then he could make a separate plan for himself and his family.

Tomás and Julián were among the first men to be called out in the spring of the year when María began her real pottery-making. They were assigned to work on the upper part of the ditch, before it entered the community lands around the pueblo. Other men worked on the lower sections of the ditch, but the hardest work was up at the head gates, where they made sure that the water ran right from the beginning. Desidéria's husband was working with Tomás and Julián, and Ana's was on the next stretch below them, so the whole family was together in this work.

Since the men were too far from the houses and too busy to come in for their dinners at noon, the women took food out to the workers. They got everything ready, and when the time came, they went from their houses, carrying covered bowls and baskets and pans of food, marching together to the places where their men were working. Up

175

at the head of the line one of the women began to sing, a glad song because it was spring and the work for the crops had begun. All the women took up the song, and so they went, singing and marching and carrying food, into the fields where the men waited for them.

The meal was not a feast or a great gathering. The members of each family sat together and ate their meal in a group. The little groups, together making one big gathering, were scattered out along the ditch. When everyone had finished eating, some of the men sang while they rested. When the eating and resting and being together ended, everybody went back to work. The men dug and cleaned on the ditches, and the women returned to their houses to wash the dishes and start getting another big meal ready for the men to eat in the evening.

When all the ditches were cleaned and the people were ready to plow and plant, came the time to dance the Pintito—the dance of the little paints. This dance was for the men who had done the hard ditch work. When they danced it they forgot the slime and mud and dirt at the bottom of the ditches, the wading in cold water and the hardness of bending; and they thought only of the water the ditches would bring and the corn that the water would cause to grow.

The men danced all day in the plaza, coming out four times and saluting each of the four world corners four times. The dancers and singers wore evergreen boughs on their heads and necks and arms. A square of little cedar trees was planted around the black stone in the plaza. The fields are square and the world is square, and the water is the cedar blue-green of the fields and the sky.

Everything in the dance had a meaning, even the little rings of white paint against the black paint background on the dancers' legs. Those were little white rounds, like snowflakes or raindrops falling on the darkness of the earth. So the workers became dancers, and the time of the year and the work to be done at that time became colors and patterns for the dancers to wear and the women to see.

After the Pintito had been danced and the rain that always followed it had fallen, the people settled down to the biggest work of the spring. Tomás and Julián were gone from their homes from before daylight until long after dark, and María and Reyes took this time to clean and plaster and calsomine their houses. María had done the work when they came back from Pajarito in the fall, but spring was the usual time for doing it, and she wanted to get back to doing things in the usual ways. She and her mother and sisters worked together, taking each house in turn. In that way the work was not hard for any of them, and they finished it quickly.

The dances and the work and the things that went with spring followed along so much in their usual patterns that María forgot about other matters. She was so settled back into the regular pattern of the days that it was a surprise to her to look out of the window one morning and see two white men coming towards the house. She ran quickly to take off her apron and smooth her hair, but there was knocking at the door before she was ready to be seen by strangers. She wished that Julián were there to talk to the men, but when she opened the door, she found that she knew both of them. It was Jack who stood nearer the door, but the head man stood just behind him.

"Good morning," they both said in Spanish. María answered them in that language and asked them to come in. Because there were two of the men, she did not mind sitting in the room with them, even though they were not relatives.

"Are you back for the summer?" she asked them, and the head man said yes. Then he asked, in his turn, "Where is Julián?"

"Out with my father, planting," María answered. "He'll be back pretty soon, though."

"That's good," said Jack, his face lighting up. "We want to see him. He's the first of our friends that we want to see."

"Do you want him to go to work again?" María questioned.

"Yes," said the head man, "if he can come, we want him again this summer."

"I guess he can," María said. "It's up to him. You'll have to ask him when he gets back."

"Will you come, too?" Jack asked.

"I don't know," replied María. "I didn't think about it. Maybe I will. I guess I'd rather stay home, though. I like it here."

"What will you do if you stay home?" asked the head man. "Make pottery?"

"I already made some," said María, laughing. "I made some for you."

"Did you?" the head man asked. "The kind I wanted? Where is it?"

"I got it right here," answered María. "Wait a minute. I almost forgot I made it, it's been so long."

She left the two men and went into the kitchen. From the place where she had put them, high up on a shelf, she took down the three good pieces of pottery. They were wrapped in old cloths, to keep them clean, and she carried the bundles back into the living room and set them on the floor before the two men.

"There," she said. "I want you to look at it. Maybe you won't like it."

When she turned back the cloths and stood back away from the vessels, she waited a long time for the two men to say something. Then the head man drew a deep breath, and leaned down and touched the pottery gently. "Why, María," he said, "it's beautiful. It's just perfect."

"You didn't say how many you wanted," María reminded him.

"How many did you make?" he asked.

"These and two others," María replied. "Five altogether. Those others were spoiled, though. They were spoiled in firing."

"It's too bad that you lost them when these are so good," said the head man.

"It couldn't be helped, I guess," said María. "We always plan to lose some when we fire them. My aunt taught me that."

"Maybe you can work out another way of firing," Jack suggested.

"Maybe," said María. "We always do it the same way, though. That's the way we fire the pottery."

"We wanted it fired in the usual way," the head man agreed. "That was the idea, Jack. We wanted to know if it could be done in the open fire, you know. This proves that it can. Did you do the decoration, María?"

"No," María told him, "I didn't. I'm not any good at designing.

Julián did the decorating. He's good at painting, like last summer when he painted up all that paper you gave him, remember?"

"That's right," said the head man, "he did. Did he draw a pattern for this, María, to make the design fit the bowl?"

"No, he just made it fit in his head," María replied. "He sat and looked at the pottery, and then he took his brush and made the designs, that's all."

"They're beautiful," said the head man again. "Perfect. María, I told you I'd try to sell your pottery, but this I want to buy myself. If you and Julián make some more like this, I'll try to sell that. You make the pottery, and I'll find the people to buy it."

"All right," said María, "we can try. If you like it, we're glad."

"I do like it," said the head man. He picked up the first bowl. "How much do you want for this one, María?"

"I don't know," said María, surprised. "I never sold a piece of pottery before. We just trade them for beans or work or things. I don't know what it's worth in money. Whatever you think is right."

"I don't know either," said the head man, laughing. "I never ordered a piece of pottery before. How long did it take you to make it, then?"

"I don't know that," said María. "I worked some and Julián worked some. We both worked some, different times. I don't know how long it took us. We were working on all those pots together. I'd work a while and let it dry a while, so I could cook lunch or take care of Adam, or things like that. Then I'd come back and work some more."

"You must have some idea," the head man insisted. "How long? Guess. One day, four days, a week——?"

"Well," said María, considering, "do you mean the time we went for the sand and clay, too, and the time for firing? And the day Julián went around asking everybody in the pueblo for guaco? All those things?"

The head man threw his hands up over his head. "I don't know, María," he laughed. "I really don't know whether you ought to count those things or not."

"Maybe you could get at it this way," Jack suggested. "Figure what you would pay for a bowl like that if you bought it in a store."

"A bowl this size?" asked the head man. "Then you'll have to decide whether it's a fine Chinese porcelain bowl, or an ordinary crockery mixing bowl, or something in between, you know."

"No, that doesn't help much," said Jack. "María, how much would you pay for one of these bowls, if you were buying it?"

"In money?" asked María, and Jack said, "In money."

"I guess I'd pay two dollars for that one," said María, pointing to the bigger bowl. "That's a good size for a yeast bowl, and it's hard and will last a long time."

"Is that a fair price?" asked the head man, and María thought the matter over for a while.

"I guess so," she said then. "It seems fair to me."

"When you're selling the bowl, too?" demanded Jack, and María laughed and said, "Yes."

They agreed on a dollar and a half for the smaller bowl and three dollars for the big jar, and the head man paid María six silver dollars and two quarters. She sat and looked at the money for a while, then tied the coins in one of the cloths she had wrapped the pots in, and slipped the package into the front of her dress.

"A long time ago when I was a little girl," she said, "a woman told me to tie my purse in my handkerchief, because cloth sticks to cloth and you can't lose it. So I still do."

They all laughed, and then Jack sighed a little. "I wish those other pieces hadn't been spoiled in the firing," he said. "I'd like to have some pottery, too. María, can't you make me some?"

"If I stay home this summer, I can," María promised.

"Maybe you'd better stay," said Jack, "and think about pottery."

"You get just plain pots, then," María warned him. "Julian has to do the designing on them."

"María," Jack said, "I have an idea. Why don't you stay home this summer and make the pottery? Then you can have it ready for Julián to decorate when he gets back from the Pajarito. That will be work for him to do in the winter when he finishes in the fields."

"It's all right with me," said María, "but it's up to him. He's got to say if he wants to or not. That's his decision."

The two white men laughed at that. María did not think it was a funny thing to have said, and she was still wondering why they had thought so when the door opened and Julián came in. He smiled when he saw his friends, and his face was bright with pleasure because they had come. Then he saw the pottery on the floor in front of them.

"Hello," he said, "you buy those pots? Those some old pots we dug out of the ruins. You don't want to buy those old pots."

The Selling

Jack leaned his head over on one side, and looked at the pots and then at Julián.

"We like these pots all right," he said. "They aren't bad pots. I bet that big one will even hold water. We just don't like the decoration on them. All those fine lines and things, who thinks they're pretty?"

For a minute Julián looked at him with the smile going off his face and his eyes drooping like those of a child who has been scolded. Then Jack threw back his head and laughed, and after a minute Julián laughed too.

"You make jokes," he said. "I thought for a minute maybe you don't like my painting."

"Sure I make jokes," Jack said cheerfully.

"This is no joke, Julián," said the head man. "We think there ought to be more of this pottery. Jack wants some, and the others will, too, when they see these. We think María ought to make a lot of pottery this summer, so when you come back in the fall, you can decorate them. That way you'll have pots ready to sell next summer."

"Do you think they can sell?" Julián asked.

"I know it," said the head man, "I just bought these. María, show Julián the money."

Julián shook his head. "That's hers," he said. "In our way, that money belongs to the lady."

"I'll divide," said María. She took out the money, and gave one silver dollar to Julián. "You can have that," she said, and Julián said, "Thank you."

"Now let's make a plan," said the head man briskly. "María, have you what you need to make a lot of pottery?"

"No," said María, "that little fine sand is all used up."

"Then you'll need some more," he said.

"We need guaco, too," said María. "Pretty soon is the right time to pick it."

"And yucca for brushes," Julián added.

"All those things," said Jack. "I want my pots. How long will it take?"

"Maybe two days," María said, "maybe three. It depends."

"Well," said Jack, "if Julián and I work together at it, we ought to be able to get it all in two days. Then we can leave, and you can work."

"All right," agreed María. "We can start getting ready tomorrow."

"Good," said Julián, and the other men repeated, "Good."

20. Part of Living
(1909–1910

Reyes had always taught her daughters that it was the woman's part of living to hold things together. Men could build up or tear down houses and ditch banks; but women put clay and sand together to make pottery, or cooked several foods at one time to make one dish. That was part of a woman's life, to make things whole.

Because Julián was a young man, he was whole, and he did not need to be put together. He held himself with his own strength. María was not conscious, in the first years that they were married, of any need to help him in that way. It was later, after the girl baby's death, that his need for help began and that he had to draw on María's strength. It was hard to say, she thought, who had more need of strength in a family. The man needed his power for singing and ceremonies and work; but the woman, as her mother had taught her, needed her power for the man. Neither could live a complete life without the other.

In the winter after the girl baby died, María was more and more conscious of Julián's need for her strength. He had begun to change. He worked hard with Tomás, or for the white men on the Pajarito, or in his own fields, but a sort of spring had gone out of him. There was the time he fell down drunk in the plaza, too. María did not see him drunk again, but once or twice he went on winter evenings to visit his Spanish friends and came home smelling unpleasantly of vinegar. María hoped it was vinegar.

Reyes was sick a good deal of the time lately. She was pregnant, and she was really too old to have another baby. It hurt her and tired her. With all the older girls married and settled with their own families, she was at home alone with Tomás, and he was too busy with farming to help her much. María went up the hill every day to help as much as she could, but she was big again herself, and the walk was hard for her.

182

"I've been thinking," Reyes said to her one morning.

"What have you thought?" María asked.

"Well," said Reyes smiling, "here are two women, and neither of us good for much except helping the other a little. What we ought to do is live and work together until each of us can take care of herself."

"That's a good idea," María agreed.

"It seems like the only thing to do," Reyes continued. "I think you and Julián should close your house and move up here with us."

María hesitated a moment. "I don't know," she said. "Maybe it would be better if you and Father moved down with us. Then we wouldn't have such a big house to take care of. If we needed other help later on, Ana or Desidéria could get there easily."

"Yes," said Reyes slowly, "this is a big house, and it's alone and lonely. We'll come down and stay with you. There's room enough."

For the rest of the winter they lived like an old-fashioned family of mother and daughters and sons-in-law. Reyes and María worked together, and Ana and Desidéria helped them. Often they all cooked together, and when the husbands came home in the evening, all four families ate supper at María's house. After supper they all sang or told stories, as they had in the evening when the girls were children.

María's baby, was born first. María was glad that he was born while the weather was still cold, so that he could get a good start in life before the hot weather came. Reyes' baby was not born until he was well grown and María was beginning to take care of her house and family again. They all teased Reyes about it. María said that she was waiting until the boy grew up enough to take care of his aunt or his uncle, and Reyes joked back. Then all of a sudden one evening Reyes stopped talking and sat still, looking startled and hurt.

"I've held off as long as I can," she said to María, trying to smile but with her face twisting with pain.

Julián went for Desidéria and Tomás went for Ana. As Juanita, who was living at Ana's, was too young to help much in other ways, Desidéria took her children to her sister's house for Juanita to take care of. The three older sisters worked together to help their mother. There was not much that they could do. Reyes helped them by telling them what she needed as long as she could; then she lay quietly and looked at things that she wanted, until her daughters gave them to her.

"I think we need help," Ana said, towards morning.

"I'm going for our aunt," María said, reaching for her shawl. As she turned, with the wrap in her hand, she saw her mother's eyes looking at her, and she handed the shawl to Desidéria.

"You go," María said. "Mother and I have been together in all this until now, and I want to stay with her."

Tía Nicolasa came back with Desidéria, and they all watched and waited. They built a cedar fire to steam Reyes, to make her pain less. It was full daylight after a black, long night, when the baby was born.

"Is it a boy or a girl?" Reyes whispered.

"A girl," María said.

"You take care of her," her mother breathed. She turned her head a little on her pillow, to look at Ana. "You take care of Juanita," she said.

"We'll take care of them, Mother," María answered. She was surprised at the way her voice came out of her mouth; it was so quiet and steady. "We'll care for them till you're ready to."

"I won't be able to," Reyes answered. "I want you all to say a Rosary for me now."

Tía Nicolasa laughed, a high titter like a young colt whinnying. "Of course you'll care for them, Reyes," she assured her sister. "You'll sleep a while and rest a while, and then you'll care for your children."

"Someone else will care for them," said Mother. "I thank God they can care for each other. Say your Rosaries now."

They knelt there beside the bed, and together they said the Rosary. When they looked again, Reyes was asleep.

"That's the best thing," Tía Nicolasa said. "She needs the rest. She has to sleep for a while. Then we'll give her some *atole,* and she'll be all right."

"I hope so," María said. She bent and touched her mother's forehead. It was cool. "I never heard her talk like that before."

They went about the work they had to do, cleaning the room and bathing and naming the baby, and getting things ready for the rest of the day. Desidéria made coffee, and they all drank it gratefully. Then Tía Nicolasa went back to the bed and bent over it. She, too, touched her sister's forehead. For a moment she stayed there notionless; then she straightened herself.

"She knew, girls," she said. "Your mother knew. Now you have no mother."

That was the worst day María ever remembered. She did the things that needed to be done. Friends came and asked if they could help, and did little things, and went away. Some of the oldest women sat in the living room and cried. María could not cry, although sometimes a mist got in the way of her sight, and when she wiped her eyes, her hands were wet. Still the day went on. Late that evening men came, not relatives but friends, with a wagon hitched behind two horses, and took Mother away.

María waited until the men had gone and the family was alone. Then she made a bundle of her mother's clothes and little things. Julián came and got the package and rode off with it, up into the hills to throw the things away.

When he came back, Desidéria and Ana had gone home to their own families, and María and her father were alone with the two babies and Adam. Julián came in and sat down by the fire, facing Tomás.

"This is a bad day," Julián said.

"There has never been a worse one for me," Tomás replied. Then they were all quiet. María gave each of the men a bowl of *atole* and took one herself. Very quietly they ate the gruel.

"You will want to stay here for a while," Julián said to Father.

"I will want to stay with some of my children," answered Tomás. "I think I would rather stay in my own house, though."

"Our house is yours," María said.

"Thank you," her father replied. "I'd rather be in the old house, I think. That land belonged to my father, and your mother and I built the house when we were married. That's where we made our lives. It's where you children were born. It's my place. An old man belongs in his own place. I would rather both of you lived there with me."

"Thank you, Father," María said.

"What shall we do with this house?" Julián asked. "This is where we started our lives together."

"You'll make a life in the old house, I think," Tomás answered. "That's a good house to live in. We can all be happy there, and be together. You can give this house away, or keep it for later, for your children."

"That's the best way," María agreed. "We'll keep it for our children, when they need it."

When they began moving, María was surprised to find out how much they had. She had thought they owned very little furniture and not many clothes, but putting everything together in the wagon, and later putting it all away in the old house, showed her how much there was. It was a lot of work, and they were all tired when the four days of moving ended.

Julián went down to the village store on the evening of the fourth day to get some lard. No one in the family had had time to butcher, and the supplies were running low.

"Get a big measureful," María told him, and Julián smiled and said, "Don't worry. I'll get you plenty."

It seemed to María that he was gone long enough to slaughter the pig and render the lard. Supper was over when he left; and at first she was busy washing the dishes and putting the babies to bed for the night. Then she sat down beside her father, who was smoking by the fireplace, and she thought that the house was strangely quiet. She realized that it was quiet because Julián was not there.

"He's been gone a long time," she said.

"Maybe he met somebody and stopped to talk," her father suggested.

"Or went to see his mother," María agreed.

"That might be," Tomás said, and just then the door opened and Julián came in. He tripped over the doorstep as he entered the room, and when he straightened up from that, he leaned over so far in the other direction that he hit the wall. He had a big tin pail in his hand. The weight of the pail seemed to pull him towards the wall, and slowly down, until he sat on the floor looking up at them.

"Got you some lard," he said, trying to lift the pail. It was so heavy that it seemed to pull his arm to the floor, and then in against his side.

"You got a lot," María said.

"You said get plenty," answered Julián. His voice was funny. It sounded as if he meant it to be fast and hard, but the words tripped and fell over each other as his feet had.

Tomás leaned forward and looked straight at his son-in-law. "Where have you been?" he demanded. "What have you been doing?"

"Went by to see Spanish Pete," said Julián. "Old friend of mine. Used to ride together. Haven't seen him in a long time." This time, when he opened his mouth, the sharp, vinegary smell that María remembered came out of it with his words.

"What did he give you?" Tomás asked sternly. "What have you been drinking?"

"Just a little wine," said Julián sulkily. "Little red wine. Pete makes it himself. He drinks seven, eight glasses every evening. He doesn't get drunk. I drank one glass, two glasses, maybe. I couldn't be drunk."

Tomás frowned. "I think you are," he said.

"Couldn't be," Julián insisted. "Didn't drink as much as Pete. Couldn't get drunk on just a little red wine."

"An Indian can get drunk on the smell," Tomás told him. "You're drunk. Go to bed."

"I don't want to go to bed," Julián snapped. "Want to sit here and sing." He threw back his head and began to sing a coyote song. Most times he was a good singer, but this time his voice wandered around, so that sometimes you could recognize the coyote song and sometimes you could not. It was bad.

"Go to bed," said Tomás, and he got up and pulled at Julián's arm. Julián was a young, strong man and Tomás was an older one, but Julián came up off the floor in one piece, like a doll, and went falling through the bedroom door in one piece, behind Tomás. The door closed behind them. María still sat by the fire, facing the bucket of lard where it lay after it had pulled Julián down to the floor.

It was a long time before Tomás came back. Then he shut the door behind him, and sat down and looked straight at María. "This is a bad thing," he said.

"Why did he do it, Father?" María asked. She could not seem to make herself understand what had happened. She felt the way she had the day her mother died.

"I don't know," said Tomás. "Maybe he didn't mean to do it. He isn't used to it, like Pete. Maybe it was an accident."

"Then it won't have to happen again," said María. "That's what Juan Gonzales said the time before."

"Then it has happened again," Tomás said. "That means it may keep on happening. There are lots of reasons why men drink—sometimes because they are sick and sometimes because they're afraid."

"Why would Julián be afraid?"

"It might be for a lot of reasons," said Tomás slowly. "Maybe he doesn't like the way he's living, or the things he's doing. Maybe he's afraid to take care of a family. Maybe of being sick or dying, and nobody's taking care of the family for him. There are lots of reasons."

"Those things can happen to anybody," said María slowly. "Those aren't things to be specially afraid of."

"Not to you or me," Tomás answered, "that's true. They're part of living, for us. But you're afraid of horses, and to Julián and Ana and me horses are part of living. That's the difference."

"What are you afraid of, Father?" María asked. She felt that she needed to know his fear.

"Nothing in this life," Tomás answered. "I am afraid of not meeting your mother again when this life is over."

"You'll meet her," María cried. "All you have to do is to live the way she taught us to."

"There," said her father, "that's what I mean. That's part of living to you. You're sure that if you live the way your mother taught you, you'll meet her. I'm not sure I can live that way. It's like that with everyone. We each have some fear."

"You don't drink," said María.

"I don't need to," Tomás answered. "I know what I'm afraid of, and I say it. When a man is afraid and doesn't know why, he can't always face the fear. Then he may drink. Fear is worse than something to fear."

"Yes," said María.

"Well," Tomás went on, "maybe this isn't fear at all with Julián, and maybe it is an accident. That would be best."

"I don't want another accident," said María. "This makes two."

"I don't like to interfere with what another man does," Tomás said, "but you're my daughter and Julián's your husband. I'll speak to Pete about it tomorrow and ask him to be careful the next time Julián visits him. You say nothing; not to Julián, or Pete, or your sisters, or Juan, or anyone. We'll try to act as if it hadn't happened. If we can all forget about it, it will be an accident."

188

21. The Drinking
(1909–1910

For a long time things had not gone well for the pueblo and its people. Trouble began when the big trees in the mountains were cut down, but it did not end there. More and more of the young men went away from their homes to work, and with each one who left there were more problems for the people who stayed at home. At first only the young, unmarried boys left. They went away because, with the fields and ditches suffering from the floods that the mountains sent down, their families did not have enough food for everyone. It was better for the young men who were able to work to go away and to send back some of the money they made, than for them to stay at home and drag down their parents.

The single men went wherever they liked. Some went into Santa Fé and found jobs there and stayed near their homes. Others kept on going until they got to Albuquerque and went to work for the railroads in that town. Still others went north, into Colorado, where they worked in the beet and bean fields in harvest time, and found town jobs when the weather got colder.

Having the young men gone changed many people's lives, but the pueblo itself was not hurt until the married men began to go. Some of them went to the same kinds of jobs that the younger men took, and others worked for the white men at Frijoles in the summer. There they made enough money to carry their families through the winter.

Having the men gone was bad because it made a difference in the ceremonies. All the religious acts of the pueblo needed men. Some ceremonies needed to have a certain number of men to be given at all, and all the dances needed men to be complete. As long as the men were working in Santa Fé or at Frijoles, they could get home for their ceremonies, but the men who were farther away found that it was hard to leave their jobs and come back to the pueblo when they were needed there for one or four or eight days.

Another thing that hurt the pueblo was the number of men who started drinking while they were away. At home they were protected by the law, which would not let white people sell or give them liquor. They were protected by their own rules, also. Nobody in the pueblo liked a man who was drunk. The people did not like to see him or smell him or be around him. There were rules forbidding men who drank from taking part in the ceremonies, and not to take part was punishment for anyone.

While they were at home, the men did not seem to want to drink much. They were busy with the fields and with their families, and there were many things to do at home. They had little time to think about drinking or to want liquor. It was when they went away and were lonesome for everything that was the pueblo—it was then that they started to drink in order to forget their lonesomeness. They spent the money they had earned to help their families on something that harmed them. Then the men felt badly about what they had done, and drank more to get over the bad feeling.

When they came home, the men who had learned to drink wanted to keep on drinking. They could not get whiskey or wine from the people who knew them, but evil white people who did not care about the law began to move near the pueblo. Soon it was almost as easy for an Indian who had money to buy liquor as it was for a white man. Then things began to break down for everybody.

María worried about all this. She still hoped that the times when Julián got drunk had been accidents. At the same time, she was afraid an accident would happen again. Julián might get to be like some of the other men, who liked to get drunk. That would make matters worse for her and for the children.

That was why she worked so hard making pottery the third summer that Julián was at Pajarito. She wanted to have a lot of jars and bowls finished when he came home, so that he would be busy all winter decorating them. She sent for Juanita, often, to come stay with the children and help with the cooking and housework. Then she could spend more of her time at the pottery.

After a while Juanita offered to help her with smoothing and polishing the bowls, and they worked together getting the pottery ready for the winter. María would sit making the coils and building up the vessels, then hand them over to Juanita for finishing. The sisters worked that way all summer, and when Julián came home in September, they were ready for him.

The Drinking

One of his first questions after getting home was, "Did you get any pottery made?"

"Yes," María told him, "we made a lot."

"How many?" Julián wanted to know.

"Oh, a lot," María repeated. "They're out in the storeroom. You can go and look at them."

Julián went out to the storeroom. María heard him open the door, and then she heard nothing at all. Then she heard Julián begin to laugh. He laughed and laughed, and when he came back into the living room, he was still laughing.

"Do you know how many pots you have out there?" he asked.

"No," she said, "I don't. I haven't counted them."

"You've got about two hundred," Julián said. "That's a lot of pottery. What are you going to do with it all?"

"Sell it," María answered. "All those white men wanted pottery. If they want it, other people will. You can decorate it all this winter, and when spring comes, we'll fire it and have it ready to sell."

"I don't know," said Julián slowly, "I don't believe I'll have time to do much decorating this winter."

"What do you mean?" María asked. She was afraid of his answer, but she had to know.

"They want me to work in town," Julián said. "The head man is going to open a museum in town, and he wants me to work there."

"What's a museum?" María asked.

"It's a place to put the things they dig up, so people can come and look at them," said Julián.

"That's a good idea," María said. "Then people can study and learn about pottery, can't they?" Another idea came to her. "Where will you live in town?" she asked.

"They're going to have the museum in the old Palace," answered Julián. "There's a room I can live in there. I'll live where I work, and take care of the floors and the cleaning, and learn about the boiler, and all those things."

"It's a good idea," said María again. "Why don't you take some pots into town with you? You can decorate them when you aren't doing other things. Maybe you could sell some. If people come to see the old pottery, they might like to buy some new pieces to take home with them."

Julián laughed at her. "You always wanted to be a trader," he said. "Even when you were a little girl, you wanted to have a store and sell things. Your father told me."

"Well," María argued, "people make a lot of money that way."

They talked about it for several days, until Julián agreed to take some pots to town and decorate them there. He asked the head man about it, and Jack, too; and they said it was all right. He could work on the pottery in his spare time. Jack even helped María to wrap some of the vessels in Julián's bedding, and he promised to bring them back to the pueblo for firing when the decorating was finished.

"Then I'll get some more to take back to him," he said. "That way we'll keep him really busy."

"Yes," said María, "I want him to keep busy all his spare time. I don't want him to start drinking like some of these other boys."

"Keeping him busy is a good way to prevent it," Jack agreed. "If you're so worried about him, why don't you come along, María?"

"I don't want to leave home right now," María said. "I got these two babies, and maybe there might be another one. It's bad for babies to be away from home."

The Drinking

"That's right, too," said Jack. "You think it over, and if you want to come to town to live, that's all right. We'll try to keep Julián busy this winter and keep his mind off drinking."

María felt better about Julián's being in town after that. It was not as if he were going off by himself like some of the other men. He was with friends, who would be good to him and help him.

Jack made three trips out to the pueblo during the fall, to bring decorated pots to María and to take undecorated ones back to Julián. After Jack left the first time, there was a clear, still day and María decided to fire the finished pots. They turned out just right, without any smoke smudges. The designs were clean and distinct. The next time Jack came, she had the finished pottery waiting for him.

"You can take these, too," she said. "Maybe Julián can sell them."

"I want to buy two of them myself," Jack said. "Shall I pay you?"

"Yes," answered María, "you pay me. I'll put the money away and keep it safe."

Jack paid her, and when he came again, he brought her more money. "This is for the pottery," he said. "Julián said it belonged to you."

"Yes," said María. "Where's Julián's money, though? I thought they were going to pay him for working."

"It's like working at Pajarito," Jack informed her. "They'll pay him when the job is finished. He'll get all his money at once."

"That's a good way of doing," said María. Then she asked, "Who buys the pottery?"

"The people who come to the museum," replied Jack. "They all like it, and most of them buy some."

"I'm glad they like it that well," María said.

She waited for the next time, and when Jack came again, she asked him, "Are people still buying pottery?"

"Yes," said Jack. He looked a little embarrassed. "Here's the money, María." He handed her a bundle, wrapped in one of Julián's handkerchiefs. "There isn't as much as there was before," he added.

"What's the matter?" María asked. "Didn't he sell so many pots? Don't people want to buy pottery?"

"People want to buy pottery and Julián sold a lot of it," said Jack. "That isn't the reason." He hesitated, and got red in the face. "Julián used some of the money," he said.

"Oh," said María. Then she asked slowly, "What did he use it for?"

"He got drunk," said Jack. It seemed as if he could not get the words out of his mouth fast enough. "Look, María. You'd better come back to Santa Fé with me. I think Julián needs you there. I'll help you get things ready so you can go. There's another room at the museum that we can fix up for a kitchen for you, and you can live there. He'll be all right if you're with him."

"I don't know," said María. "That's bad, what he's done. I don't think I ought to take the children and go there. It's bad for them, seeing things like that and knowing about them."

"Look, María," Jack said again, "what you say is right. I know that. But it isn't all the right there is. If you're there, Julián won't want to drink. He'll be ashamed to. And he'll be too busy. You can find things for him to do. This way, he finishes his work for us early, and when he's got all the pottery decorated, he has nothing much to do. He just sits around, without people he knows to talk with or be with. If you're there, it will be different. He's a good man, María. He's a good man. You don't want to let him spoil himself this way."

María sat still and looked at the floor for a long time. All sorts of thoughts were running crazily through her head. The pueblo that was so ruined that the people went away, and then was more ruined because they were gone. Julián's limp body and the way his face changed when he was drunk. The children and what would be best for them and make them happiest and healthiest. Her father, who had been good to her and trusted her, and would be alone if she went to Santa Fé. Herself, and whether she could live with Julián if it meant living with drinking, too. Then she remembered her father's words. These things are part of living, he had said, and not all of living is easy. She made her decision.

If having money is what makes Julián get drunk, she thought, having money and being alone, then I've got to be with him. I can hold off the lonesomeness and take care of the money. I can protect him. She turned to Jack, who waited. "I'll go with you," María said. "The children and I will go. Then we can have our family together, and things will be all right. Wait till I get some clothes for us. We can take the rest of the pots and some clay and sand with us, too."

22. The Black Pottery
(1909–1912

Being at the museum was nice in some ways, but María never felt at home there. She could not explain to herself why some of the young men, who had been away from the pueblo and had come back, wanted to leave again. To María, being away from home was being away from a part of life that was bigger and more important than herself. She needed to feel the pueblo around her to feel that she was safely alive.

Even having Julián and the children with her did not give her the same feeling. They were part of home but not all of it. She had felt the same way during the years that she and Desidéria were at school, but what she felt now was stronger than the feeling she remembered. Here she and Julián and the children were; and there, away from them, was the pueblo that should have been all around them. It was as if they had stepped aside from the main part of their lives and were living in time that belonged to somebody else.

Taking care of two rooms and a small family was not much work for María now. During the daytime Julián was busy about the museum building, but he could come into their quarters and say "hello" whenever he passed the door, and most of the time María knew what he was doing. In the afternoon one of the young men museum workers, who was studying Indian languages, came to their rooms for lessons in Tewa. He would ask Julián what an English word meant and then write down the Tewa meaning when Julián explained it. One afternoon María, who was in the next room, heard him ask, "Julián, how do you say, 'I went to town,' in Tewa?"

There was a pause; then María heard Julián say something, rather indistinctly, and under his breath. She waited a minute, trying to make sure in her mind of what he had said. Evidently the white boy felt uncertain, too, for he asked, "What did you say? Please say it again."

This time there could be no doubt about Julián's answer. Slowly and carefully he repeated the Tewa words: "Kiss me, please, darling."

"Julián!" María cried "Julián! You mustn't say that! That's a bad thing to say!"

"Why is it?" Julián asked. "You don't mind when I say it to you."

"That's different," María retorted. Then she said to the white man, in English, "You make him say that over again."

This time Julián meekly translated "I went to town" into Tewa.

That kind of thing—the games and the teasing—that was the fun of being at the museum. Running water in the house, a cookstove, and the electric lights that went on and off when you turned a button were good. Having the water indoors seemed to make the housework so easy that María had hardly started before it was finished. Having the electric lights so she could see well in the evening gave María an idea. She thought about it for a while, and then she asked Jack, "Are you going back to the pueblo?"

"Why, I don't know," Jack said. "It's kind of hard to go in the winter time, like this. Do you want something from there?"

"I guess I don't need it," María said.

"Well, what is it?" Jack asked. "If you tell me, I'll know. Then if I do go, I can bring it back with me."

"I'll tell you," said María. "I left some clay and some sand in my storeroom. If you ask Desidéria or my father, they'll take you in there and you can get those things and bring them back to me. I've used all I brought with me."

"Will you make me a pot if I do?" Jack asked, and María said, "Sure, I'll be glad to make you a pot."

It was more than a week before Jack could make the trip out to San Ildefonso, but when he came back, he had the sacks of clay and fine sand with him. María could go on working on pottery in her spare time, getting it ready to fire. Julián helped her with the polishing, and in the evenings he worked at the decorating.

Late one afternoon the head man came in and found them both hard at work. "You've got a lot of pottery here," he said, looking around the room.

Julián laughed. "We've got too much," he said. "I don't know what we're going to do with it. Pretty soon we'll have the bed full of it. Most times we could sleep on the floor, but with the floor full of pottery already, I don't know where we're going to sleep."

"Why don't you fire it and then sell it?" the head man asked.

"We got no place for firing," said María. "At home we have a place fixed up in the back yard, but here it's different."

The Black Pottery

"You can build a fire in the back yard here," the head man said. "Nobody will mind if you fire pottery there. We'll give you some wood from the wood pile for it."

"We can do that Saturday," said Julián. "Then maybe we can sell some of this stuff before the bed gets full."

Firing in the back yard of the museum went all right. They had a good, clear day to begin with—without any wind and not too cold. By now they both had had enough experience to know just what they were doing. When the pottery came out of the fire, everything was just right. Not one vessel was spoiled by breaking or fire-clouding.

The head man took the pottery to his office, where visitors to the museum could see it and buy it. He seemed to be as proud of the work as María and Julián were, and he liked selling it. María tried to get him to take some of the money from the sale of the pottery, but the head man would not do that.

"You both worked hard for that money," he said. "It belongs to you."

After that, both María and Julián worked steadily in their spare time at the pottery-making. Every piece they made sold at the museum. One day a man who had a shop on the plaza came to see them.

"I'd like to buy some pottery for my store," he said in Spanish.

"All right," said María, "you can go talk to that man in the front office."

"I have talked to him," replied the shopkeeper, "and he sent me to you. He said for me to ask you about something."

"What is it?" Julián asked.

"This is it," said the shopkeeper. "I can sell some of your pottery in my shop, I know. I think that in summer, when the tourists come, I can sell a lot of it. But it costs me money to run that shop. I have to pay for the lights and the building and all those things. If I buy the pottery here and then sell it for the same amount that I pay for it, I can't make enough to pay for a share of those other things. So I thought maybe you would make me a special price on pottery for the store, what we call a wholesale price. You can ask the same price here that I do, if you want to. That way I can buy more pottery and I can sell more."

"Will that help us?" María asked.

"Well," said the shopkeeper, "it might. If you are in the pueblo, you can probably sell your pottery to any people who come there. If you are here, you can sell pottery to people who come to the museum.

Still, you miss a lot of sales. People go to my shop who would **not** come to the museum or go out to the pueblo. If you let me have **the** pottery, you'll sell to a lot more people, and you'll get better known all the time."

"I guess that's right," Julián agreed.

"I don't know," said María. "We don't care about being well known or anything. Pueblo Indian people don't think about things like that. We all just want to get along in this world and be together."

"Well," argued the shopkeeper, "even if you don't care about being well known, there's another way to look at it. After a while all the people who come to the museum or go out to the pueblo will have bought pottery. Then there won't be anybody left to sell to. But there are new people coming into my store all the time. It's right there on the corner of the plaza, and everybody who comes to Santa Fé goes by it. It's easy for them to come in and buy pottery from me. I can keep selling and selling to new people all the time."

María sat and thought things over for a while. "I guess we can do that," she said. "I want to make some extra money. If we have the money, we can plant fruit trees, and maybe get a cooking stove."

Julián turned and looked at her. "Why do you want a cooking stove?" he asked her. "You always cook in the fireplace at home."

"A stove is easier to cook on," María informed him.

"I don't mind," said Julián, amiably, but still surprised. "It's all right with me if you want a stove." He turned back to the man. "We can sell you some pottery, I guess," he said. "You offer us a price."

It took them a long time and a lot of talking to agree on prices. Julián got the head man and consulted with him; and he helped them all figure the prices. When the storekeeper had gone, the head man said, "You don't have to go on selling to him after this first lot, if you don't want to. All you have to do is try him and see how it works out. If it doesn't go right, you can stop."

María nodded. She had thought of that. "Maybe I'll open a store of my own some day," she said. "Then I can sell to everybody myself."

"Maybe you can," said the head man. Then he went on, "María, this summer when the students come here, would you be willing to show them how to make pottery? They will learn a lot if they can see somebody really working at it. You can work here at the museum, or I'll bring the students out to the pueblo. Then you can sell them the pottery, if you want to. We'll pay you for your time anyway."

María bent her head down while she thought. She was shy about having people watch her while she worked, but the head man had been good to them, and she wanted to do the right thing.

"Well, all right," she said, after a long time.

Julián laughed at her. "First you want a store and now you want to be a professor," he said. "All the time, the main thing you're thinking about is that cooking stove."

"A stove would be a good thing to have," María insisted. Now that she really thought about having a stove, she knew she wanted it.

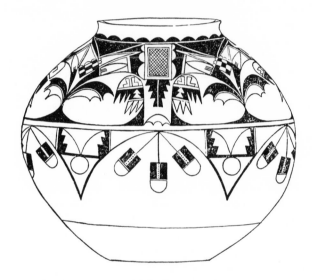

When summer and warm weather came, it was time for Julián to leave the furnace he had taken care of all winter and go back to the pueblo to help Tomás in the fields. Julián spoke about it to the head man.

"Why go back?" the head man asked him. "You can stay here and go on with your other work, and with the money you earn here and what María gets from her pottery, you can hire a man to help your father-in-law and still have money to save for the stove. It's better that way, I think."

Julián went back to the quarters and talked with María about it.

"Which would you rather do?" she asked him.

"I like it here," Julián said. "I like this kind of work, and I can do it all right. When I'm working in the fields, I'm not very good. Your father can do more than I can. Then I get ashamed, because he's an old man and I'm a young one, and I ought to be the one to do more."

"You'd better go and tell him," said María. "He's expecting you. I'll give you some money for him, so he can hire a Spanish boy."

"All right," said Julián. He went to tell the head man what they had decided.

"That's good," said the head man. "I'll take you to the pueblo tomorrow. Go see if María wants anything from her house, so we can bring it back to her."

When he got back to their quarters, Julián found María talking to the storekeeper.

"He wants to buy some more pots," said María.

"We haven't any," Julián said to the man. "We sold them all."

"I need some," said the storekeeper. "They sell so well I can't keep them in the store. Here it is almost summer and the tourists are beginning to come to Santa Fé, and I need some pottery to sell them."

Julián turned to María. "The head man said he'd take me out to the pueblo tomorrow and we could bring back anything you need," he told her in Tewa. "Maybe there's some pottery we could bring back."

"I don't remember any," María answered, "but you can look in the storeroom and make sure if you want to. You can ask Desidéria and Ana, too. Maybe they have some they'd like to sell."

"It ought to be your pottery," protested the storekeeper, when they translated for him. "People are getting to know your work. They come in and ask for your pottery."

"It all looks alike to white people, my sisters' and mine," María reassured him. "That won't make any difference. You can sell it all just the same. You don't have to say who made it."

"No," said the man doubtfully, "I don't suppose I do."

"It all comes from San Ildefonso," María went on. "It's all just alike in each pueblo. It's the pueblo that makes the difference, not the woman who makes the pottery."

"I guess so," said the storekeeper. "All right, Julián. You can bring me some pottery from María's sisters, if you want to. I'll pay them the same that I pay María."

"I'll tell them," promised Julián.

He came back late the next evening, with a big blanket-wrapped bundle of pottery in the back of the car.

"They sent it," said María.

The Black Pottery

"Yes, they sent it," Julián said.

"Did you find any of ours that we weren't using?" María asked.

"Well, yes, I did," answered Julián.

"I didn't remember any," María said thoughtfully. "I thought we brought it all into town a long time ago."

"Well, you just didn't remember," said Julián, "and I did. I found it, too. I'm a good hunter—in storerooms."

"What is it?' demanded María. "Let me see it."

"I'll show you," said Julián. He untied the bundle, and began taking out the pieces of pottery one at a time. María could recognize each one as he unwrapped it and set it on the floor.

"That's Ana's, and that's Ana's" she said, "and that's Desidéria's. My, they've been working as hard as we have! Who made that one? It doesn't look like any of the others."

"Juanita made it," said Julián. "She's been working hard, too. You didn't say anything about her, but she wanted me to bring some of her pottery, so I thought I would."

"That's all right," said María. "Are there any others? Where are mine that I don't remember?"

"Here's one of them," said Julián slowly, and he carefully took out a pot that was wrapped separately, with the ends of the cloth folded underneath so that it made a different kind of bundle from the others. He set the package on the floor and began unwrapping it. When the cloth was off, he looked at María with his eyes laughing, and María laughed back, aloud.

"The black pots!" she said. "The ones that were spoiled. We can't sell those!"

"Why not?" asked Julián. "All that man wants is pottery. Those tourists won't know the difference."

"Maybe they will, though," María insisted.

"I think they won't," retorted Julián. "We can try it, anyway."

The storekeeper came back the next morning. They showed him the pots Ana and Desidéria and Juanita had made, and he looked at them carefully. He agreed to take the pottery.

"I know I can sell them," he said. "They look just like yours."

"I don't think so," said María. "We all make them a little bit different."

"Nobody will notice," said the storekeeper. "Have you any of your own? Did you find any?" he asked Julián.

"We found some special ones," Julián said. His face was sober,

201

but his eyes were laughing again. "They're so special that we didn't want to sell them, not for a long time. They aren't like most other San Ildefonso pottery."

"Let me see them," the storekeeper requested. Solemnly Julián unwrapped the black pots and set the vessels out before the white man.

"Those are different, all right!" said the storekeeper. He sat and looked at the pottery for a long time. "I like them," he said, finally. "I'll take them. How much are they?"

Julián started to answer, but María spoke first. "They cost more than the others," she said. "That's because they're different."

"All right," said the storekeeper, "I can charge more for them, too."

When the white man had gone, Julián looked at María and laughed and laughed. "I guess you've got your store already," he said. "It won't be long till you get that stove to go with it."

María laughed, too. "I wanted your joke to be good," she said.

Before she had finished the breakfast dishes the next morning, the storekeeper was knocking at the door of their quarters.

"Have you any more of that black pottery?" he asked.

"Why, no," said María. "We made only those two pieces."

"Can you make some more?" the storekeeper demanded.

"I guess so," said María. "Why? Can you sell it?"

"Yes," answered the storekeeper, "and I want some more, right away. I sold those two pieces before I could get them into the shop, and people who have seen them are already coming in and asking for some more. Can you make some right away?"

"Not for a while," said Julián. "We'll make them for you when we can."

"That's all right," said the storekeeper. "As soon as you get it ready, let me know. I can sell all you can make of that kind of pottery."

When he had gone, Julián turned to María. "We made a new kind of pottery," he said. He sounded excited.

"We did," said María, "but it was an accident."

"I don't mind that kind of accident," said Julián.

"No," agreed María, "I don't, too. It sure cuts down the work. Now we don't have to be so careful about the firing. It won't matter about smoke smudges on the black pots." She looked around the room, at all the pots they had made in the last few weeks. "Get some wood and manure ready," she said. "We can start firing tomorrow. I'm sorry you painted designs on these, that's the only thing. They don't show when the pots are black. The next ones we can just leave plain, I guess."

23. The Work Goes On
(1913

There was never any doubt in María's mind about where she belonged in the world. Whatever happened; wherever she went and whatever she did, her home and her place were in the pueblo. During the three years that she and Julián were living at the museum in Santa Fé, she was never quite complete inside herself.

At any time that she wanted to during those years, she could close her eyes and see things she had left. She could see the lines of the irrigation ditches, laid out in their neat pattern of squares around the fields, and the lines of the houses of the pueblo, laid out in their neat pattern of squares around the plaza. There was the Black Mesa rising beyond everything else, making its own pattern against the others. From its steep, square sides, her mind's eye would drop to the flat squares of the village, and the patterns would begin to form themselves all over again.

Any change in one of the patterns changed all of the others, and that was one reason why, after three years, María decided that they should go back to the village and stay there. Her mother's death had changed things, and her father's aloneness changed them even more. People were going out of their lives, and she wanted to hold fast to what was left. In the second year even the Corn Dance was changed. There were so few people left in the village who could dance at all that the council had sent out word for all those who were living away to come back for the ceremony. Those who had outside jobs got excused from them, or made plans to find new jobs after the Corn Dance.

The village had the full four days of preparation before the dance, and the people danced all the Corn Dance day in the plaza, as usual. Even so, the chorus was so small that the dancers could hardly hear the singing, and there were so few dancers that they seemed to be crowded together, as if they were hanging to each other to be safe

203

from things that were too strong and dangerous for them to understand. No one of them could protect himself from changes without the help of all the others.

After the dance was over, María spoke to Julián. "We'd better stay on here," she said. "We can live with my father in the old house again and help him with his work."

Julián nodded. "Yes," he agreed. "They need us here. Only the thing is, how are we going to live, if we stay? I made enough money for us at the museum, but here, with all of us living off your father's land, we can just get by. I don't see how we can manage, with Clara and our little boy and all."

"We can sell pottery," suggested María.

"Where are we going to sell it?" Julián asked.

"We can sell some of it here at the house," said María thoughtfully, "and the museum people will keep on buying some, if we tell them what we want to do, and that man at the store in town wants some. Maybe some of the other stores will want it, too."

"How are we going to send it to them?" was Julián's next question.

"Some of them will come out and get it, I think," answered María, "and we can take some of it to town in the wagon."

"I don't know," said Julián. "We might make enough money that way, or we might not. You can't tell. Maybe I'd better keep on working at the museum. You and the children can stay here if you think that's best."

María shook her head. She did not want to do that. She was sure that if Julián were alone in town, he would start drinking again. She wanted to prevent that.

"Families belong together," she reminded him. "It's not good for children to grow up without a father to watch them and teach them, especially boys. I think we all ought to be together, wherever we are. I think the best place is here."

"We can try it," Julián said doubtfully. "If we do need more money, I can go back to the museum, I guess."

"Let's figure it out a little," María said. "We can add up what you made at the museum and what we made together on the pottery, and see if it's enough."

That evening they sat down with pencils and paper and started adding. It was like doing arithmetic sums, María thought. She remembered how careful Miss Grimes had always made her be about the way her papers looked, and, remembering, she was careful to get all the figures down just so, in neat columns with one line under another. When they had worked out their sums, she turned to Julián, and smiled. "This is like old days," she said, and he answered, "Yes, like the time before we were married. What have you got, now it's all added?"

María looked at the figures. "It's all right," she said. "We made more money from the pottery than we did from the museum. We can afford to live at home and keep on working. You can tell the head man that."

The head man, when Julián told him what they had decided, was understanding. "I think you're doing the right thing," he said. "We hate to lose you, Julián. You have done good work for us. But I think Indians should be together in their own place. That's the most important thing for them. If you can make enough money this way, you should stay. We'll help you. We'll keep on selling pottery for you, and we'll arrange to send somebody out to get it, from time to time."

"Will you tell that man at the store about it, so he can send for it, too?" Julián asked, and the head man said that he would.

Four days later the man from the store came to the pueblo to see them.

"Got any pottery made?" he asked, as soon as María opened the door.

"Not yet," she answered. "We haven't had time yet."

"I still have a lot of orders for that black stuff," said the store-keeper. "Why don't you make some more? There hasn't been any since those first two pieces."

"We're going to make it right away," said María. "That's the first kind we're going to make."

As soon as the man left, she turned to Julián. "Now you've got to get busy," she said. "You go right away and get the fire ready. It's a good clear day."

"What are you going to fire?" Julián asked.

"I've got all these polished pieces ready," María said. "We'll start with those. Then I can make some more."

"Just plain?" asked Julián. "You're going to fire them like that?"

"I don't see why not," said María. "You don't need to decorate them, because when they're black, the decorating won't show."

"All right," said Julián. He went out and got the fire ready. To-gether they carried out all the vessels and arranged them on the bed of cedar and broken pottery. They heaped up the cedar and dung around the pottery, and set fire to the pile. Then they waited for the flames to die down. It was a fine, still day, and the smoke went straight up in the air.

"I don't know," said Julián, watching the smoke. "I don't believe those are going to be black pots. They aren't getting the smoke."

"I think they'll be black all over," María argued. "I think that means it's going to be good."

"All right," said Julián again. He seemed to be willing to agree with her, but he watched the smoke doubtfully all the same.

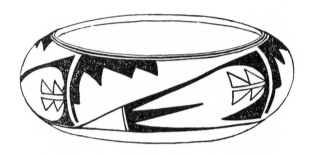

When the smoke had died away and the flames were gone and the fire was really out, Julián began feeling in the ashes with a forked stick. Gingerly, he lifted out the first pot. It was a clear, even red in the sunlight, without a single fire cloud to spoil its color. It was a beautiful vessel, not just like any they had made before, but it was not black.

"Maybe it's red with the heat," said María, studying it. "We can wait and see if it gets black when it's cool."

"I don't think it will," said Julián. He lifted out the rest of the pottery and ranged the pieces in a straight row before her. Every vessel was the same clear, even red, except those from the bottom of the pile. They had little smoke clouds up their sides, but they were still red vessels with black smudges.

María stood and stared at the row of bowls and jars. "Something went wrong," she said, finally.

"I don't think so," Julián said. "I think everything went just right. That's the trouble. We did too good a job of firing."

"We've got to do something," María protested. "What are we going to do? That man wants black pots. Maybe it was the guaco in the designs on the others that made them black. Maybe we should have painted these with guaco, so they would be black all over."

"That's a lot of work," argued Julián. "I still think it's the firing. I think we should fire them differently." He shook his head. "We can figure it out," he said. "You did the arithmetic and it came out right. Now I'm going to figure this out. You wait."

He sat down on the ground, leaning against the woodpile, with the row of pots in front of him where he could look at them.

"I'm going to sit here and think about them," he said. "This has to be studied out."

"Well, you can sit there and think as much as you like," said María. "I'm going in the house and start making some more pots."

"Go ahead," said Julián, absent-mindedly. She went into the house and left him sitting there looking at those pots as if they were the most interesting objects in the whole world.

From time to time during the afternoon, María looked out of the window. Julián was still sitting by the woodpile, still looking at the pots with his eyes half-closed. María could tell by the way he breathed that he was not asleep, but there was nothing else to show that he was not taking a siesta. At supper time she had to go right up to him and speak straight at him to make him hear her.

"All right," said Julián, "I'm coming in." He got up off the ground and followed her into the house, but his mind was still on the pottery. He put salt in his coffee and sugar on his beans, and never knew the difference, not even when María told him.

"You cooked the beans differently tonight," he said after the meal was over. "I think I like the old way better."

María shook her head and washed the dishes. Julián sat by the window and looked out at the pots. When María went out and brought the vessels in at dusk, he turned his head and looked at her. "I think I know," he said, and went to bed without another word.

The next morning Julián got up with a determined look on his face. "How many pieces did you make yesterday afternoon?" he asked.

"Four," María told him.

"It's not very many, but I guess I can try," said Julián. He went out and began getting a pottery fire ready.

"They're not dry enough yet," María warned him, when he came in and began gathering up the pottery. "They ought to dry three or four days."

"This is just to try," said Julian.

"They'll be ruined," María protested. "They'll all break."

"I've got to know," answered Julián. "If they aren't right, you can make some more."

"It's a lot of work to spoil," María observed.

"Well, maybe then we won't spoil any more," Julián replied. "You can come and watch if you want to. You will have to bless the fire, anyway."

María followed him outdoors. He had built a small fire, and now he set the pots on the firebed and covered them with cedar and dried dung just as he always did. María sprinkled the meal and said a prayer, and Julián lighted the fire.

He let it get a good start, until the flame was blazing clearly. Then he turned and picked up a sack from the ground. "Stand back, now," he warned her. "This might make you sneeze."

He dumped the contents of the sack over the fire and a cloud of powdered manure fell on the flames, smothering them. Julián picked up his shovel and began heaping the manure that had fallen to the ground over the fire. There was a thick, choky cloud of yellow smoke.

"You're getting dirt on it," María cried, watching the shovel.

"That won't hurt," Julián answered. "What I want to do is to smother this fire but not put it out."

"You're doing it," said María.

They stood and watched until the smoke was gone and the fire was burning brightly again. When the flames had gone out there was a big pile of ashes left, and Julián said, "We've got to wait for it to cool."

"It's almost dinner time," María reminded him.

"I want to see what's going to happen before I eat," Julián replied.

María went into the house and gave the children some cold *tortillas* and beans to eat. When she came back, she brought some of the cold food with her, and she and Julián ate it, waiting and watching beside the cooling ashes.

"Now," said Julián, when they had finished their meal. "I guess we can take them out now."

He dug in the ashes gently with his forked stick, and began lifting out the vessels. Slowly, one at a time, he set them on the ground. Then he blew the ashes away. The color was right. It was a deep, shiny, gleaming black.

"They look like Santa Clara pots," said María.

The Work Goes On

"Yes, but they're shinier," Julián answered. "This is the way they ought to be. Do the people at Santa Clara smother their fires?" he asked.

"I don't know," said María. She tried to remember. "I guess they do. They must, because their pottery comes out this way, too."

"We should have remembered," Julián said. "Then we could have gone across the river and asked somebody, and saved all that thinking."

"It wouldn't have saved any time," said María. "It would have taken a whole day to make the trip over there."

"It would have saved me a headache," retorted Julián. "I never thought so hard in all my life."

"Now we know, though," said María. "We can get to work."

"You can get to work," corrected Julián. "There won't be anything for me to do till it's time to fire, if you're just going to make them plain."

"You can help with the polishing," María suggested.

"Men don't polish pottery in the pueblo," answered Julián. "I'm going up in the field and see if I can help your father." He turned, and wandered away.

24. In the Business

(1915

Along time afterwards, María tried to remember how the pottery-making got to be a business. She found out then that she could not recall the details. It had just grown, quickly on the whole, but so steadily that she lost track of the steps.

One step that she did remember was the trip to San Diego. Jack was working on another world's fair there, and he wanted to build a pueblo, for the western people who had never seen a pueblo, so that they would know what one was like.

Jack had always been interested in the broken pots that people at San Ildefonso put on top of their chimneys. These pots were always old, because it took a big pot to make a big draft, and big pots did not wear out in a hurry. One way of seeing what kinds of pots people had used in their houses in bygone years was to look at the broken ones they put on their roofs.

It would be expensive and wasteful, Jack decided, to buy whole pots and knock out their bottoms to make chimney pots for his world's fair pueblo. Therefore, he hired María and Julián and Ramoncita to come to San Diego and make the chimney pots there.

María worried about making the big jars. Up to that time she had made only comparatively small pieces of pottery. Her biggest bowls had been about the size of the mixing bowls in the stores, and the largest jars she had made were the right size, the white people said, to hold flowers on tables or mantelpieces. She could build vessels like those quickly and easily and could be sure that they would be firm and good.

When it came to making the larger pieces, however, it was different. She brought the clay and sand with her from San Ildefonso to San Diego, big sacks of each. As Jack had promised to get them cedar wood and cow dung, she did not have to bring those. She was sure that she could write home for more clay and sand when she needed them. Ana or her husband would see that they were sent.

210

In the Business

Jack had arranged a good place for them to work at the world's fair. The weather was warm, so that they could be outside all day, and he had picked a quiet corner, away from the other workers, for María and Ramoncita. Since Julián was to be working on the building, María and Ramoncita could work as much alone as if they were at home in the pueblo. Even being quiet and alone did not help with their work at first. Again and again María and Ramoncita would start the big pots. Halfway up the sides the coils would begin to weaken, and the vessels would cave in. Then there were just piles of wet clay, and they had to start the work all over again.

María thought that their failure might have come because the air in San Diego was wet all the time. She wanted to wait for a dry day, the kind of day that was best for pottery-making at home, but Jack explained to her that here near the ocean the air was always damp, and a dry day would never come. There was no way of going back to the pueblo and making the pots there, now, so she and Ramoncita just had to go along with what they were doing as well as they could.

Julián came up one evening and sat and watched them for a while. María was building up the sides of a big jar, and she had got them about a third of the way finished. Everything was going along smoothly, and she had added one big thick coil after another very carefully. She built on two more rows; and suddenly, without any warning, the pot fell in. She looked at it, ready to cry.

"Does it always do that?" Julián asked.

"Every time."

"Do you always work it the same way?"

"Yes," answered María, "we do. We work just the same way we would in making any other pot. You can see for yourself it's not any different. It's just bigger."

"Maybe you ought to work it differently, all the same."

"I don't know any different way to do it."

Julián sat and thought for a while. "I tell you," he said then. "You make a little pot just the same way as you do the big one, and the same shape, and let me watch you."

"What good will that do?" María demanded. "I'm not making a little pot; I'm making a big one."

"Well, try it anyway," said Julián.

"All right," said María. She took some of the clay that had started to be a big pot and thumped out a *tortilla* of it between her palms. Then she put the clay down in the base of an old bowl, which she was using as a form, and began to spin out a coil of clay for the sides. When the coil was long enough to go around the edges of the *tortilla,* she flattened it a little by slapping it with her palms. She took the flattened coil, tipped it on edge, and shaped it around the base of her jar, smoothing the join with moistened fingers. She made more coils, one at a time, and built up the sides of the vessel until it was a deep bowl.

"Now what happens?" Julián asked when she reached this point.

"Now I have to bend it in."

"All right."

María shaped another coil, first long and round like a sausage, then flat like a ribbon. Just as she had done with the others, she fastened it to the lower coils.

"Now stop," said Julián.

María took her hands away from the jar, and waited. Julián ran his fingers over it, outside and in, lightly and carefully. He felt the last coil more strongly than he had the others, and nodded.

"Do you know what you did here?" he asked.

"Just what I did with all the rest," said María.

"No, you didn't," said Julián. "You think you did, but you've done it so often that you don't know. You made this one just a little, little thicker than the others. Now go on working."

María went ahead and finished the jar. It was slender, and it had a long, straight neck. From time to time Julián stopped her, so that he could feel the pottery. When the jar was finished, he smiled at her. "It's like building a house," he said. "All the weight rests on the foundation."

"That's the base," said María. She was getting tired of having him inspect her work and tell her all about it.

"The base is one foundation," Julián said. "It's the foundation for the bottom part. There's another foundation, though. This middle coil, where you begin bending for the shoulder. That's the foundation for the top part. All the upper part and the neck rest on that. That's why you made it thicker than the other coils. Now you work it that way with the big pot. Something else. Do you make the coils for the big pot the same size as for the little one, or are they bigger?"

"They're bigger," María answered. "It's a bigger pot, so they're longer and thicker."

"Well, they have to be longer, of course," said Julián. "You have to make them go clear around. I think you ought to make them thinner and make more of them, so you can guide them better, that's all."

In the Business

"I don't see that it makes any difference."

"Maybe it doesn't," said Julián, "but you try it anyway." He yawned. "I'm hungry," he said, "let's have supper."

María left the pottery and went to work getting supper. She had a cookstove here, like the one at the museum in Santa Fé, and cooking was easy and a pleasure.

The next morning María and Ramoncita went to work on the big pots again. This time they followed Julián's advice. They used small coils and built them carefully up to the shoulder. Then, for four rows, until the edge of the shoulder was completely turned, they used coils that were nearly twice as thick as, but were narrower than, those on the rest of the vessel. When the day was over, there were two strong, solid jars standing on the ground, waiting to be scraped and smoothed the next day.

After that, things went easily. María and Ramoncita finished the big chimney pots without any more trouble, and then settled down to work on smaller pieces to be sold to visitors. The people who ran the fair were paying them all money to stay at the fair and make pottery but, in addition, it had been agreed that all the money that came from pottery that was sold there would belong to the workers.

It was hard, at first, to get used to working with people looking at your hands. Julián had finished his part of the building, and he decorated the pottery that María and Ramoncita made. Nothing seemed to trouble him. Julián could work with no one around the demonstration space, or he could work with a hundred people leaning over the railing and watching, and never be troubled at all. He could even talk to the watchers and answer their questions.

Because he did not mind the watching and talking and questioning, María and Ramoncita left all the talking to him. Soon the guides who took people through the buildings were saying, "You can talk to Julián, here. The ladies don't understand much English."

Julián would look up and grin and say in English, "What you want to know, lady? Me heap big chief. Me know everything." And all of the people would laugh, and ask him questions.

Some of the questions made María and Ramoncita angry. Many people wanted to know if they were both of them Julián's wives. Sometimes Julián said they were; sometimes he said that Ramoncita was his wife and María was her grandmother; sometimes he said, "Me no got no wife, lady. Me look for one. You marry with me, huh?" And then the ladies would giggle and blush and go away. María and

Ramoncita did not think it was funny, but Julián and Jack did and would sit around in the evenings inventing new things for Julián to say to the white people the next day.

Sometimes during that fair they had a day off. One time they went into town shopping, and bought things to take home to the village as presents. Another time they went to the zoo. Julián stood and stood and looked and looked at the monkeys.

"What do you want to stare at those old things for?" María asked him. She was ready to look at some of the other animals.

"They're just like people, but different," Julián answered. "I like looking at them."

"Well, I don't," said María. "I can look at you, and I don't see much difference."

She wondered sometimes why she was so cross. They were making a great deal of money. People they knew were nice to them. She was together with her cousin, and they had a good house to live in, in the pretend pueblo. Once she decided that she was unhappy because the pretend pueblo looked more like Taos than like San Ildefonso. Then she knew what the matter was. She was lonesome. She wanted to go home. That night she spoke about it to Jack, and he nodded.

"You're homesick," he said, and María agreed, "That's it. I'm sick for home, here in my heart."

"You can go soon," said Jack. "The fair will be closing in another month. Do you think you can stand it that long?"

"I don't know," said María doubtfully. "A month is a long time."

"It is," agreed Jack, "but you ought to stay if you can, María. You're making good money here, and you're getting better known all the time. Now that you're in the pottery-making business, it's good to get well known. It's like advertising, like paying the newspapers to print stories about what you have to sell, only you don't have to pay them. This is part of your business."

That was true, and María knew it. "Couldn't I just stay at home and pay the newspapers?" she asked.

"You could if you wanted to," answered Jack. "I think this is cheaper, though. You just sit here and work, and get paid for doing what you'd have to spend money for otherwise. It won't be long. You stick it out."

María stuck it out after that, until the end of the month was there and she and Ramoncita and Julián could go home. They would have had to go anyway, because they had used all the clay they had brought with them. Ana had sent them some clay from home, but they had used it, too. María did not want to send for any more, because it did not seem worth bothering Ana about it for such a little while. For the last week that they were in San Diego, she and Ramoncita made pottery all day and then tore it up in the evening, so that they would have something to work on the next day. Julián laughed at them, but he went on decorating what they made, even when he knew his designs were going to be part of a pile of clay in the morning.

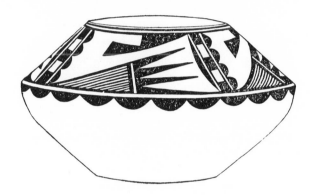

On the trip home they counted out their money, and María and Ramoncita divided it. One third went to Ramoncita and two-thirds to María and Julián, because they had all worked equally.

"What are you going to do with your money?" Ramoncita asked.

María looked at the pile of coins and bills in her lap. "It's a lot of money," she said. "I think I'll do a lot of things with it. What are you going to do with yours?"

"Buy that five-acre field of Spanish Pete's. We need more land to farm," Ramoncita said promptly. "What are you going to do with yours?" she persisted.

"I'll tell you one thing she'll do," said Julián. "She'll buy a cooking stove."

María nodded solemnly. "I'll buy a cooking stove and a sewing machine," she said. "Those things I always wanted."

"But what else?" asked Ramoncita.

María thought some more. What Jack had said came back to her. "Well," she said, "if we're in the pottery business, we ought to have a business place to be. The way we are, when people come to the pueblo to buy pottery, they come right into our house. I'm going to make a room for them to come to. Then they won't be tracking dirt all over the floor, and seeing what I'm cooking for dinner, and playing with the children all the time. The family can be off to itself, and still there will be a place for people to come. I'll fix it up nice, and put pictures and things on the walls, and they'll like it. It'll be like a store for them to come to."

"We might get some canned goods and meat and cheese and kerosene," Julián suggested. "Then the Indians will come and buy things when the white people aren't around, and we'll have company all the time. I'm going to be lonesome for all that company we had at the fair." He sighed deeply, but his eyes were smiling.

"I think we had too much company at the fair," said María. "I'm tired of all that company. That's why I want a separate selling room. If you get so lonesome you can work in the new room. That's where you can do your decorating. You don't mind having people watch you work."

"No, I don't mind," said Julián. "I think it's fun. All right. We'll get the cookstove and build the room, and then we'll be in the business sure enough. In another year we'll be millionaires."

"You'll be the only people in San Ildefonso who are, then," said Ramoncita. "Everybody else there just gets poorer and poorer."

"We'll sell pottery for the others," said María. "They can get as much money for it as we do, if they work as hard. We'll sell yours and Ana's and Desidéria's—all our sisters' and cousins'."

"That's good, thank you," said Ramoncita. "How are you going to do it? Pay us a little and sell for a lot, like the stores in town?"

María shook her head. "No," she said, "not that way. The stores in town have to pay for rent and lights and all those things, but we have our house and we'll just be open in the daytimes, so we won't have to pay extra. No, you bring your pottery to our house to sell. Then what we get for it is yours. It won't cost you anything. You ought to feel glad about it."

"I think everybody will feel glad, if it works that way," said Ramoncita.

25. The Invention

After their return from San Diego, things went better and better for María and Julián. Those were busy years, and they both worked hard, what with the pottery-making and the children. María sometimes got so busy with other things that she neglected the pottery for days at a time. Just now, though, she had worked steadily for three days. She wanted to get as many pots as she could ready to fire. Julián was working in the fields with Tomás, and was good help, but he seemed to be getting restless. Late in the afternoon, when the men came back from gathering the corn, he sat down on the floor where María was working. She got up and went to get supper, leaving him sitting there.

When she came back to call Julián for the meal, María stopped and stared without speaking at what he was doing. He had one of her new, polished pots in his hand, and he was painting a design on it with the slip that she had mixed to polish the pottery.

"Why are you doing that?" she demanded.

"Oh, I don't know," said Julián, looking up at her. "I guess I just wanted to paint a design. Do you mind?"

"No," answered María. "It's all right. I don't know what will happen when you fire it, that's all."

"I don't either," said Julián. "We can wait and see."

Two days later, when all the corn was in, they began firing. Julián had collected a lot of dried manure. Because most of the cow and horse dung had been used on the fields or made into dry cakes for burning the pottery, he had to use sheep manure to smother the fire. When he poured it on the flames, the smoke cloud was thicker and yellower than ever.

"That's the best smoke yet," Julián observed. María moved back from the dense cloud.

"It certainly is," she agreed. "I never saw so much smoke anywhere before."

217

María

The pottery was as black and shiny as it had been the time before. Julián had put his decorated pot in with the others, and it came out black, too; shiny black where it was polished, and dull black where he had painted over the polish with the slip.[1]

"It's different looking," said María, and Julián laughed and said, "Well, nobody ever saw a pot like it before, did they?"

When the storekeeper came from Santa Fé the next week, they had the black pottery lined up and waiting for him. The white man stood and looked at the vessels and admired them.

"Those are the right kind," he said. "I can sell those, all right. That's what people keep asking for. How do you do it?"

María opened her mouth to tell him, but Julián shook his head. "We know how," he said. "That's the way we make it. Other people here don't do it that way. They'd laugh at us if they knew what we do. We don't want to tell anybody. We don't want to be laughed at."

"All right," said the storekeeper, "I don't blame you. You don't have to tell if you don't want to. It's your secret."

"It isn't really a secret," María said, "but they would laugh if they knew."

"I don't care," said the storekeeper again. "It's all right with me if you don't tell. What did you do to that one on the end? How did you get the design painted on it? That's another new kind."

"You don't have to take it if you don't want to," said Julián. "We were just trying out something."

"Oh, I'll take it," said the storekeeper. "I can try things out, too. I'll let you know if I sell it. And you get some more black ones ready for me. I'll be back in a couple of weeks."

When he was gone, María looked at Julián and laughed. "I guess you're an inventor," she said. "I guess you're an inventor, like that Robert Fulton they used to write about in the schoolbooks."

Then María got the new cooking stove. She chose it from the mail-order catalog, being careful to consider all that was said there about stoves. She finally decided on one that had a tank on the back, to heat water for the dishes, and an oven on top, so that she would not have to lean over in order to watch through the mica window the food that was baking.

María herself wrote the letter to order the stove from Denver.

[1] The exact date of the invention of black-on-black pottery at San Ildefonso has not been determined. The discovery took place in 1918 or 1919, according to Mrs. Martínez. The first piece of whose sale there is a record was accessioned in 1920 by the Museum of New Mexico.

The Invention

Julián took the letter into Española to mail, instead of giving it to the postman, and then they settled down and waited for word that the stove had come. Finally the freight office sent them a postal card saying that the stove was in Española, and Julián drove in with the team and wagon to get it.

He came back the next day, with a big wooden box filling all the back end of the wagon. There was hardly room left for the box of dress goods and groceries that María had asked him to bring her from the store. She and the children went out to see Julián's arrival, and he grinned down at them from the wagon seat.

"Here you are," he said. "Anybody that lives here want a stove?"

"Everybody does," said María, laughing back at him. She looked down the hill, and saw Ana and Desidéria, with their husbands, hurrying up. "Here comes help," she told Julián, and he nodded and got down from the wagon.

"That's good," he said. "It took two men to help me load it, and I know I can't get it off alone. Why did you pick the heaviest stove in the book, anyway?"

"It said there it would hold heat because it was cast iron," María answered. Then she stepped back, out of the way, while the three men unloaded the stove and carried it into the kitchen.

It took them a long time to pry off the boards and take the case to pieces, and when they had done that part of the work, the men still had not finished. The stove was inside the case, but it was in parts. There were many little boxes packed around the main stove. All of them had to be opened. The smaller boxes held the pipe lengths and the different little parts of the stove. Away down in the bottom of the box there was a brown paper envelope, and in it the screws that would fasten the whole thing together.

Julián laid out all the different pieces on the kitchen floor, and looked at them. "I thought they would send a whole stove," he said sadly, "not just little pieces of one. A fireplace is easier to put together. I think I'll just build you a new fireplace."

"No you won't," said María. "I waited a long time for this stove, and now I'm going to cook supper on it tonight. You hurry up and get it put together."

The three men went to work, matching the parts with each other, and figuring out where each one was supposed to go. There was a book of instructions in the box, with pictures of the stove parts and how they fitted together, and the men followed the pictures. Sometimes when they could not quite figure something out, they would call María, and she would read parts of the book to them, spelling the words out slowly. It had been a long time since she had tried to read aloud from a printed book.

When it was all finished and the bolts were as tight as he could make them, Julián cut a hole in the roof of the kitchen for the stovepipe. He ran the pipe through the hole, sticking up above the roof, and then he nodded to María.

"It had better be a good supper," he said.

Everybody stayed for supper, and the new stove cooked a good one. The stove was so quick that María almost burned the beans, but she got the pot off in time, and the food was all right. After supper they all sat and looked at the new stove and enjoyed its heat. People began coming in to see the stove, and María made a big pot of coffee and some *sopaipillas,* so they could all see how it worked.

"Now you have this," Julián said, "I guess you're going to be satisfied, aren't you?"

"I'm satisfied with the stove," María replied. "What I want next is a sewing machine."

"Well, try to get one that's already put together," said Julián. "I don't want anything else that comes in little pieces."

About four days later Isabella and Tonita came to see María. They had both been making pottery for a long time. They had learned from

220

The Invention

their mothers at about the same time that María and Desidéria learned from Tía Nicolasa.

"Come in," María said, when they knocked. She was sitting on the floor in a corner of the kitchen, making pottery. "Sit down," she added. "Please excuse me if I go on working."

"That's all right," Tonita answered, and Isabella added, "That's what we want to talk to you about."

"The pottery?" asked María.

"Yes," said Tonita, "we want to talk to you about the pottery."

"What is it?" inquired María. She was not sure that she could tell them anything about pottery, because they both knew as much as she did to begin with.

"It's like this," Isabella said. "Everybody in the village, almost, makes pottery."

"Yes," said María.

"They all make about the same kind," Isabella went on.

"Yes," María said again.

"But you can sell yours," said Tonita, taking her turn at the talking. "You sell it, and you get enough from it to buy new cooking stoves, and sewing machines, and everything like that."

"It pays pretty well," María agreed. She thought she knew what was coming, and she was thinking about what she ought to say when the words were spoken.

"Well," Isabella resumed, "we all started learning how to make pottery at about the same time. We were even. Then you began to sell yours and get ahead of the others."

"That's right," said María.

"We were thinking," Isabella said again. "We thought maybe some of the rest of us could sell pottery, too."

"Times are hard," Tonita suddenly interrupted. "It isn't easy to get along these days. My father had three fields, and he made good crops from them. He could sell his wheat and alfalfa and corn for enough money to buy clothes and flour at the store, and what we put up from the garden would feed his whole family with some left over to help people who were old or poor or not so lucky. Nowadays my husband and I have those same three fields and we aren't even getting by. We make just enough crops and gardens to feed ourselves in good years. In bad years we have to get help from other people. That's not right. We work hard and it makes us ashamed not to be able to buy good clothes for our children and give them the things they'd like to have."

221

Corn Dance

The Invention

"It's that way at my house, too," said Isabella. "Our fields are ruined with these floods. The ditches wash out in the spring, and it takes all summer to get the banks fixed so they'll carry water. Then by that time a drought has set in and the water has stopped running, so there isn't any to fill the ditches. Then fall comes and the water floods and tears out the ditch banks again, and the men have to start all over. All I have to feed my children most of the time is beans and *tortillas*. I can't get them nice clothes. I try hard, but my children look poor. It makes me ashamed." She stopped talking, and she and Tonita sat and looked at María.

María thought. Her hands were resting on the bowl she held, and her eyes were on the new stove. Outside the window she could see her two boys and Clara, their little aunt, playing in the yard. The children looked clean and well fed, and their clothes were new and good. María knew what was the right thing for her to do.

"I tell you what," she said to Tonita and Isabella. "A long time ago, when my aunt taught me to make pottery, she told me something. She said that pottery-making belongs to everybody. Everybody who came to her and wanted to learn to make pottery, she taught. She said that was the way it was supposed to be. I want to do things right, the way she told me. You already know how to make pottery. Go home and make some and I'll send it to the store to be sold with mine."

"Thank you," said Isabella, but Tonita said, "You say your aunt taught you how to make pottery. We know from our mothers how to make the kind she made. But you're about the only one in this village who knows how to make the black kind, and that's the kind that sells best. Will you teach us how to make that kind?"

Again María thought. "Julián worked that out," she said. "He's the one that knows the most about it. I think he'll feel the same way I do. He'll be willing to teach you. You go home and make your pottery and when it's ready, bring it to us to fire. You can watch and help. That way you'll learn the firing."

"Thank you," said Tonita and Isabella together. After a little more talking, and watching María as she worked, they went back to their houses.

When Julián came in from working on the ditches that evening, for even pottery-painting did not excuse a man from ditch work, María told him what had happened. Julián listened, and sat and thought for a while.

"What did you tell them?" he asked finally.

"I told them we would teach them what we know," María answered, and Julián nodded.

"That's right," he said. "That's the right thing to do. This isn't a secret. If it helps one family, it can help all the families. Everybody has to work together on the ditches, and everybody ought to work together on other things. You did right."

"Will you teach their husbands about firing?" María asked him.

"If they want to learn," Julián replied. "I don't want to have things other people can't have. If you have the best things and begin to get famous and rich and all, then nobody's happy. Other people can be jealous and begin not to like you, and it's not good. I'll teach anybody that wants to learn, the way your Tía Nicolasa taught us."

"That's good," said María. "Maybe some of the young ones will want to learn, too," she went on. "I can teach them. They can work with me, and help with polishing and scraping. Then they'll see and know the things I do."

"That's a good way for them to learn," Julián agreed.

Tonita and Isabella were back with their pottery sooner than María had expected them. They had twelve bowls apiece ready to fire, and María counted and found that she had twelve herself.

"You leave the bowls here tonight," she said, "and tomorrow come over early in the morning and we'll fire them."

"Thank you," said Tonita and Isabella.

When they took the bowls out to the fire pit the next morning, Tonita and Isabella watched carefully. When the time came to sprinkle the corn meal on the wood, each of them took a pinch of the meal, and sprinkled it with a prayer as María herself always did. Then the two women stood at one side and watched while Julián piled on the cedar branches and the dung cakes.

"That's the way I always build a fire," said Tonita when the pile was ready to be lighted. "I don't see any difference between that and an ordinary pottery fire."

"Wait," said María. "It will be different. Wait."

When Julián and María spread the powdered manure over the fire, their friends understood the difference.

"It looks easy," said Tonita, watching.

"The hard thing is knowing when to do it," Isabella observed.

"Yes," said Tonita. "We'll have to watch again two or three times, to be sure we know the right time to do it."

After the fire had gone out and the ashes had cooled, Julián began lifting out the pottery with his forked stick. He set each piece on the ground carefully. All of the bowls were perfect. None had broken in the firing.

"You'll have to be careful now," Julián said. "It would be too bad if you got mixed up and couldn't tell one bowl from another."

Tonita laughed at him. "We can tell," she said. "We can always tell."

"How?" Julián demanded.

"It's easy," said María. She bent over the row of bowls. "These thin ones at this end are Tonita's. She always makes hers thinner than anybody else's. Then there are some of mine. You can tell them by the way they turn in at the rim. These are Isabella's. They aren't as thin as Tonita's and they don't turn in like mine. The rest turn in a lot, so they're mine again."

"That's a good way of telling, and you can pick them out," said Julián, "but what about other people? What if they want to know?"

"Pottery-making belongs to the pueblo," said María, repeating again what Tía Nicolasa had told her when she was a little girl. "As long as they come from San Ildefonso, that's what counts."

"I guess so," said Julián.

When the storekeeper came out from Santa Fé at the end of the next week, he was surprised to see how many black bowls were waiting for him.

"You must sit up all night to make these, María," he said. "This is more than I ever got before at one time."

"I had help with them," said María.

"You must have," the storekeeper replied. "Nobody could tell it, though. They all look just alike."

"They're all good bowls," María answered. "Do you want us to make some more?"

"I don't think so," said the storekeeper, considering. "Not for a while, maybe. Bowls sell all right, but this is such a lot of them I think you'd better make jars for a while. Like *ollas,* but smaller. The white ladies like to have them to put flowers in. And, María, did you ever make any plates?"

"No," said María, "just flat sort of lids for *tinajas.* Indians don't make plates."

"Try making me some," suggested the storekeeper. "People keep asking me for plates and I haven't any. Make them like lids, but flatter."

"We'll try," said María. "Come back and see how they work, pretty soon."

Isabella and Tonita had seen the storekeeper drive up and then leave. They came in almost as soon as he was gone.

"Well?" asked Isabella, and Tonita said. "What did he say? Tell us."

"He thought I made them all," María answered. "I told him I had help with them, but he said he couldn't tell the difference; the bowls were all just alike."

"Did he want some more?" asked Tonita.

"He wants jars the next time," María replied. "That's enough bowls for now, and he can sell some jars. He wants plates, too."

"We don't make plates," said Tonita.

"That's what I told him," María assured her.

"Are you going to try?" Isabella queried.

"I can try," said María slowly. "I never did, but I can try."

"You try the plates," said Tonita, "and we'll make the jars. How big does he want them?"

"Like water jars only smaller, to put flowers in," said María.

"Maybe like the brass ones on the altar in Santa Cruz church," Tonita suggested. "They ought to be easy."

"Yes," said María. She added, "He always brings me the money after he sells the pottery. Next time he comes I'll have some money for you."

"Good," said Tonita. "We'll go home and make some jars right away. Good-bye."

"Good-bye," said María.

After her friends had gone, María sat down and thought about plates. She took a china plate out of the cupboard and studied it. It was made the same way the covers of the old jars were. All she had to do was to make jar covers, but to make them a little larger than the old ones.

She was working on the first one when Julián came in.

"What's that?" he asked. "I thought all your jars had covers."

"These are plates," said María. "That white man wants some plates."

"Oh," said Julián. He looked at the new shape for a while. "All the plates I ever saw had designs painted on them," he said.

"You can paint designs on these if you want to," María offered.

"I'll wait and see how they turn out," answered Julián. "They may change shape when I fire them."

226

26. The Signatures
(1923–1926*

María could never tell, in her own mind, what happened in each single year after San Diego. Time and the seasons ran together for her. The important things were the little boys, as they were born and grew up (or died), and as she watched them.

The children and the pottery were almost her whole life. Her time was divided between them with little left for anyone else, not even for Julián. A pattern had made itself for their lives, and almost without thinking they followed it.

Julián did not work in the fields now, but he got up as early as any farmer. He built the fires and brought in water from the well while María got breakfast. While she cleaned the house and washed the dishes and put the beans or stew on the stove to simmer for dinner, Julián took care of the animals and the garden. Then they both settled down to work.

At first they worked in the kitchen, just as they always had. It was comfortable in there, and they were used to it. If Tonita or Isabella or Rosalia were helping with the pottery, they felt free to come into the kitchen and work, or to go home when they had other work to do there. María and Julián could go on with their own working, no matter who else came or went.

People who wanted to buy pottery or groceries came to the door of the new room and knocked until Julián heard them. Then he would stop whatever he was doing and go wait on the customers, coming back to the kitchen after the people had left. One afternoon he came in late and sat down before his work-bench with a weary sigh.

"What's the matter?" María asked him.

* This date, too, cannot be definitely established. Jars signed "Marie" were collected in 1923; unsigned jars date from as late as 1926. The "Marie and Julian" signature first appeared about 1925. In telling of the use of the signatures, however, Mrs. Martínez apparently described a single incident.

227

"That's the sixth time," said Julián. "Six times this afternoon I've had to get up and down. It's hard on my legs. It hurts them."

"It's too bad," María agreed.

"Maybe you ought to take turns," said Tonita, looking up from the bowl she was polishing.

"He's good at that part," María replied. "I'm not. I'm shy with strangers, but he can talk to them."

"Maybe he ought to work in the other room," Tonita suggested. "Then he'd be nearer things, if people wanted them."

"Maybe I could do that," said Julián.

"It's kind of friendly, all working here together, though," said María.

"It doesn't have to be unfriendly if I work in there," said Julián. "We can leave the door open, and talk sometimes, the way we do now. Then when people come in, I can close the door till they leave."

"You'll still have to get up and down if you do that," María reminded him.

"I won't sit on the floor in there," Julián answered. "I'll get a regular table and chair and put them by the window, and not sit on the floor. Then it won't be so hard to keep on working."

That was the way they worked it out. It was easier for everybody, especially after summer came and the tourists started visiting the pueblo. At first the white people came to watch the dances, but before they left the watchers always seemed to come up the hill to the house and buy pottery to take home with them. The white people liked watching Julián at work, as the people in San Diego had, and they would stand around him, with their eyes fixed on his brush, while he painted. Some of the strangers asked Julián if he ever painted pictures. When he said that he did, they wanted to buy pictures as well as pottery. Julián got out the old water-color set Jack had given him when they camped at Frijoles, so long ago, it seemed, and sometimes when he was tired of decorating pottery, Julián painted pictures to sell.

When it was an Indian who came into the store, to buy a can of tomatoes or some sugar or flour, then Julián would look up from his work and say, "Go ahead. Help yourself." Their friends would take what they wanted from the shelves and put the money down on Julián's work table. Then they would talk for a little while, without watching Julián's work, and go away. That was all, and it was easy and did not interrupt.

It was about two years before some of the other women started to work for themselves. The pottery was selling well, and people began to write in from far-away places, like New York and Boston and California, to order pottery for their homes or their stores. There was a lot of work to do, with the orders and everything, and Julián spent some of his evenings packing pottery to be sent away.

Then one morning Tonita came in and sat down facing María. "I've been thinking," she said.

"What about?" María asked, spinning a long clay coil between her palms.

"Well," said Tonita, "there are lots of people who want to buy pottery. Sometimes, even with all of us working in spare time, you don't have any ready to sell. I've been thinking I'd like to work full time in my own house, and have pottery to sell too."

"Why don't you?" María asked.

"I wanted to talk to you first," said Tonita.

"It's hard work," María warned her. "It isn't easy, with all the people and everything. And you have to work steadily and all the time, to make enough to sell." She set the bowl aside to stiffen a little before she smoothed it, and began to slap out a *tortilla* of clay for the bottom of another vessel. "You have to plan and work and go ahead all the time, no matter what you'd rather be doing. Some days the clay won't go right, but you have to go ahead anyway. And the people come and go and talk. You can see what it's like here."

"I've seen it," Tonita agreed, "but I think I can do the work. I can build pottery pretty fast, and Juan likes to paint and decorate it. Lots of the men like to do that work. Cresencio and Alfredo have been doing it about as long as Julián."

"Yes," said María, "and they're good at it, and Juan's good. Well, you go ahead. Make your pottery and sell it. Your house ought to be a good place for selling, right there at the entrance to the village."

"You don't mind?" asked Tonita.

"Why should I mind?" María inquired. "If you can do the work and make some money, that's good. It's helping your family, and that helps the pueblo. Go ahead."

So Tonita and Juan started their pottery-making, and soon after that Cresencio and Ana, who had been selling their things with María's and Julián's, decided that they would like to have a shop, too. Then Rosalia, after thinking it over, decided that maybe she would have a place. María actually felt relieved that they were going into the business. If other people were working full time and there were plenty of places to buy pottery, some of the tourists could go to the other houses. She and Julián could work on the orders that came from far-away places and be quiet and happy at home. It seemed a good idea. They were making as much money as they needed for their own family. Adam and Clara and Juan had nicer clothes and more of them than any of the other children in the Indian school in Santa Fé. She had a good cow, so that the little boys at home were getting all the milk they needed. Julián had bought a team and a fine green Bain wagon, to use when he made trips to get clay and sand, and María had bought herself a sewing machine with fancy ironwork legs. Still she had money saved up and put away, and none of them wanted for anything. They even talked about buying a truck, so that they could get bigger loads of sand and clay, and make better time on the trips, than they could with the wagon.

María seldom went for clay and sand herself, now. She left that part of the work to Julián. While he was away, Juan and Clara ran the store, although they usually came shyly into the kitchen to call María if white people came to buy pottery. With the Indian customers, whom they knew, the children went ahead and sold the groceries just as if they were grown up.

One such day, when María was working steadily in the kitchen, she looked up to see the children in the doorway.

"White man," said Juan.

"Government car," said Clara.

Both together they said, "You'd better come."

María set aside the *tinaja* on which she was working and got up from the floor. There was clay on her hands and wrists and on her apron, but when she slipped the apron off over her head, the front of her dress was clean. She dipped her hands in the wash basin to get off the worst of the clay, and ran her palms over the top of her head to smooth her hair. Then she went into the front room, where the white man waited.

"You want to buy pottery?" she asked. She had got over her feeling that it was rude to ask a direct question of a white person, although she still never asked one of an Indian.

The white man turned towards her. He did not look straight at María, but beyond her, at the wall. His blue eyes and pink skin looked like those of a young boy, she saw in a quick glance, but his hair was white. The man was not quite smiling; his hand was outstretched.

"Maybe," he said. "Are you María Martínez?"

The Signatures

"Yes," María answered. She wondered if the man could be a relative of Miss Grimes'; his coloring was so like the school teacher's.

"I heard about you," the white man said. "I was up on the Arapaho Indian reservation in Wyoming, and I heard about you there. You are famous, María."

"Am I?" María asked. She glanced beyond him, at the government car parked in the yard. The man had come alone. He must have other business than pottery.

"Yes," he said. "Your pottery is very well known. I was the superintendent of the Arapahos, and I heard about it up there."

"That's nice," María said.

"Then I was sent here, to be superintendent in Santa Fé, at the school," the stranger went on. "There I heard more about it, and I saw some of your pottery for sale in the shops in town. I wanted to see it and to meet you."

"That's good," said María. "You sit down."

The white man sat down easily in Julián's chair by the window and glanced around the room. "Is this all yours?" he asked, looking at the pottery on the long table against the wall. María's eyes followed his.

"It's all made here," she evaded. She recognized some of Tonita's work, and a bowl of Rosalia's that had not sold, and several pieces of Desidéria's work. "It's all made in San Ildefonso."

"Did you make it all?" the white man persisted, "every piece?"

"I made some of it," said María.

"Who else makes it?" he wanted to know.

"Oh," María said, "Tonita makes it—that's her house down the hill on the south side of the plaza—and my sisters make it, and Rosalia and Isabella—oh, lots of the ladies make pottery. It's all San Ildefonso. It's all made right here."

"Can you tell your own pieces?" the white man asked.

"Sure," María told him. "I made this one and this one and this one, and this is one of my sisters', and this is Tonita's—she makes the best pottery of all, I think."

"Can other people tell?" the white man demanded.

"Sure, if they know," said María. Then she asked, "You been to see the governor?"

"Oh, yes," said her visitor. "I saw him first off. That's the right thing to do, you know. So I saw the governor and some of the councilmen. Then when the business was finished, I came to see you. Are these your children?" he asked, nodding his head sidewise at Juan and Clara, who were peering around the kitchen door.

"It's my little boy," said María. "The other, she's my sister. I'm raising her."

"Do they go to school?" asked the Superintendent.

"In winters they go," said María. "Last year my sister and my oldest boy went to Santa Fé. I guess this year they'll go again. They like it pretty good there. They make good grades, too. Lots of 'A's' on their cards."

"Fine," said the Superintendent. "I'm glad to hear it. When they come back this fall maybe they can make all 'A's'."

"Maybe," María agreed.

"Not enough of the Indian children go to school," the white man went on. "Do you know why that is, María?"

"Is easy," María said. "Their families don't got enough money for clothes. They're too ashamed to send the children without nice clothes."

"But the government gives all the children clothes," the Superintendent reminded her. "Why do they need others?"

"Government clothes aren't pretty," María informed him. "They all look alike. Parents like to see their children look pretty, all dressed up right. Maybe Sundays they go visit the children; take them to town to buy ice cream cones. Then they like those little ones to look nice so they proud of them."

"I see," said the white man. "The Arapahos felt that way, too. Why is it that some of the families are so poor here? What's happened? The Pueblo Indians were always supposed to be good farmers and hard workers. What's the matter?"

"You better talk to the governor about that," María said.

"I have," answered her guest. "I want to hear what you say, too. I know what the governor and the council think."

"It's when the trees were cut," María said. "Then the water and the dust spoiled everything. Families where the ladies make pottery, or the mens sell pictures, they do all right. It's the other families have hard times. Something ought to be done about that tree-cutting."

"You're right there," the man agreed. "Do you think the families that make pottery will be all right, María?"

"Pottery is good," María informed him. "We got enough money for a cooking stove, a sewing machine, a wagon, a cow, the children's clothes—everything. All from the pottery. Others does it too. It's good."

"How do you sell your pottery?" the Superintendent asked next.

"Most times to people who come here," María replied. "Sometimes to stores in town, when they send somebody out to get it. Now we get orders from long ways away: New York, Boston, California, all those places. We send them pottery and they send us back money."

"What about the other ladies?" the man went on. "Do they do the same thing?"

"Most of them sell here in the village," said María. "When somebody comes out from town or writes an order, they sell some to us if we don't have enough to make out for what's ordered."

"So when it goes away, it all goes from this house," said the Superintendent thoughtfully. "People who don't buy in the pueblo must think that it's all your pottery, then."

"I guess so," María answered.

"Well," said the Superintendent, "do you know what I think you ought to do, María? When a white artist paints a picture or carves a statue, he signs his name to it. Then the people who buy it know it is his work. I think you ought to sign the pottery the same way. Could you do that?"

"Sign with my name?" María asked, wonderingly.

233

"Yes," said the Superintendent. "You went to school and learned to write, didn't you? You speak good English."

"I can write," María said. "Where should I sign, though?"

"Maybe on the bottom," suggested the Superintendent. He picked up a bowl and turned it over. "Here, on the flat place. There's room to write your name there."

María looked carefully at the bottom of the bowl. "There's room," she agreed. "I should write my name there? Maybe with a polishing stone?"

"That's a good idea," said the Superintendent. "Write it with a polishing stone, good and clear. Maybe it would be better to write 'Marie' than 'María', too. Put an 'e' on the end of the name instead of an 'a'."

"Why?" María questioned. "That's my name, María."

"White people are more used to saying 'Marie,' and I think it will be easier for you to write," was the reply.

"What about Julián?" María went on. "Should he write his name, too, on his paintings?"

"Why, yes," said the Superintendent. "I think he ought to do that."

"And on the pots when he decorates them?"

"Yes, on the pots, too, if he does the decorating."

"But he can't write," María said.

"Can't you show him?" the white man asked. "You could write his name for him on a paper, and then he could copy it."

"I guess so," said María.

"Then, when people want to buy a piece of María Martínez' pottery, they can turn it over and see if it's your work," said the Superintendent. "They'll know what it is then."

"But it's all San Ildefonso pottery," María protested. "I don't see that it makes much difference who makes something. The pottery all comes from here. It's all made the same way. It doesn't matter if it's mine or somebody else's."

"Maybe not to you, and maybe not to the other ladies," said the white man. "And if people come here to the village for pottery, they know whose they've bought. It doesn't matter to them whether the piece is signed or not. But people who buy away from here want to know."

"All right," said María amiably. "We can do that, I guess. We can try." She laughed a little. "Always white people are showing me about selling pottery," she said. "That head man at Frijoles, he showed me what to charge in money when people wanted to buy. And the store man in town, he showed me about making special prices when people buy pottery and then sell it again. Now you show me about signing it. I sure have a lot to learn about these things."

"We all have a great deal to learn about everything," the Superintendent agreed. "We have to learn and study all our lives, and then we only know a little part of what there is in the world to know."

"That's what my mother and my teacher always said," said María. "Keep learning, keep learning, they would say. There are still things to know, they said."

"And they were right," said the Superintendent, getting up. "They were wise ladies. Good-bye."

"They were wise ladies," said María reflectively. "Good-bye." She held out her hand, and the man laid his palm briefly against hers. "Come again," she said. "Come when Julián's here, and talk to him."

"I will," her new friend promised. "Good-bye."

When Julián came home that night, María told him about the visit, and about what had been said. Julián listened thoughtfully.

"Should the other ladies sign their pottery, too?" he asked.

"I guess so," said María. "He didn't say anything about it."

"It's all right," said Julián, "but suppose you sign your work and they sign theirs, and then theirs doesn't sell, what will they do then? Won't their feelings be hurt?"

"They might be," María said. She had not thought about that. "That would be bad. It isn't nice, to hurt their feelings."

"No," said Julián, "we don't want to do that. It would be awful if people got mad at us because their feelings were hurt."

"We could do this," said María, consideringly. "White people can't tell much about pottery anyway. If the other ladies want me to sign their pottery, and they ask me to, I will. It's up to them. They can have it the way they like. I'll do what they want me to."

"We can tell them so," said Julián. "Now, you write off my name so I can draw it on the pictures. You can write both names on the pottery. I couldn't draw with a polishing stone."

Part IV: The Finished Bowl

27. The Breaking
(1923

The pueblo was something in and to itself, a whole that was greater than the sum of its parts. Where human lives grew like grass, the pueblo grew like the old cottonwood in the plaza, slowly and through many years but without stopping. Always, too, it grew with direction, without deviation from an ordained pattern.

Therefore the pueblo was what it was meant to be—a wall and a shelter for its people. Within it they were safe with one another; to it they returned when they had been outside for a time. The need for physical defense against the Apaches or the Spanish or the Anglo soldiers had gone long ago, but against whatever shocks might come upon its people from without the pueblo still stood as a barrier.

In spite of the fact that she herself had been away from the pueblo to school, and had lived at the museum, and had gone to world's fairs, María sometimes wondered if it were right for her to let the children go away. She wanted her sons to have all the schooling they needed and would take, and she had promised her mother that she would take care of Clara. That meant that one child should have the same chances as the others. Clara and Adam went to school together, although Adam was the older, and they both studied and learned well. They were both smart.

That was why María was surprised when Clara began to get bad grades. When the report cards were sent home at the middle of the second year that Clara was in school at Santa Fé, her grades were poor. As she and Adam had always made about the same marks and they had the same teachers, María did not understand why Clara's grades changed and Adam's didn't. She showed the cards to Desidéria.

"That is funny," Desidéria said, looking at the cards.

"Something's happening," said Julián through the doorway of the salesroom.

"It's bad," María added. "It worries me. Something's wrong."

"Maybe she isn't trying," Desidéria suggested.

"I think she tries all right," said María. "I think maybe she isn't happy. She likes it at home. Maybe she wants to come back here."

"I don't know," said Desidéria. "We went away from home, and we made good grades."

"It's a bad age for a girl to be lonesome, about twelve," said María. "We were both there together and seeing each other every day. That makes it different."

"Yes, we were," Desidéria agreed, "but Clara has Adam there. Still, a boy would be different, and he isn't even her own brother."

"That's just it," María nodded, "I think I'll go down and talk to the Superintendent. Julián, can you take me to Santa Fé tomorrow?"

Julián was putting his brushes away, and now he came and stood in the doorway, looking worried. "I guess so," he said. "There's a council meeting tonight, and it may last pretty late. If it does, will the day after tomorrow do?"

"Why, yes," said María. "I'd like to go as soon as we can, that's all."

"We'll do that," said Julián.

Desidéria got up from her chair. "Well," she said, "if there's a council meeting, I'd better get home and start supper early, so we can be ready for it. Good-bye."

María smiled, after her sister had left. "You'd think she was on the council herself, instead of her husband," she said. "I'll get supper, too, so we can be ready."

"Thank you," said Julián. "I'll take care of the chores." He went out to the corral without saying anything more.

It was a quiet supper. María was worried about Clara, and Julián had something on his mind. Juan, who was a little boy, was quiet and good and went straight to bed without being told. María started to wash the dishes, and Julián stood for a minute with his hand on the doorknob.

"I may be late," he said. "Don't wait for me." And he was gone.

María went to bed because she was tired, and she could think best about Clara as she lay still in the dark. She had been settled in bed for only a short time, it seemed, when she heard the outside door open and Julián come in.

"That didn't take long," María said through the darkness. Julián was moving about the room, very quietly, getting ready to go to bed himself.

The Breaking

"No," he answered, "it didn't take long." His voice sounded as María had never heard it before, so tired that it was without life, and it fell from his mouth like a tired arm falling against a bed.

"What is it?" María asked him. "Is something wrong?"

"Lots of things are wrong," Julián replied. "You'll know soon. I can't tell you now."

That was all. Something was wrong with Clara, and María was worrying about that; something bigger was wrong outside the family, and was deadening Julián. Neither of them spoke, and neither of them slept.

In the morning, Julián got up and harnessed the horses to the big green wagon. The team was waiting by the time María had breakfast ready.

"We're going to Santa Fé," Julián told Juan. "We'll be gone until day-after-tomorrow night. You can eat and sleep at your Aunt Ana's."

Juan puckered up his face. "I don't want to go there," he said. "I want to go to Aunt Desidéria's. Aunt Ana's as cross as a bear sometimes. She just growls at us, she's so bossy."

"That's all right," said María. "You can go to Aunt Desidéria's. We'll drive by and tell her you're coming, on our way."

The pattern of the winding road beside the river was the one that María remembered from all her life. The river had flowed and the road had moved beside it just this way, always. New houses were built by the roadside, and new faces came to some of the houses when old ones left them, but there was an unchangingness about the landscape that was a part of María's life.

Only on this day her feeling about the road and the river was a different one. Traveling in this way had always been happy before; there had been lightness and excitement in the wagon with her, even when it was an old, creaking wagon and the horses that drew it were old and slow. Now it was a fine new wagon and the horses were young and spirited, but there was no happiness in the wagon. She and Julián and an unhappiness sat there together, without speaking.

There were rooms for visiting parents at the Indian School, and they spent the night there. It was too late to see either of the children when they got in, but the next morning, in the dining hall, María saw Adam as he came in to breakfast.

"Come and talk to me as soon as you've eaten," she said, and the boy nodded. María stood watching him until all the children had gone in. She could not see her sister anywhere.

Adam came over to her chair as she was finishing her coffee. María set down her cup, and they went outside together.

"Where's Clara?" María asked.

"In the infirmary," Adam answered. "She's been there about a week now."

"What's the matter?" María demanded. "Where's she sick?"

"She isn't sick," said Adam. "She's funny. She seems like she doesn't hear things."

"She doesn't hear things!" María repeated. "That is funny. She always did hear. She could hear as well as anybody. She's a good singer and dancer for a little girl."

"She doesn't hear," Adam insisted, scowling anxiously. "She knows what I say when we talk Tewa. But when the teachers talk English, she doesn't hear."

"I'm going over there," said María. "You go on to school. We can see you at lunch time. Father can go to the shop and look at the wood-working students."

She pulled her shawl up over her head, as she walked across the campus to the infirmary. She could not let people see how strange and worried she felt. A woman had to be strong, Reyes had told her. She must not let people know, ever, when she was being weak.

There was a young nurse in a stiff white uniform sitting at a desk in the lobby of the infirmary. She looked up when María entered. "Visiting hours from two to four this afternoon," she said briskly.

"I got to see Clara Montoya," María said.

"This afternoon, from two to four," said the nurse, smiling with the front of her face.

"She's sick," María explained patiently. "I got to see her now. She's a little girl and she's got no mother."

"If you'll come back at two this afternoon you can see her," the nurse said.

"I got to see her now," María repeated, and she stepped forward into the long hall beyond the desk. The nurse put out a hand to stop her, but María brushed it aside with the corner of her shawl, and went on down the hall. The doors of the rooms were open, and she looked in through each one until she came to a door near the middle of the hall, and through it she saw Clara lying on a bed by a window. There were three other beds in the room, with three other little girls lying in them. María smiled at the children and went over to her sister. Clara looked all right. Her color was good, and her arms and legs were round and plump and healthy. She smiled when she saw María, and María went solidly across the room and stood looking down at her.

"What's the matter with you?" she asked, in English. "You don't look sick. You look all right. Why are you here?"

Clara smiled and smiled and held out her arms. She said in a whisper, in Tewa, "My older sister."

"You're all right," María said, still in English and not raising her voice. "There's nothing wrong with you. You don't have to be here. Get up; you ought to be ashamed."

Still Clara smiled, so quietly, and still she held out her arms and whispered in Tewa. One of the other girls spoke up behind María. "It's not any good talking English to her. She don't hear you. Say something to her in Indian."

María bent forward across the bed and spoke, this time in Tewa, as quietly as Clara herself. "Do you want to go home?"

Tears formed in Clara's eyes and moved silently down her cheeks. She nodded. "I want to go home," she said in Tewa. "I want to go home with you."

There was a stir at the door, and María turned around to see the white nurse entering. Behind the nurse was the Superintendent, and with him was another white man. The Superintendent came forward, and shook hands with María.

"Come to the front office, María," he said quickly, without giving the nurse a chance to speak. "I'm glad you got here."

In the front office, he said, "This is the doctor for the school. He was going to send for you this week, to talk with you about Clara."

"What's the matter with her?" María demanded. "She don't look sick."

"She isn't, really," the doctor said reassuringly. "She's unfortunate in a way, but she isn't really sick."

"Then what is it?" María insisted. "She's a smart little girl. Her grades are bad this time, but that's a mistake. She's smart, not dumb."

"She's a very smart girl," the Superintendent said. "If she hadn't been so smart, we would have found out sooner that there was something the matter with her. Clara's lost her hearing, María. Her grades are bad because she can't hear what the teachers say. She is deaf."

"How did she get to be?" María asked. "She could always hear. She could sing and dance and everything."

"We think it started this winter," said the doctor. "She had a bad cold. It must have made an infection inside her ear and stopped her hearing. That happens sometimes."

"Will it get better?" asked María. "Can she get over it?"

"We don't know, yet," the doctor answered. "Sometimes children get over that kind of trouble and sometimes not. It's hard to tell. A lot depends on finding out about it in time. It must have happened slowly, so that Clara didn't notice it herself right at first. It wasn't until her grades got so bad that we knew there was something wrong."

"Couldn't they watch her, after she was sick?" María asked the Superintendent.

"I wish they could have," he replied. "The infirmary was full of sick children then, and some of them even died. If they seemed to be getting a little better, the doctors and nurses paid less attention to them, and more to the sicker ones."

"I see," María said. "So just nobody knew what was wrong. Except Adam. He knew. Didn't he tell you?"

The Breaking

"He told the nurse, I think," the doctor said, "but everybody was so busy—"

"And he was a young boy," María added. "Sometimes grownups don't listen to boys." She sat for a minute, with her hands folded in her lap, looking beyond the doctor at the blank white wall. "What can we do now?" she asked. "We got enough money to do what we need to do. She can have any kind of medicine she ought to have. What do we do?"

"There's nothing we can do now," the doctor told her. "Nothing anybody can do. You take her home where she will be comfortable and happy, and keep her there with you. At the end of a year you can bring her back and we'll examine her. And you can watch her. If there is any change, either better or worse, in her hearing, bring her back here right away. You can tell about those things better than we can."

"All right," María said. She stood up, and drew her shawl around her. "I'll do that. When can she go home?"

"Would after lunch be all right?" the Superintendent asked. "That will give you time to get her clothes from the girls' building, and for the doctor to make a final check of her ears for his records."

"That's all right," said María. She turned to the doctor. "I'll watch her good," she said. She went out of the office without even looking at the nurse.

On the infirmary steps, the Superintendent put his hand on her arm, briefly. "It could be worse, María," he said quietly.

María nodded. "Yes," she said, "she could be blind. Not to see sunlight—that would be the worst thing, I think."

"Or not to know that she was seeing it," said the Superintendent. "Her mind is still good, María, remember that. Even if she is slow to understand things, she *can* understand them if you give her time. Get books for her, and newspapers, so she won't forget how to read. She is good at figuring. Let her keep the records about the pottery."

"We never had any records," María said.

"Then you ought to," answered the Superintendent. "That is another thing for you to learn about pottery. You need records. Let Clara keep them. Then you'll always know how many pieces you shipped to each dealer, and who owes you money, and how your business is going."

"That's a good idea," María agreed. "I'll do that. Are there books to get about it?"

"I'll get them and send them out to you," the Superintendent promised. "That will help."

"Thank you," María said. "Good-bye."

She found Julián still in the woodworking shop, after she had packed Clara's clothes and had everything ready to take home. She told him what had happened.

"She'll be better at home," Julián said, watching a lathe turn and turn, dizzyingly. "Can she understand Tewa?"

"That's the funny thing," María said. "She understands that, and she wants to talk it. She seems to hang on to it. I guess because it belongs to home."

"She's always known it," Julián said.

"She needs to be home," María insisted. "She needs to be back in her own place."

They sat at the same table with Adam at lunch, but they all talked very little. Afterwards Adam came with them to the infirmary, and he and Clara shook hands shyly. The last they saw of him, as they drove away from the school, was his straight back, going soberly and stiffly across the campus to the boys' building. He might feel pretty bad, María thought, but even she would never know for certain just what he felt about it all.

"We'll stay at Tesuque tonight," Julián said when they had gone through Santa Fé and were out on the road. He spoke in Tewa, slowly and distinctly but quietly, and after a minute Clara nodded.

"We can stay with our friends at Tesuque," she said in her small whisper.

"Why do you whisper, Clara?" Julián asked her. "Why don't you speak out loud?"

"I do," said Clara. "Are your ears wrong, too? I speak the way I always did. My throat feels the same way."

María shook her head at Julián above Clara's. "His ears aren't so very good," she said, speaking carefully as Julián had. "He can hear me call him to dinner, but he can never hear me tell him to go and feed the horses." Clara laughed.

It was a little like being at home to be at Tesuque, and to feel the sureness of its adobe walls around them, shutting them in from the outside. The Tewa their friends spoke was not quite the same as their own, but it was enough like it for even Clara to understand the words. She brightened more and more as the evening went on, and by bedtime she was like herself again.

The Breaking

Going along in the wagon the next morning was a good time for María. Clara could understand and reply to what people said, even people outside her own family. The child turned her head to watch a flight of grackle go crackling across the road, and smiled a little.

"Why don't they make any noise?" she asked María. "I always thought they were noisy birds."

María's heart darkened again for a moment. This was a reminder. But Clara had been better at Tesuque, and surely when they got her home, she would be all right. Once she was inside her own pueblo, with her own people around her, everything would be safe for her again. It made no difference to María that their own house stood outside the walls of the pueblo itself. That was not important. What was important was to know that the pueblo was there and that they belonged to it. That was their great security—the pueblo's wholeness within itself.

They came at last to the turn-off from the main road. Clara, who had been drooping drowsily against María, wakened and straightened herself on the wagon seat.

"Now we are getting home," she whispered.

María glanced across at Julián, with a smile in her eyes because Clara was happy. Julián sat straight on the wagon seat, his face set on the road before him. He was not smiling and he did not speak. He did not even drive, but held the lines loosely and let the horses find their own way.

They came to the east wall of the pueblo, and Julián turned the horses south, towards their own house. At the top of the hill the horses stopped to breathe, as they always did; and as she always did, María turned to look down at the village.

"Why," she said, surprised, "Somebody's building a new house there, between the south wall and the kiva. Two new houses. Four." She laughed a little. "It looks like a whole new plaza," she said. "San Ildefonso will be like Jémez, pretty soon, with a south plaza and a north one."

"It is a new plaza," Julián said. "It's like a new pueblo," he added, under his breath.

"There can't be a new pueblo," María said impatiently. "Just one is all there ever was. That's private land down there, between the south wall and the kiva. That family always owned it and had their corn fields there. They can build new houses, but they can't build a new pueblo."

247

"There will be new houses and a new kind of life," said Julián. "It was decided at the council meeting. I can't tell you any more."

Juan had seen the wagon turn up the hill, and now he came running and panting upwards in his turn.

"Father!" Juan called. "Father! Something is happening. The men are doing something. They tore down that old house on the south side of the plaza, in front of the cottonwood tree. They tore it all down, Father. In one day. There's just a hole there now."

Clara was sitting still beside María on the wagon seat. Her face had brightened when she saw the little boy, but now it was puzzled and twisted with a frown of trying to understand.

"What is it?" she whispered, "what happened? Is something wrong? Did something break?"

María laid her hand on her sister's arm. "Yes," she said, "something has broken. There was something whole, and it broke. I don't know why it did." She turned to Julián. "I wanted to bring her home," she said. "You'd better go on up to the house."

28. The Breach in the Wall
(1933

Tearing down the house on the south side of the plaza and opening a passage where there had been a solid wall before had let evil go through into the pueblo. There was no way of stopping it now. As long as the wall of houses and the wall of people stood firm against the evil that was outside, life in the pueblo was safe. Now that that unity was broken, safety was gone.

María watched every change as it happened. Their house on the hill above the round kiva overlooked both the plazas, and she could see the people come and go below before her eyes. For a long time all the movement was in building, and the houses of the new plaza quickly rose and took form. Then the building was finished, and people settled down once more to living in their houses. Then, indeed, the view from the house on the hill seemed strange, with the movements of everyday life going on in the space where there had been only dancing and gardening before.

Through all the years that María could remember, there had been some Spanish families who lived in the pueblo. Some of them had intermarried with the Indian families, and all of them were a settled and normal part of living.

The Spanish people who lived in San Ildefonso went to Mass at the church with the Indians, and shared saints' days and other white men's holidays with them. These Spanish-Americans knew that when the Indians had a ceremonial dance, it was for themselves alone. Two or three days before such a dance started, the cacique sent his messenger to visit the Spanish homes and give their people warning. Then the Spanish families stayed inside their own houses for as long as the dance went on. They minded their own business and did not interfere. Everybody knew them and liked them and respected them.

For a long time, however, other Spanish people had been moving into the country around the pueblo. Some of them were farmers. Like

249

the old families, they stayed at home and worked, and nobody minded having them. Still other Spanish people opened stores near the pueblo. Now that cars came driving through from Santa Fé and Española, two Spanish men had opened filling stations. One even had his marked "Garage," but whenever the drivers of cars stopped for repairs, this man said that his repairman had gone out to lunch. Once he admitted to Julián that he had put the garage sign up just so people would stop and talk to him. He came from Santa Fé, and he got lonesome sometimes, now that he was living out in the country.

Stores and garages were all right. Nobody in the pueblo minded having them. It was when still others of the newcomers began to open *cantinas* that María got worried. *Cantinas* were supposed to sell liquor only to the Anglos and the Spaniards. Some of the barkeepers remembered the law and were careful not to sell anything to the Indians. Others were not. It was like the old days before there was national prohibition, when the Indians bought liquor in Santa Fé and Albuquerque. Then there had been a time when there was prohibition for everybody, whites as well as Indians. Now that was over, and the whites could buy liquor, so the Indians said they were going to buy it also. They said that it was wrong to make laws that worked for one people and not for another.

María did not think much about that part of the law. She was convinced that any kind of law that made liquor-selling possible was a bad one, and she did not care how it worked, or for whom. She made up her mind about this after Julián began drinking more and more often. First she spoke to the Superintendent about it.

"There are bad men around here," she said to him.

The Superintendent had driven out with some ladies from the East who were visiting the school in the pueblo. The ladies were look-

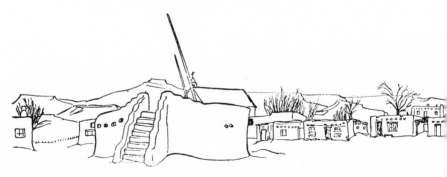

The Breach in the Wall

ing at the pottery in María's salesroom, with Julián explaining things to them, and the Superintendent had come out to the workroom to talk to María.

"There are bad men in most places," he said now. "Who are the bad men here?"

"Some of the Spanish men. They are being bad to the Indians."

"In what way? How are they bad to them?"

María stopped working. Her face was still above her quiet hands, as she looked directly at the Superintendent.

"They sell them whiskey," she said.

"Can you prove it?" the Superintendent asked. "We can't do anything about it unless we have proof."

"Julián gets drunk," said María.

"I've heard about that," said the Superintendent. "He used to do that a long time ago."

"It's now. It's more than ever," María told him. "He scares me, and he scares the boys. It's bad for boys to be scared of their father. They don't respect him the way they ought to."

The Superintendent sat quietly, looking at the row of half-finished pots stiffening on the floor before them. "It is bad," he said.

"It's bad for everybody," María said. "When you came here first, it was all whole. There was one plaza; the people danced once when they had ceremonies. Now if one side dances the Buffalo Dance, the other side dances the Humming Bird Dance. If one side has a ceremony, the other side has a different ceremony. They have their own kivas. They don't hold things together any more. There's a hole in the wall, and there's holes in people's hearts. They've got to be together again."

"It's all bad," the Superintendent repeated.

South Plaza

"Was a time," María went on, "when all the people was poor. They was poor together; they helped each other out with what little they had. Now some of us are rich; we have cars; have food; have good clothes. We could help the others more, but the people who aren't rich won't let us. They're proud. Won't take from us. That's not right. If the pueblo was whole again, they'd take from us like we was their own sisters. They wouldn't feel no different."

"None of it is good," said the Superintendent.

"Then they drink," said María. She had put away her tools, and she folded her hands against the apron on her lap. "Then they hate. If they didn't drink, they'd be unhappy; but they wouldn't hate. If people's unhappy, you can help them; but when they're hating, they're people broken to pieces. There isn't any real person left to help. If the liquor was gone, maybe we could bring things together again."

"We can try," the Superintendent agreed. He rose, at the sound of the ladies saying good-bye to Julián in the other room. "I'll send the Indian police out. We can try."

After the Superintendent and the ladies had gone, Julián got up and left the house without saying good-bye. He did that often now, and María knew what it meant. She got supper for herself and for the children; she put away the remains of the meal and cleaned up the kitchen; and then she said her Rosary and went to bed. There was nothing else for her to do. Julián would come back sometime; when it would be was in God's hands. She hoped God would strengthen the Superintendent's hands, and she closed her eyes and rested, if she did not sleep.

She waited two days for Julián to come home. She had put away his brushes and the other tools he worked with. It was tourist season and so many people came to the house that she gave up trying to work on pottery herself, and spent her time selling the pottery and answering questions. It was a slow, tired two days, and she had a sick husband to put to bed and nurse at the end of it. She asked no questions. Long ago she had learned not to ask questions.

There was a knock at the door late in the third afternoon, and when María opened, in answer to it, the man who stood facing her was not a tourist but an Indian. He wore high-heeled cowboy boots, and there was a gold star pinned to the front of his dark blue flannel shirt.

"María Martínez?" he asked.

"Yes."

The Breach in the Wall

"I'd like to talk to your husband."

"Are you going to arrest him?"

"No," said the policeman. "I got to talk to him, though."

Julián was up out of bed. He had seated himself in his usual work place by the window, with his paints and brushes and an *olla* before him on the table, but he was not painting and he still looked sick and shaky. The policeman stood beside him, and though he was not a tall man, the newcomer seemed to touch the ceiling, he was so angry and so sure in his anger.

"Where did you get it?" he asked in Spanish.

Julián looked up at him, sidewise. "You Apache?" he asked.

"Jicarilla," the policeman informed him. "I'm asking you. Where did you get it?"

"I can't tell you," said Julián.

"You mean you won't."

"I mean I don't know."

"You mean you don't want to know."

"I mean I've forgotten."

The policeman turned to María. "I guess you'll have to tell me," he said.

"I don't know which place," María answered him. "When he goes out like that, he goes alone. There are lots of places. Why don't you arrest them all, all those men?"

"I got to have evidence," the policeman answered stolidly.

"What's evidence?"

"I got to see him buy it, or he's got to go to court and swear they sold it to him."

"Does it have to be him?" María asked fearfully. A court was a strange place and a bad place to her.

"Well," answered the policeman, "it's easy with him. He's been drinking. You can tell that to look at him or smell him. If he swears to me who sold it to him, I can arrest the man. Then he can swear again in court, and we can lock that man up."

"I don't remember," said Julián stubbornly.

"I can tell you names," offered María.

"You do that, then," said the policeman. "Then I'll watch them."

María told him three names. Then she stopped. There was another name; there was Spanish Pete's. Pete had lived in the village a long time. His was one of the oldest Spanish families there. He was a neighbor. He made wine for his own use, and he gave some to his friends. He did not often sell it, as far as she knew. She did not want to make trouble for Pete and his wife.

"That's all," she said.

The policeman was watching her closely. "You know more," he told her.

"That's all," María repeated, stubborn as Julián.

"I'll watch those, then," said the policeman. "If there are any more, I'll find out about them, too. You'd better tell me. It makes things easier."

"That's all," María said. Her mouth closed.

"Good-bye," said the policeman. "If you have more trouble, you'll have made it for yourself, remember."

When he had gone, Julián looked up at María. "You didn't tell him about Pete," he said. "Why?"

"I'll talk to Pete," María said. "You and the boys and Clara can get supper. I'll be back after while."

She went into the bedroom and closed the door. She took down the picture of San José from the wall, and, with the point of her sewing scissors, dug out the adobe behind it. When she had opened the *nicho* she had made there long before, she took out the two big rolls of bills that she had hidden in the wall. Then she dressed herself carefully in her best clothes and put the money, tied in a handkerchief, in the front of her dress. She drew her shawl over her head and went out without speaking to anyone, walking carefully so as not to soil her high white moccasins. Julián looked up as she passed through the room where he sat. His eyes followed her to the door, but neither he nor María spoke.

All the way to Pete's house, María was telling herself that she should plan what she was going to say. She could not do it. Words would not come into her head; she knew only what she was going to do, and she trusted that words would be sent to her when she was ready for them.

Pete's wife opened the door for her. "Come in," she said.

María followed the Spanish woman into her house, and when her hostess gestured to a chair, she sat down.

"Will it rain?" Pete's wife asked.

"I don't know," María replied. "When things are bad, the rain is bad, too. Sometimes it doesn't come."

"Are things bad?" asked the Spanish woman.

"Very bad," María replied. "Is Pete here?"

The Breach in the Wall

"He's out feeding the horses. He'll be here in a minute. Will you wait?"

"I'll wait," said María. She sat with her feet squarely on the floor in front of her, looking at her hands that rested in her lap. It seemed a long time until the door opened and Pete came in.

"Hello," he said.

"Hello," said María.

"Will it rain?" Pete asked, as his wife had.

"I don't know," María answered again. Then she said. "I need to talk to you."

"All right," said Pete, sitting down in a chair by the table. "What is it?"

"We've all been neighbors a long time," María said. "We've got along all right. We don't want trouble with our neighbors."

"Nobody wants that kind of trouble," said Pete's wife.

"That's why I came here," said María. "You don't want trouble. I don't want trouble. I want to fix up all this trouble we had, and make things whole again if I can." She pulled the package of bills out of the front of her dress and held it in her hands, unwrapping it slowly. "I want to buy your house, Pete."

"This house?" Pete asked.

"I want to buy this house," María reiterated.

"I don't want to sell," said Pete. "I like it here. My family always lived here. I don't want to go."

"Pete," María told him, "you got to go. You can't stay here any more. This is enough of things. There's too much drinking. I always have tried to be a good neighbor. I want to keep on that way. I'll buy your house. How much do you want?"

"A thousand dollars," said Pete defiantly. "You pay me a thousand dollars now, this minute, and I'll move."

María drew a deep breath. She had enough money; for a moment she had been afraid that he would want more than she had with her. She took one of the rolls of bills from her lap and held the bundle out to him.

"You count it," she said. "Your wife can watch."

Slowly, one at a time, Pete and his wife laid the bills down on the kitchen table. There were ten of them, ten one-hundred-dollar bills.

"There," said María. "That's yours, that money. Now you can go, tomorrow morning."

Going back to her own house, María moved slowly. There was a light in the kitchen window, where Clara was probably washing the dishes. There was a government car standing by the kitchen door. She wondered if the policeman had come back to question Julián when she was not there. But it was the Superintendent who was waiting for her when she opened the door. He stood up and held out his hand.

"Hello," he said. "I came to ask you if you would teach a pottery class at the Indian school this summer. Julián said you had gone out."

María took off her shawl and folded it over the back of a kitchen chair. Her hands surprised her by not shaking.

"Yes," she said. "I went out. There was a farm for sale, and I went to buy it. The boys are growing up, and we have to look out for them."

29. Growing Away
(1934–1939

Through all the changes in the pueblo and all the changes in the world outside, the one thing that did not change was María's love for her children. All four of them who had lived were boys, and when she thought about it, she was glad that they were. She wondered if a mother would not have to love differently to love girls. It made things simple and uncomplicated to do your loving all in one single way.

Adam was a good deal older than the other three. Tomás, his grandfather, had died when Adam was a little boy, and sometimes María wondered if her father's spirit had not come back to this son who was a good farmer and a good man; who wanted to live in the pueblo in a plain, old-timey sort of way.

Adam was a grown man and married, while the others were still youngsters. He stood beside María, and together they watched the younger boys diving into the irrigation ditch like three round, brown, spraddle-legged frogs, and they laughed together. No one, in these later days, was as companionable for María as Adam. She could trust him to help with business as well as with farming, in a way that she could not trust his father. More and more, as time went on, she consulted with Adam about the younger boys.

"What do you want them to be?" he asked her, and María answered, "Good men and good farmers, like my father."

"Not rich artists?"

"No," María replied. "Getting rich is all right in some ways. It helps make the children strong, if you can buy a cow and give them milk to drink. And they look better if they wear good clothes. When you have money, you can hire men to build up the ditches and keep the water going right and save the fields. You can help out people who are unlucky, if you have money. All those things are good. But there are other things that money buys that aren't good. It looks as if you couldn't have the good things without getting some of the bad ones, too."

"They go together," Adam said.

A little at a time Adam became the man of the family. He was the one who was there, the person you knew where to find. Sometimes, now, Julián was gone for many days at a time, and María would not know where he was. Since Spanish Pete had left the pueblo and the policemen had arrested some of the men who kept *cantinas* near by, Julián had to go farther and farther away to get liquor. At first it worried María; then she began to get used to it. She was alone in her life, as Reyes had warned her that she might be. There was nobody to help her but God and the Saints, until They sent her Adam.

In the year when two of the boys were in the Indian School at Santa Fé, one of them starting and the other finishing, the Superintendent made a suggestion that surprised María.

"I think you ought to send Juan away to school, María," he said.

"Why?" María asked. "He's finishing high school now, and he's smart and knows a lot. Why should I send him away?"

"There are two reasons," said the Superintendent, setting his finger tips together in a way that he had. "One is that he is smart and knows a lot. He ought to go to college somewhere and learn more."

"To be a teacher?" María inquired.

"Maybe to be a teacher," said the Superintendent, "but maybe to be something else. His skill is in his hands, like yours and Julián's. He can be an artist or an engineer. That's one reason for sending him away."

"What's the other?" María asked.

"The other is that when a boy is getting to be a young man he ought to see the best things going on around him," answered the Superintendent. "If he is at home in the pueblo he will see some ugly things happening, María; you know that. It's better for him to be older before he sees them."

"He can stay with Adam," María offered.

"That won't help," said the Superintendent sternly. "A boy ought to be with his own family, either his parents or his wife, or clear away. Being in his brother's house won't make it any better."

"All right," said María. "I know. Is there a college?"

"I'll arrange it," said the Superintendent. "I think we can get him a scholarship, so that it won't cost anything but his food and clothes."

"You don't need to do that," said María. "We got money for our boys. Maybe somebody else hasn't. You fix it for those other boys to go free, and we pay for him. We do it that way."

258

Growing Away

So Juan went away to study engineering, and was gone for most of five years. The people at his college liked him and liked the way he studied. They wrote María good letters about him and about his grades and his work. It was all good, and it made her happy. Juan was coming along.

After the younger boys were both in school in Santa Fé and Juan was working there, María felt herself more alone than she had ever been. Her sisters, except for Clara, who still lived with her and Julián, had their own families. Clara lived a little away from people, even people whom she loved, in a silent world of her own. Julián, too, had his own world, and belonged less and less to other people. Adam's family was growing up, and María loved them, but she did not want to make Adam's world hers. They were all one family and all part of her family, but they were spreading out into the world.

"Aren't you lonely sometimes, María?" the Superintendent asked her once. She had come to Santa Fé to give a pottery demonstration at the school, and he had come to talk with her after her work was finished.

"I'm lonely," María answered, gathering up her polishing stones.

"Fame is a lonely thing," said the Superintendent.

"It's lonely not having your family together," said María suddenly. "If I could have them all with me, it would be different. Even Julián is like gone, nowadays."

"Maybe we could get him to come back," the Superintendent suggested.

"I don't know," said María. "When it's like that, when the liquor gets hold of them, the person you knew is gone. It's a stranger who comes, then. How can you bring back the one you love?"

"Maybe if you took him away somewhere," the Superintendent said. "Just the two of you by yourselves. I have a letter about sending some potters to a world's fair in Chicago. Would you like to go?"

María sat looking at her tools. "Maybe we could," she said. Then she laughed. "Always world's fairs," she said. "When we went on our honeymoon after we were married, it was that St. Louis World's Fair. And when we were inventing the pottery and the ways to make it, it was San Diego World's Fair. Now there's another. How many worlds are there to make so many fairs?"

The Superintendent laughed, too. "Only one world, we all say, but many people in it. All of them can't travel to the fairs, so the fairs have to be brought to them. Would you like to go?"

María

"I don't want to leave home, but if we went, just Julián and I, it might help," said María.

That was the way the traveling began again for them. First there was the Chicago World's Fair. There never was a fair like that one for working and making money! Everything was fixed just right! They even had a room that was shaped like a big milk bottle, with a chimney for a ceiling, so that they could fire pottery indoors. They took in so much money that María was not sure what to do with it all. Once she looked up and saw a lady she knew, who lived in Santa Fé, leaning over the guard rail and watching them work. María was so glad to see a friend that she put down the jar she was making and shook hands without wiping the clay from her fingers. The two women had a long talk, and as they were saying good-bye, an idea came to María.

"Wait," she said. "Please, will you do something for me?"

"If I can," said the lady.

María went back to her work table and took up the sack of money that lay there—all the money they had earned in four months at the fair. She had kept it herself, and she had never told Julián how much there was. He had had no chance to spend any of it.

"Send this to Adam, please," María said. "He can take care of it and use it for the farm."

"But, María," the lady protested, "you can't do this. You can't just give your money away like this."

"No, no," María said, "I'm not giving it away. You send it to Adam, please."

And a week later a letter came from Adam, saying that he had the money and was putting it away in the bank.

There were potters from all over the world at Chicago. They made pottery in all the different ways of their different countries and fired their wares in a big electric kiln so that the pottery would be hard and good. One of the men who took care of the kiln wanted María to fire her pottery there like the others.

"I think we ought to," Julián said, his eyes gleaming as they used to when he was a young man. "I'd like to know what would happen to it in that machine."

María thought for a while. Julián loved experiments, and she had made this trip as an experiment of her own, to see if she could bring him back to himself and to her. There were good reasons for trying the electric firing. Then she shook her head.

"No," she said, "I guess not. If the Superintendent found out about it, his feelings would be hurt. He says Indian pottery is for Indians, and it's got to be made the Indian way. That would be wrong, when he sent us here to show how to make Indian pottery. We couldn't do that."

"I guess not," Julián slowly agreed.

Yes, Chicago was good. They were together and they stayed together, and they did things in company. There was no drinking. It was a good life, and it seemed right for both of them.

It was best to be at home, though, when the long months were over. Their own house felt right and good around them, like a house where a family lives.

"It worked for him," María told the Superintendent when he came to see them. "He's like himself again."

"Good," said the Superintendent. "Four months is a long time, too. If you can keep him going right for a year, it may all be over, María."

"Maybe we ought to go away again," María said thoughtfully.

"That's what I came to see you about," the Superintendent answered. "I've been asked to take a group of Indian artists east, to Washington, D. C., and then on down to Atlanta where the commissioner used to live. About eight people, I think. Will you go?"

"I don't know," María said. "It's good to be here at home again." She looked out of the window. Two of Adam's little boys were diving into the irrigation ditch and were splashing happily in the chilly September water. "Brown frogs," said María, watching them. "My own boys used to do that. I'd miss seeing these grow if we went away too much."

"But going away is helping Julián grow, you know," the Superintendent pointed out. "You have to think about his growing, too."

"Yes," said María. "I've got him to think about. All right. We'll go."

The first night out on the trip, they stopped in Texas. As they were traveling in government cars, they could take their time and see everything. Julián got up early in the morning, and when María dressed and went out to find him, he was sitting on the ground by a flower bed in front of their tourist cabin. He had picked up a handful of earth from the flower bed, and he was working the clay with his fingers.

"I believe we could make pottery out of this," he said, showing María the sample.

María took the piece of clay between her fingers and felt it. "I guess so," she said. "Not good pottery, though."

"Maybe not good," said Julián, "but I think it would work."

"We could take some home and try it there," said María. She got a paper sack from their wastebasket, and they put the clay in the bag. Julián drew a star on the sack, because they had heard Texas called the Lone Star State and that would show them where the clay had come from after they got it home.

"We can get clay from every state and try them all," Julián said. "That way we can tell which clay is the best."

More and more Julián was acting like himself. He sang in the car, and he played jokes on everybody. Gathering the clay was no joke to him, though. He got a lot of paper sacks from a grocery after breakfast, and he watched the side of the road as they went along. The driver of the car had to tell him whenever they crossed another state line, so that Julián could look out for clay beds. Then the driver had to stop when they came to a place that looked right, and Julián would get out and scoop up a sackful of clay.

Mr. Roosevelt was not at home when they reached Washington, but Mrs. Roosevelt was, and they all visited at the White House. Mrs. Roosevelt shook hands with everybody and then made them a speech.

Growing Away

She said that Indian art was important to all Americans, that it was priceless and could not be replaced, so they must take care of their crafts and teach them to the coming generations.

"That was a nice speech," said María to Mrs. Roosevelt, when it was finished.

"Thank you," said Mrs. Roosevelt, "I'm glad you liked it. You are one of the important ones. We have a piece of your pottery here in the White House, and we treasure it and show it to visitors from overseas."

"Thank you," María said in her turn, "I'm glad you like our pottery."

They went on to New York then; and María got to see all that Miss Grimes had told her about: the Statue of Liberty, and the Battery, and Fifth Avenue. She sent Miss Grimes a postal card from the Statue of Liberty. She saw things that had been built since Miss Grimes had been in New York: the Empire State Building, and Rockefeller Center, and a new museum that was called the Modern Museum. María wondered why. All the museums looked newer than the houses in the pueblo, so they all had to be modern. Why name just one of them that?

"Do you like this?" asked the Superintendent, "Is it pretty?"

They were standing at the corner called Wall Street, and the buildings went up around them like canyon walls. María did not want to hurt her friend's feelings, but she had to be honest.

"It's all right," she said. "I like better to look at the Black Mesa, though."

By the time they reached Atlanta, they were all tired. There was a message for them there, from Adam. "Come home now," said the telegram. "There is business about the land and fixing the ditches. We need all the men. Father must come home." It was the best news that María could have had.

On the trip home, they still got out of the car sometimes and gathered up sacks of earth, but Julián was not thinking as much about his experiment as he had been before. He was thinking and talking about the land and the ditches and what ought to be done for them. María had never heard him talk so much about those matters before. It was wonderful for her, as wonderful as the news that the pueblo wanted and needed him to help settle things.

She left the business of the land and the ditches for the men to decide, because she found out when she got home that Juan wanted

263

to get married. He wanted a church wedding, and they had it, but there was no Indian wedding to go with it. María was disappointed about that. She had the younger boys sent home from school for the celebration, and she did not like having them disappointed.

"Remember," she told them seriously, "most people only get married one time. You ought to do it just right, and be sure you have permission for it from your parents."

"That's right," said Adam seriously. "You ought to get permission from them, and do everything the way it's supposed to be."

After the wedding was over, María began making pottery out of the different kinds of clay they had brought home with them. She put each piece down on its sack, in order that the different ones would not get mixed up, and in his spare time Julián painted the state designs on the little bowls she made. Some of the clay was good and easy to work with, but some of it was bad and the bowls turned out funny-looking.

"Let's give these to the Superintendent for Christmas, to show him how much we enjoyed the trip," suggested María.

"Good," said Julián, and later, when the time came, they gave the Superintendent the bowls. He promised to treasure them until he died, and then give them to a museum.

"Which place did you like best, María?" he asked, admiring the bowls.

"Tennessee," María answered promptly. "It has the best clay."

Now that she was at home, María knew that she was tired. Julián was like himself, busy about the land and the ditches and his painting. She could sit still and rest, making pottery, and watch the children grow again. She was home to stay.

And then, the first thing she knew, Julián went away for four days, right after all the land business was settled. When he came back, María asked no questions; she said nothing. It had happened again, another one of those bad accidents. It seemed as if she had to keep him traveling, to keep him living and acting right. All the bad things were beginning again, and they were worse because Julián was older. A young man could fight poison with his body, but an older man's body was not strong enough to fight.

But when the invitation came to go to San Francisco for another world's fair, María hung back. She felt safer within herself at home. It was better here, in spite of everything. Then she thought about Julián.

Growing Away

"I guess we'll go," she said to the young woman who had come from the Indian Agency to talk with her about it. "We won't have to stay long, will we?"

"Just a month," the young woman answered.

María had seen the ocean when they went to San Diego, and another ocean when they were in New York. It had always seemed wasteful to her, to have so much water in one place when it was needed everywhere, but it had not worried her. In San Francisco they lived on one island and worked on another, and there was water all around them all the time. The ocean bothered her now, when she knew she could not get away from it.

They had come to San Francisco on the train, but María decided that she did not want to go back that way. She wrote home to Tony and asked him to bring the new station wagon that Julián had ordered before they left, to drive them home. That would be better. They would be together and be a family, that way. Perhaps they could stop and get clay from different states as they went along.

It was a joy to her to look up from her work and to see Tony standing by the railing. There was an Indian girl beside him, a girl from San Juan Pueblo, whose parents María knew. She was smiling and holding out her hand. María wondered how the girl got there.

"Mother," Tony said, laying his hand on the girl's arm, "meet my wife." He sounded glad and excited.

There were people all around watching them, as María got to her feet. She stooped under the rail, and took the girl's hand in her own, and led her away. She knew she was not crying, but there was a mist before her eyes so that she could not see. When her vision cleared, she and the two children and Julián were in their room on the island, and she herself was saying aloud, "We've got to go home. We've got to go home. We should always have stayed where we were, in our own place."

Julián was asking questions about the wedding, and how the girl's parents were, and what the trip to San Francisco had been like, but María hardly heard him.

"We've got to go home," she was saying to herself. "We've got to go home. Everything bad comes from going away. Now my boy's got married, and I wasn't even there. That's the worst thing. We've got to go home."

Now Julián and Tony were beginning to plan the trip back; when they could start and how long they could travel each day. María let them plan. How they traveled did not matter. She knew only that they had to go home. She shook her head a little, to try to clear her mind so that she could think; and then she saw the girl, sitting little and alone and quiet beside her while the two men made their plans. María put her hand on her new daughter-in-law's arm.

"It's all right," she said. "We have room for you in our house. There's enough for everybody, till you get your own house built. But we have to talk to your parents and bring the families together. That's all. Everything will be all right, and we'll all be happy. But we've got to start home tomorrow morning."

30. The Governor
(1940

The governor of the pueblo was an important man because he was the one who met and talked to and worked with strangers. He stood between the people of the pueblo and the people outside it in business ways. Some governors were men who held other positions, in the religious life of the pueblo, perhaps. They were more important for being themselves than for being governors. Other governors were chosen because they had white friends and were used to being around white people, so they were right for that kind of job.

Julián knew many white people, and most of those whom he knew were his good friends. They liked him and he liked them. That was a good reason for his being made governor. Even so, María was surprised when he was chosen. In her father's time, or in the days when she was a young woman, a man who had any bad habits at all could never have been the governor. It seemed to be a good thing to have happened to Julián, at that. He was conscious of his responsibility and proud of it. He hung the gold-headed cane that President Abraham Lincoln had given the governor of San Ildefonso as a badge of office back in Civil War times on the wall of the salesroom. People could see it as soon as they came through the door. No stranger could doubt that he was in the house of the governor, when he came in and saw that cane hanging there.

Now the salesroom was more than a store. The Indians still came there to buy "pop" and kerosene and groceries and tobacco, and the white people came there to buy pottery, but many other things went on in that same room besides the buying and selling.

Julián sat at his table by the window, facing the outside door. He could see people who were coming to the house, and he could see them as soon as they came into the room. If they were Indians coming on official business, Julián would lay down his paint brush while they told him why they were there. Then he would pull his glasses down on his nose and look over them while he said what he thought. These glasses a white artist friend had given him in San Francisco, and they were not very strong, but Julián felt comfortable and like an official artist when he was wearing them.

After he had given his opinion, Julián would open the drawer of his work table, and give all the Indians cigarettes. He seldom smoked himself, but he always had lots of cigarettes around. White people who came to the house gave him the tobacco. Julián would smoke a cigarette to be friendly, and then put the rest of the package away until he needed it for his friends.

It was not an easy time to be governor. There was fighting going on in some parts of the world, and that seemed to mean that there was a lot of talking about it for the government to do. María remembered the last war, and how sick some of the men from the pueblo were when they went overseas on ships, and she hoped that nothing like that would happen again. The war talking was bad enough.

A lot of the talking was about hunger. People in the fighting countries had no time to plant, and their fields were being torn up and destroyed. Women and children were going without food and were starving for it. María remembered back to the years before the pottery-making, when sometimes there was not enough food for everybody in the pueblo, and her heart hurt her with thinking about it. She gave a roll of bills to Julián.

"Send this to the people overseas to buy food," she said. "I don't want to think about children not eating."

Julián pulled his glasses down on his nose and looked at her, with his dignified, official, governor's look.

"Which people?" he asked.

"I don't care," María said. "Anybody that's hungry. They all need it over there."

"All right," Julián said, "I guess we'll send it to the Chinese. They look like Indians."

"Some people say the Indians were Chinese once," María added. "Yes, send it to them."

Julián sent the money by the next government worker who came to the pueblo, and after a while they got a letter from the United China Relief Association, acknowledging their contribution. It was a fine letter, with beautiful Chinese designs all around the edges. María put the letter away and saved it carefully.

One day the new superintendent came to see Julián. Because it was official business with the governor, María shut the door of the salesroom. She told one of Adam's little boys to sit in front of the house, and to tell any visitors that they were to go to the kitchen door if they wanted to buy pottery. Nobody came, and it was a long, slow, quiet afternoon, with the sound of the men's voices, heavy and tired and anxious, coming to her without words, from the other room. Late in the afternoon, Julián came out in the kitchen.

"I've asked him to stay for supper," he said, jerking his head towards the door of the salesroom. "He's got to see the council afterwards."

There was no time for María and Clara to cook a special supper, so they served what they had in the house. The new superintendent ate beans and *tortillas* with them, and afterwards thanked them for the food. The members of the council began to gather before the meal was over—tired men, coming quietly out of their fields into the big salesroom, and sitting quietly there until the Governor was ready to meet with them. As soon as Julián and the Superintendent had finished eating, Julián led the way into the council meeting. The door of the room was closed behind them.

"What is it?" Clara whispered, and María shook her head.

"I don't know," she said, forming the words with her lips so Clara could see them. There was nobody there to hear her if she spoke aloud. The two women sat down and polished pottery while they waited for the meeting to end. It was late when María heard the door open and the Superintendent's car drive away. Still she waited, while the men of the council said good-bye and left. Then the door opened, and Julián came out into the kitchen. His face looked as if it had been carved out of pottery clay, it was so sharp and still.

"What is it?" María asked in her turn.

"It's the war," said Julián. He walked over to the water bucket and filled a dipper. Stillness hung in the room and filled its air while he drank. "The war is coming soon," he said, and set the dipper down with a little clink against the side of the bucket.

"Here?" María asked.

"Maybe not here, but it is coming to us," Julián said. "We have to send our young men to it. They are having a draft. All the men under sixty have to sign up. Then, if they're called, they have to go."

"Only if they're called?"

"They can go without calling if they want to," Julián said. "They can volunteer, if they want to have it that way."

"Nobody is excused?" María asked. Four of them, she thought. Four sons, and none of them is forty. They will all have to sign up.

"Some of them may be excused," said Julián. "If they're sick, or if they're needed for farming, or maybe if they have big families, the government will excuse them. But they have to sign up anyway, so they can be counted. The government has to know how many men there are of the right age."

"If they're going to excuse them, why bother about counting them?" demanded María.

"They may need them later," replied Julián. "I'm going to bed."

When she lay still in the dark, María understood what he meant. The first ones may be killed, her mind said. Then they will need all the others. She could not believe it. She did not. Nobody from San Ildefonso was going to be killed. All of her boys would be excused. Adam was a farmer, and Juan had a family, and Tony's wife was going to have a baby soon; no, the only one that could be taken was Felipe. And he was still too young. They would never take him.

In the morning, she tried to find words to speak to Julián about the boys. But Julián had put on his glasses as soon as he got up, even before he put on his shirt, and whenever she started to speak to him, he pulled the glasses down his nose, and looked at her above them. She could not find words that would get past that glass barrier to his ears, no matter how hard she tried. All day, without speaking, she tried to think of words to say.

Julián had the registration desk set up in the salesroom. He sat by the window, with the gold-headed cane resting on his table, instead of a bowl or a jar, and an American flag hanging on the wall facing the door. The young men came in to be signed up. There was a young woman there from the government, to write out the registration cards, and it was very frightening to María to hear the woman's voice through the kitchen door. "Name?" she would ask. And, "Age?" And then, "Occupation?" All these questions being asked in her own house of boys María had known all their lives.

The men in the pueblo were all signed up within the first two days, and then those who had been away from home began coming in. Felipe was one of the last of these. He came home from school at Santa Fé on Saturday, and María did not know he was there until she heard the government woman ask, "Name?" And Felipe's voice as he answered, "Philip Martínez."

The salesroom was a government place now, and María knew she should not go in from the kitchen. Instead, she got her shawl and went around to the front of the house. There she waited, outside, until Felipe finished and came out. She knew that he would use this door and not go out the wrong way, through the kitchen. When she saw him, María tried to smile.

"Is it over?" she asked. "Did you get signed up?"

"It's all right," her son answered. "They registered me."

"Are you home to stay?" inquired María.

"Till tomorrow night," said Felipe. "I have to go back on the school bus then. They were sending a lot of the boys home to register —Santa Claras and San Juans and Taos boys—and I came, too. We all go back on the bus tomorrow night.

"Oh," said María. "Come and have some coffee. Clara made *biscochitos* this morning."

Clara smiled at Felipe and set the coffee and the little cakes before him without speaking. With those whom she knew and loved, Clara seldom needed to speak.

"Why did you do it?" María asked.

"I wanted to," Felipe answered. "All the boys I know are being registered."

271

"They're older than you."

"They aren't as big," said Felipe, grinning. "You fed us right when we were little boys. I look as grown up as any of them."

"You've got to wait. You're too young," María reiterated.

"I'm volunteering," the boy said. "I might just as well. I don't see any sense in waiting."

"No!" María said. Suddenly she was angry. "No! That isn't right. If you wait, you may never have to go. All the fighting may be over before you're old enough."

"I've got to have your permission, and Father's," Felipe said. "Why don't you want to give it? I'm young and strong and healthy. Why shouldn't I go? I think I might like to go, anyway. I'd get to see a lot of new countries."

"You'd get to see a lot of trouble and suffering," María said. "No, you shouldn't go. I won't give you permission. You'll have to wait."

"I don't want to wait," Felipe said. He set his jaw sullenly. "I want to go now and get started."

"You'll have to get the Governor's permission for that," María said.

"I'll go and get it," Felipe answered, standing up.

"And I'll talk to the Governor, too," María told him. She wrapped her shawl around her, and marched squarely across the floor to the outside door of the kitchen. Clara stood back against the wall, watching, her face drawn and twisted with worry and not understanding.

At the door of the salesroom, María stood back. "You can go first and do your talking," she said. "Then it will be my turn."

"I will," Felipe answered, and he walked stiffly ahead of her into the salesroom. The government woman had gone home now that her work was finished, and Julián was alone. Felipe stood for a minute and looked at the flag on the wall, and then he turned to face the Governor.

"What do you want?" Julián asked. "You've already signed up."

"I want your permission to volunteer," replied Felipe.

"Why?" Julián demanded. "You know you're too young. You told the woman how old you were."

"I don't want to wait," said Felipe. "I'm young and strong. I want to go ahead."

"Do you want to fight?" Julián asked him.

"Not specially," said Felipe, "but if anybody's going to, I can. I don't farm and I haven't got a family. I'm the kind that ought to be doing the fighting."

The Governor

"That's right for the ones older than you," Julián agreed. "But any-way there isn't any fighting yet, you know. Just drilling. There may not be any fighting."

"I don't like the government school," said Felipe. "I don't seem to get much out of it anyway. And drilling is a kind of studying. Why can't I go to army school that way?"

"Maybe you can," said the Governor. He looked at María. "Why are you here?" he asked her. His hand rested for a minute on the gold head of his cane.

"I came to ask you not to let my son volunteer," said María.

"Why?" Julián demanded of her, as he had of Felipe.

"I don't want him to go," María said. "Fighting is bad any time. It hurts the ones that are fighting, and it hurts the ones that love them. My son is young. He's just starting out. He doesn't know much about life. He should finish school and maybe go to college like his brother. Then he will have learned a little about living."

"Schools can teach some things, and living with people can teach others," Julián said slowly. "Nobody can say which things are more important. Maybe what he learns from living will teach him most."

"Then let him stay here and learn it," María said. "Let him learn it from living with his own people, not from strangers."

"Listen," Julián told her, "when you were a young woman and I was a young man, things were different. The pueblo was our world. It was all we knew, and it was good. But still you wanted to go away and learn to be a teacher. I wanted to go away and dance and sing. We had a whole pueblo, then. It was inside itself, and we were inside its walls. It shut out everything else. When we went away, we wanted to come back. We had learned about some of the things outside, like cooking stoves, and like drinking, and we wanted to bring them back with us. You say cooking stoves are good and drinking is bad, and I guess you're right. We don't always know. If your son wants to learn, he will have to do it his own way and our own way. You can't carry him on your back like a baby all his life. He's registered as one of those willing to volunteer. You'll have to wait till he's called for that. He's too young, of course. The government won't take him now. He'll have to go back to school until they think he's ready. When they say he is, will be time for you to give your permission."

"Suppose he gets killed?" cried María. "Suppose he gets hurt, with none of his own people there to help him?"

"That's the risk he takes," said Julián. "You take that risk every

273

time you go to Santa Fé; that same risk, whenever you cross the street, and there are cars. But you still go to Santa Fé."

"That's different," María said stubbornly.

"It's different," Julián agreed. "Fighting is for men, and going shopping is for women. This is men's business, and we'll have to decide it men's way." He turned to Felipe. "You have my permission," he said. "You can volunteer when the time comes." He got up and crossed the room and hung up his cane on the wall beside the flag. He came and laid his hand on María's shoulder for a moment. "Let's go out in the kitchen and have a cup of coffee," Julián said.

31. The Parting
(1943

The war times were strange and hard for María. First Felipe volunteered; and then Tony was called, in spite of his having a family. Juan was in the army engineers, making plans for buildings and bridges and camps. The only one left at home was Adam, and the house seemed very empty with all the others gone.

María seldom went to the pueblo in these days, and when she did, it was only briefly, to see her sisters. Ana and Desidéria were left to her, for Juanita had died two years after their mother. It was as if they all came together now that things troubled them. Sometimes María thought that she could hear her mother speaking in something that one or another of the sisters said; sometimes she seemed to hear her father's voice in words that Julián spoke.

Yet Julián seemed as far away from her as the boys were. He had finished his term as governor, and had given the cane and the flag to the one who succeeded him. He still painted pottery; he still painted pictures. Like all of the people, he waited. Every morning they waited till the mail man came, to know what the news was from their boys. After the mail had been read, they felt relieved, and they ate dinner. Then the waiting started in again, getting stronger and stronger until the end of the next morning.

Julián was not well. His hands were shaky sometimes, and he said that his head ached. María took him down to the schoolhouse to see the government doctor, who examined him.

"It isn't anything serious," the doctor reassured her. "He isn't a young man, and he never has taken care of himself. Time wears out bodies, especially when we don't try to build them back. Take as good care of him as you can, and don't let him drink if you can help it. That's all anyone can do."

María did what she could, but it was not easy to do anything. If he were with her, Julián seemed to be all right. Sometimes he would suddenly go out of the house, without saying anything. Then María would go after him if she could, or would send Clara to get Adam to bring his father home. Adam would bring Julián back, when he found him. They would put Julián to bed and would wait for him to get back to himself again.

It was bad, all bad—all a part of the bad times around them. The world was sick and Julián was sick. There was no cure for either of them.

The winter came, and that was a cold winter. There was ice on the water in the ditches early in October, and soon after that the first snow fell. All of the hay was not in, nor had the fall gardens been gathered, and everything froze. The *ristras* of chile froze to solid red icicles, hanging against the house walls. When the peppers were pulled away from the adobe, they left stains like blood. Blood on the ground overseas and blood on the house walls at home. It was all bad. Red was not a cheerful color any more.

It was on a cold, still, snowy morning that María realized how quiet the whole house was. Julián usually whistled softly when he worked. She looked into the salesroom and saw that he was not there. She put on her shawl, and herself went to get Adam. All that day they looked for Julián. He was nowhere to be found. He had gone.

The Parting

Adam went to the places where Julián most often stayed when he was away from home, but there was no trace of him anywhere. They asked everybody they knew, but no one had seen Julián. It seemed as if he must have flown away.

María never knew how many times she wakened in the next four nights; she never surely knew whether she slept at all. Julián was gone, and when her voice was not calling him, her mind and her heart were. Then, on the fourth night, without her willing it, her calling stopped. She fell into a deep sleep, and it was broad daylight when at last she awakened. There were footsteps and voices outside the door. She went to see who was there. Adam came in pulling off his cap.

"They found him, up on the hill," he said. "Two young boys found him, just lying there. We're going to take the wagon and go back for him. Don't worry and don't cry. It's better this way."

María did not want to cry. There were no tears in her for Julián. They had been together and had worked together for a long time. Now there was an ending. All things in life changed and ended in their own times; and lives were like all other things. She saw Adam go away with the wagon, and she saw her sisters and her daughters-in-law come into the room; and she saw all the women weep. She let them cry around her. Crying was not for her.

"How can you stand it, Mother?" Adam's wife asked her once during that day, and María said, "I have to stand it. I'm strong here, in my heart, and God and the Saints will help me stand it. That's all."

When the wagon came, bringing Julián's body, she went out to see him and to say good-bye before he was taken away, even though it was not a usual thing for a wife to do. The sickness and the trouble were gone from Julián's face, and he looked young again. María was glad of that, and she was glad to see his face once more, as she best remembered it. That was a good way for things to end. He had come to the end of his furrow and he had let go the plow-handles. In her time she would do the same thing.

It was an old-time funeral. Late that afternoon men who knew the family well but were not related to any of its members took Julián away to the hills. María would never know just where they put him. His clothes and paints and brushes—all the things he had finished with when he finished with his life—the men took away, too. They would throw those things into the river where the stream ran deepest. No one else would need or could use those things.

The Parting

Then, after Julián and whatever he might later need to use where he had gone had left the house, the family had a feast for all the pueblo. Everybody came, and they all ate and wept, and María moved among them. This feast was given to comfort her and to keep her from feeling lonely, but she found that she was the one who was comforting the others.

When the next morning came, María heard the church bell greeting the daylight. All the family went down the hill to Mass. Most of their friends went to the church with them. The priest spoke kindly to María, after the service was over.

"I don't think he suffered," the father said.

"I don't think he did," María answered. "His heart was tired, and now it won't be tired any more. It's a good thing for him to rest. Good for him and good for everybody."

She went home with Clara, then. Her house was quiet and clean, for some of the women had stayed away from Mass to have it so. Then they had gone away to their own homes.

"What shall we do now?" Clara whispered.

María was moving mechanically about the kitchen. There was a pot of coffee ready on the stove, and she found some fresh *tortillas* in the cupboard. She put the food on the table, and the two women sat down and ate their meal alone.

"What shall we do now?" Clara whispered again.

María raised her head. She heard a whishing of tires on the gravel outside the house.

"I'm going to sell pottery," she said. "People are coming here to buy it, and they expect me to sell. All my life, since I was a little girl, I've been selling things. I'm going to keep on living, so I'll have to keep on living that kind of life. I'm used to it."

She pulled off her apron and smoothed her hair, before she went out to meet the first of the day's customers.

Appendices

Table of Pottery
(as illustrated

The word "underbody" as used in descriptions of the pottery means the base or lower portion of the bowl or jar, below the design band.

PAGE

9 San Ildefonso tinaja
Signed "Marie and Julian," ca. 1934
Black on black
Height: 9¾ inches
Width: 10¼ inches
Coll. Laboratory of Anthropology, P.W.O.A.P. 10

23 San Ildefonso meal bowl
Attributed to Nicolasa Peña
Black and red on cream slip with red underbody
Height: 8½ inches
Width: 13¼ inches
Coll. American Museum of Natural History, 50.1/3518

42 San Ildefonso utility jug
Micaceous clay, with two bands of applied decoration;
fire-smudged
Height: 9⅛ inches
Width: 6½ inches
Coll. American Museum of Natural History, 50.1/3824

55 San Ildefonso utility bowl
Micaceous clay, with applied decoration; fire-smudged
Height: 7 inches
Width: 7⅞ inches
Coll. American Museum of Natural History, T/22847

283

PAGE

62 San Ildefonso storage olla, ca. 1840
Black on cream slip with red underbody
Height: 13½ inches
Width: 15¾ inches
Coll. Margaret Schoonover, Nambé, New Mexico

75 San Ildefonso tinaja, early commercial work, 1909
Made by María, painted by Maximiliana (Ana)
Black on cream slip, with two reds on underbody
Height: 9⅜ inches
Width: 10½ inches
Coll. Margaret Schoonover, Nambé, New Mexico

86 San Ildefonso storage olla
Black on cream slip with red underbody
Height: 17 inches
Width: 19¾ inches
Coll. American Museum of Natural History, 50.1/3272

105 San Ildefonso water jar
Made by Julián and María, ca. 1915
Black and red on cream slip with red underbody
Height: 6¾ inches
Width: 7½ inches
Coll. Laboratory of Anthropology, 10, 2886

114 Tesuque double-necked water jar, similar to the wedding jar
of San Ildefonso
Black on cream slip with red underbody
Height: 8⅝ inches
Width: 7¼ inches
Coll. American Museum of Natural History, 50.1/3528

121 San Ildefonso seed bowl
Made by María and Julián, ca. 1915
Black and red on cream slip with red underbody
Height: 5¼ inches
Width: 7 inches
Coll. Laboratory of Anthropology, 10, 2885

Table of Pottery

PAGE

137 San Ildefonso plaque
      Signed "Poh 've 'ka" (María's Indian name), ca. 1925
      Black and red on cream slip
      Diameter: 7 9/16 inches
      Coll. American Museum of Natural History, 50.2/1532

162 San Ildefonso tinaja
      Made by María and Julián, ca. 1927
      Black and red on cream slip with red underbody
      Height: 11½ inches
      Width: 12½ inches
      Coll. Mrs. María Martínez

178 San Ildefonso seed bowl
      Signed "Marie"; made in 1923
      Black and red on cream slip, with red underbody
      Height: 4½ inches
      Width: 8⅞ inches
      Coll. Laboratory of Anthropology, Indian Arts Fund 2349

185 San Ildefonso tinaja
      Signed "Marie"; made in 1926
      Black and red on cream slip with red underbody
      Height: 9½ inches
      Width: 13 inches
      Coll. Laboratory of Anthropology, Indian Arts Fund 653

191 San Ildefonso food bowl
      Made by María and Julián, ca. 1925
      Black and red on cream slip with red underbody
      Height: 3 inches
      Width: 9½ inches
      Coll. American Museum of Natural History, 50.2/1530

199 San Ildefonso storage olla
      Signed "Marie, San Ildefonso, N. M."; made by María and
          Julián in 1928
      Black and red on cream slip with red underbody
      Height: 15¾ inches

Width: 19 inches
Coll. Laboratory of Anthropology, Indian Arts Fund 1166

206 San Ildefonso food bowl
Signed "Marie"; made ca. 1925
Black and red on cream slip with red underbody
Height: 2⅝ inches
Width: 7 inches
Coll. Laboratory of Anthropology, Indian Arts Fund 2347

215 San Ildefonso yeast bowl
Signed "Marie"
Black on red slip
Height: 5⅜ inches
Width: 9⅞ inches
Coll. American Museum of Natural History, 50.2/4133

219 San Ildefonso tinaja
Made by María and Julián, ca. 1919
Black on black (this is the first known attempt at this style)
Height: 9 3/16 inches
Width: 12¾ inches
Coll. Museum of New Mexico, B1-40–N/39

231 San Ildefonso bowl
Signed "Marie and Julian"
Black on black
Height: 5¼ inches
Width: 7¼ inches
Coll. Te-Ata (Mrs. Clyde Fisher), New York City

244 San Ildefonso tinaja
Signed "Marie and Julian"; made ca. 1929
Black on black
Height: 11 11/16 inches
Width: 10⅞ inches
Coll. Laboratory of Anthropology, Indian Arts Fund 1316

255 San Ildefonso bowl
Signed "Marie"; made ca. 1934

PAGE

    Black on black
    Height: 6½ inches
    Width: 8¾ inches
    Coll. Laboratory of Anthropology, P. W. A. P. 15

261 San Ildefonso storage olla
    Signed "Marie and Julian"; made in 1942
    Black on black
    Height: 15⅛ inches
    Width: 21¾ inches
    Coll. Jacques Cartier, Pojoaque, New Mexico

270 San Ildefonso storage olla
    Signed "Marie and Julian"; made in 1942
    Black on black
    Height: 15⅛ inches
    Width: 19 inches
    Coll. Jacques Cartier, Pojoaque, New Mexico

276 San Ildefonso bowl
    Signed "Marie"; made ca. 1925
    Black on black
    Height: 6 9/16 inches
    Width: 8⅞ inches
    Coll. Museum of New Mexico, B1-40-1061

Chronology of the Pottery-making of María Martínez

Pre-1908   Pottery-making in San Ildefonso was on a low level. Some women made vessels for home use, or traded their work to Indian and Spanish neighbors. There were few cash sales to outsiders, although some polychrome specimens now in museum collections were acquired during this period. None of them has been identified as María's work.

1908–1912   There was a small-scale development of pottery as a home industry. All known work from this period is polychrome ware. That made by the Martínez family was usually decorated by Julián, although a few pieces have been identified by María as her own painting. The first sale of pottery at the Museum of New Mexico, and the first employment of María as a demonstrator at that museum, under the sponsorship of the late Dr. Edgar L. Hewett, took place during these years. First sales to curio shops.

ca. 1912   Development of plain black pottery at San Ildefonso. Plain black wares were known in the northern Río Grande pueblos at a much earlier date, and it is hardly likely that the invention at San Ildefonso was spontaneous. What probably happened was that María and Julián were the first to develop a plain black ware that was salable to outsiders.

1915   Work at the Panama-California Exposition, San Diego, and perfection of a method of making large vessels. Large storage jars had been fairly common in the pueblos since prehistoric times, but María and Julián had previously concentrated their own efforts on the making of smaller pieces which would be more salable to white purchasers. This was their first encounter with the making of really large pieces.

ca. 1919   Discovery of the method of making black-on-black pottery by Julián. The exact date is hard to fix. María herself says that it happened "between Juan and the little boy who died" (1915–1918). The first recorded sale of a piece of pottery of this type, as published in the Museum of New Mexico bulletin, *El Palacio,* took place in the spring of 1920.

ca. 1919–ca. 1921   Process of making black-on-black pottery kept secret by María and Julián.

1921–1922   Teaching of black-on-black method to other potters in San Ildefonso, and development of pottery-making to a full-time industry of major economic importance to the pueblo as a whole.

ca. 1923–ca. 1926   Beginning of the use of signatures. During this period it is difficult to assign exact dates to pottery specimens, as there were no marked changes in the styles or methods used. According to María's statement, she first signed her own name, afterwards her name with Julián's, to pieces made during this time. Probably not all pieces were signed by either name, as not all museum specimens known to have been bought from María during these years have signatures. One piece, in the collection of the American Museum of Natural History, is signed with María's Indian name. By 1926 the custom of signing the work was well established and had been adopted by other potters working in San Ildefonso and near-by pueblos.

ca. 1925   The split in the pueblo, from an unknown cause, and the construction of the present South Plaza on privately owned land adjacent to the old kiva.

1934   Summer spent at Chicago's Century of Progress Exposition, making and selling pottery; fall spent in travel with representatives of the United States Bureau of Indian Affairs; return to the pueblo in the winter because of the enactment of the Indian Rights Act and Julián's participation in its administration.

1939   Pottery-making at the Golden Gate Exposition, San Francisco.

Bibliography

A bibliography may serve either or both of two purposes. It may list all the printed material available on a given subject, or it may list those titles which the writer of a particular piece of work found useful in dealing with his subject.

So far as a field ethnologist is dealing with his informants' eyewitness accounts of events, he is dealing with primary sources. Written material, whether it confirms or denies the statements which he records, must be of secondary importance to him in the completion of his work. He is concerned above all with making a new source of information available to other workers in his field. He is recording the observations of those who were present at specific events.

The list that follows is therefore not intended to be an exhaustive bibliography of the literature available on the northern Río Grande pueblos, or even of that available on the Pueblo of San Ildefonso. Material from out-of-print publications not available to the general reader has been included because it throws the light of other contemporary eyewitness accounts of the same events on those contained in this book. This factor gives added value to the few accounts made by Anglo observers during the pottery revival and the subsequent development of the pottery industry at San Ildefonso. It is a source of deep regret to the present writer that more such records were not published at the time. It is to be hoped that much material on the subject will appear in print in the near future.

Adair, John. *The Navajo and Pueblo Silversmiths*. Norman, University of Oklahoma Press, 1944.

Bancroft, Henry Howe. *History of Arizona and New Mexico*. San Francisco, Golden West Publishing Company, 1889.

Bandelier, Adolf. *The Delight Makers*. Indianapolis, Dodd, Mead and Company, 1926.

Bolton, Herbert Eugene (ed.). *Spanish Exploration of the Southwest, 1542–1706.* New York, Charles Scribner's Sons, 1916.

Bunzel, Ruth L. *The Pueblo Potter: A Study of Creative Imagination in Primitive Art.* New York, Columbia University Press, 1929.

Chapman, Kenneth M. *Pueblo Indian Pottery of the Post-Spanish Period.* Santa Fé, Laboratory of Anthropology, 1945. Second edition.

Eickmeyer, Carl, and Eickmeyer, Lillian W. *Among the Pueblo Indians.* New York, Merriam and Company, 1895.

Fergusson, Erna. "Paradox of the Pueblo Veteran," *The Southwest Review,* Vol. XXXI, No. 3 (Summer, 1946).

"Fine Exhibit of Pottery," *El Palacio,* Vol. VIII, Nos. 7 and 8 (July, 1920).

Garrard, Lewis H. *Wah-To-Yah and the Taos Trail,* ed. by Stanley Vestal. Oklahoma City, Harlow Publishing Company, ca. 1927.

Colton, Harold S. "The Patayan Problem in the Colorado River Valley," *Southwest Journal of Anthropology,* Vol. I, No. 1 (1945).

Douglas, Frederic H. *Modern Pueblo Pottery Types.* Indian Leaflets Series, Nos. 53 and 54. Denver, The Denver Art Museum, 1933.

——. *Periods of Pueblo Culture and History.* Indian Leaflets Series, No. 17. Denver, The Denver Art Museum, 1930.

——. *Pottery of the Southwestern Tribes.* Indian Leaflets Series, Nos. 69 and 70. Denver, The Denver Art Museum, 1935.

——. *Pueblo Indian Pottery Making.* Indian Leaflets Series, No. 6. Denver, The Denver Art Museum, 1930.

——. *Santa Clara and San Juan Pottery.* Indian Leaflets Series, No. 35. Denver, The Denver Art Museum, 1931.

——. *Southwestern Indian Dwellings.* Indian Leaflets Series, No. 9. Denver, The Denver Art Museum, 1930.

——, and d'Harnoncourt, René. *Indian Art of the United States.* New York, The Museum of Modern Art, 1941.

Gilpin, Laura. *The Pueblos.* New York, Hastings House, 1940.

Goddard, Pliny Earle. *Indians of the Southwest.* New York, The American Museum of Natural History, 1931. Fourth edition.

Guthe, Carl E. *Pueblo Pottery Making: A Study at the Village of San Ildefonso.* New Haven, Yale University Press, 1925.

Halseth, Odd S. "Revival of Pueblo Pottery-making," *El Palacio,* Vol. XXI, No. 6 (September 15, 1926).

Harding, Anne, and Bolling, Patricia. *Bibliography of Articles and*

Bibliography

Papers on North American Indian Art. Washington, United States Department of Interior, 1938.

Harrington, John P. *Ethnogeography of the Tewa Indians. Twenty-ninth Annual Report, 1907–1908*, of the American Bureau of Ethnology. Washington, American Bureau of Ethnology, 1916.

Hawley, Florence M. "Pueblo Social Organization as a Lead to Pueblo History," *American Anthropologist*, Vol. XXXIX (n.s.), No. 3, Part I (1937).

———. "The Role of Pueblo Social Organization in the Dissemination of Catholicism," *American Anthropologist*, Vol. XLVIII (n.s.), No. 3 (1946).

Hendron, J. W. *Prehistory of El Rito de los Frijoles, Bandelier National Monument.* Coolidge, Arizona, The National Monuments Association, 1940.

Hewett, Edgar L. *Ancient Life in the American Southwest.* New York, Tudor Publishing Company, 1943.

———. *Excavations at El Rito de los Frijoles in 1909. Papers of the School of American Archaeology*, No. 10. [Reprinted from *American Anthropologist*, Vol. XI, No. 4 (October–December, 1909).]

———. *Excavations at Tyuonyi, New Mexico, in 1908. Papers of the School of American Archaeology*, No. 5. [Reprinted from *American Anthropologist*, Vol. XI, No. 3 (July–September, 1909).]

———. *Letters on the Pueblo Indian Situation. Papers of the School of American Research*, No. 6 (n.s.). Santa Fé, The Museum of New Mexico, 1925.

———. *Pajarito Plateau and Its Ancient People.* Albuquerque, University of New Mexico Press, 1938.

———. *The Puye. Papers of the School of American Research*, No. 4. Santa Fé, The Museum of New Mexico, n.d.

Hodge, Frederick W. (ed.). *Handbook of American Indians North of Mexico.* Bureau of American Ethnology *Bulletin* No. 30. Washington, Bureau of American Ethnology, 1910.

Kelemen, Pál. *Medieval American Art.* New York, The Macmillan Company, 1944.

Kidder, Alfred V. *Pottery of Pecos.* Andover, Massachusetts, Phillips Academy, 1931.

———. *Southwestern Archaeology.* New Haven, Yale University Press, 1924.

Lockett, H. C., and Snow, Milton. *Along the Beale Trail.* Lawrence, Kansas, Haskell Institute Press, 1940. Second edition.

McGregor, John C. *Southwestern Archaeology.* New York, John Wiley and Sons Company, 1941.

Mera, Harry P. "Negative Painting on Southwestern Pottery," *Southwest Journal of Anthropology,* Vol. I, No. 1 (1945).

———. *The "Rain Bird," a Study in Pueblo Design.* Santa Fé, Laboratory of Anthropology, 1937.

———. *Reconnaissance and Excavation in Southwestern New Mexico.* American Anthropological Association *Memoirs,* No. 51. Menasha, Wisconsin, American Anthropological Association, 1938.

———. *Style Trends of Pueblo Pottery.* Santa Fé, Laboratory of Anthropology, 1939.

Meriam, Lewis, and others. *The Problem of Indian Administration.* Report of a Survey Made at the Request of the Secretary of the Interior . . . . (Institute for Government Research *Studies in Administration.)* Baltimore, The Johns Hopkins Press, 1928.

Morley, Sylvanus Griswold. *The South House, Puye. Papers of the School of American Archaeology,* No. 7. Santa Fé, The Museum of New Mexico, [?1909].

Prince, L. Bradford. *A Concise History of New Mexico.* Cedar Rapids, Iowa, The Torch Press, 1914. Second edition.

Reed, Erik K. "Aspects of Acculturation in the Southwest," *Acta Americana,* Vol. II, Nos. 1 and 2 (1944).

Roberts, Frank H. H., Jr. "Survey of Southwestern Archaeology," *American Anthropologist,* Vol. XXXVII (n.s.), No. 1 (1935).

Spinden, Herbert Joseph. "The Making of Pottery at San Ildefonso," *American Museum Journal,* Vol. XI, No. 6 (October, 1911).

Stevenson, James. "Illustrated Catalog of Collections Obtained from the Indians of New Mexico and Arizona in 1879," *Second Annual Report, 1880–1881,* of the Bureau of American Ethnology, 307–465. Washington, Bureau of American Ethnology, 1882.

Underhill, Ruth Murray. *Pueblo Crafts.* Phoenix, Arizona, Phoenix Indian School, 1946.

United States, Smithsonian Institution. *Explorations and Field Work in 1912, 1913, 1914.* Washington, The Smithsonian Institution, 1914.

Vaillant, George C. *Indian Arts in North America.* New York, Harper and Brothers, 1939.

Whitman, William. *The Pueblo Indians of San Ildefonso.* New York, Columbia University Press, 1946.

Wissler, Clark. *The American Indian.* New York, Oxford University Press, 1938. Third edition.

María: THE POTTER

OF SAN ILDEFONSO

has been set in eleven point
Linotype Granjon with one
point of leading, and is printed
on a wove antique paper

UNIVERSITY OF OKLAHOMA PRESS

NORMAN